Washington. U.S. of Ameri... ... 1803.

...ut to undertake for the discovery of the course

...most convenient water communication from

...being small, it is to be expected that you

...from the Indian inhabitants. should you

...cific ocea... ...imprudent

...d be force... ...nd by sea.

...he Wester... ...be without

...; as a suc... ...t be carried

...e in that ...the credit

...authorise... ...Secretaries

...Navy of ...you may find

...le, for the ...money or

...nd I vol... ...ith of the

...all be pr... ...date they

...nsuls, agents, merchants & citizens of any

The Founding Fathers

The Founding Fathers

THOMAS JEFFERSON

A Biography in His Own Words

VOLUME 2

By
THE EDITORS OF NEWSWEEK BOOKS

JOAN PATERSON KERR
Picture Editor

NEWSWEEK
New York

ISBN: Clothbound Edition 0-88225-053-1; ISBN: Deluxe Edition 0-88225-054 -X
Library of Congress Catalog Card Number 72-92143
Copyright © 1974 by Newsweek, Inc.
All rights reserved. Printed and bound in the United States of America.
Endpapers: Jefferson to Meriwether Lewis, July 4, 1803; MISSOURI HISTORICAL SOCIETY

Thomas Jefferson, surrounded by objects representing his scientific and intellectual interests

Chapter 8

First Secretary of State

On November 23, 1789, Thomas Jefferson and his daughters returned to their native Virginia. They landed at Norfolk with servants and baggage, excited travelers who had come back eager to see old friends and fond relatives, impatient to share their experiences abroad and to learn the latest news of politics and family marriages and births. But they began their leisurely overland journey to Albemarle with different motives. Patsy and Polly concentrated on readjusting to life in Virginia; Jefferson worried about accumulating enough knowledge of changes in American political thought and attitudes to be able to represent the new government well when he returned to France.

He had not expected that the task of reeducation would be easy. In March, 1789, he had confided to David Humphreys: "I know only the Americans of the year 1784. They tell me this is to be much a stranger to those of 1789." But almost as soon as he disembarked, he learned that his reintroduction might be more extensive than he had planned. Friends and well-wishers rushed to congratulate him on his appointment as Secretary of State in Washington's administration.

Jefferson himself had received no official notification of the appointment, and as his carriage rolled from Norfolk to Richmond, he still hoped he could decline. In Richmond, he viewed progress on construction of the new capitol with satisfaction. If "finished with the proper ornaments belonging to it," he reported to William Short, "it will be worthy of being exhibited along side the most celebrated remains of antiquity." At Eppington, where Polly was reunited with her Aunt and Uncle Eppes, Jefferson received, at last, Washington's letter of October 13.

Autobiography, 1821

On my way home I passed some days at Eppington in Chesterfield, the residence of my friend and connection, Mr. Eppes, and, while there, I received a letter from the

Silhouette of Martha Jefferson

President, Genl. Washington, by express, covering an appointment to be Secretary of State. I recieved it with real regret. My wish had been to return to Paris, where I had left my houshold establishment, as if there myself, and to see the end of the revolution, which, I then thought would be certainly and happily closed in less than a year. I then meant to return home, to withdraw from Political life, into which I had been impressed by the circumstances of the times, to sink into the bosom of my family and friends, and devote myself to studies more congenial to my mind. In my answer of Dec. 15. I expressed these dispositions candidly to the President, and my preference of a return to Paris; but assured him that if it was believed I could be more useful in the administration of the government, I would sacrifice my own inclinations without hesitation, and repair to that destination. This I left to his decision.

After sending his reply on its way to Washington, Jefferson continued to Monticello. Patsy later recalled their arrival on December 23: "The negroes discovered the approach of the carriage as soon as it reached Shadwell, and such a scene I never witnessed in my life. They collected in crowds around it, and almost drew it up the mountain by hand. The shouting, etc., had been sufficiently obstreperous before, but the moment it arrived at the top it reached the climax. When the door of the carriage was opened, they received him in their arms and bore him to the house, crowding around and kissing his hands and feet—some blubbering and crying—others laughing. It seemed impossible to satisfy their anxiety to touch and kiss the very earth which bore him."

Jefferson's holiday reunion was marked by a visit from one of his dearest and most influential friends—James Madison. As a leader in the new House of Representatives, Madison was determined that Jefferson remain in America to aid the administration. He promptly wrote Washington of Jefferson's disinterest in the domestic concerns of the Secretary of State, for Congress had assigned the office numerous duties in internal affairs as well as responsibility for supervising foreign relations. Washington responded with a second letter to Jefferson, urging him to accept the appointment and confessing that: "I know of no person, who, in my judgement could better execute the Duties of it than yourself." On February 14, Jefferson conceded to Washington that he could "no longer hesitate to undertake the office to which you are pleased to call me."

Part of the campaign to persuade Jefferson to accept had been an address by a self-appointed committee of the citizens of Albemarle. His neighbors reminded him that they had elected him to his first public office, as a burgess from their county, and they urged him to continue in the national councils, for he had demonstrated a "strong attachment . . . to the rights of mankind." They concluded that "America has still occasion for your services." Jefferson had already made his decision when he delivered a heartfelt response of acceptance and rededication, which Dumas Malone has described as "one of the finest expressions of the thoughts and hopes of a philosophical statesman."

[Feb. 12. 1790]

The testimony of esteem with which you are pleased to honour my return to my native county fills me with gratitude and pleasure. While it shews that my absence has not lost me your friendly recollection, it holds out the comfortable hope that when the hour of retirement shall come, I shall again find myself amidst those with whom I have long lived, with whom I wish to live, and whose affection is the source of my purest happiness. Their favor was the door thro' which I was ushered on the stage of public life; and while I have been led on thro' it's varying scenes, I could not be unmindful of those who assigned me my first part.

My feeble and obscure exertions in their service, and in the holy cause of freedom, have had no other merit than that they were my best. We have all the same. We have been fellow-labourers and fellow-sufferers, and heaven has rewarded us with a happy issue from our struggles. It rests now with ourselves alone to enjoy in peace and concord the blessings of self-government, so long denied to mankind: to shew by example the sufficiency of human reason for the care of human affairs and that the will of the majority, the Natural law of every society, is the only sure guardian of the rights of man. Perhaps even this may sometimes err. But it's errors are honest, solitary and short-lived.—Let us then, my dear friends, for ever bow down to the general reason of the society. We are safe with that, even in it's deviations, for it soon returns again to the right way. These are lessons we have learnt together. We have prospered in their practice, and the liberality with which you are pleased to approve my attachment to the general rights of mankind assures me we are still together in these it's kindred sentiments.

Wherever I may be stationed, by the will of my country, it will be my delight to see, in the general tide of

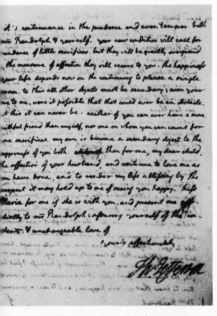

Second page of an April 4, 1790, letter to Martha from her father, concerning the duties of a wife

happiness, that yours too flows on in just place and measure. That it may flow thro' all times, gathering strength as it goes, and spreading the happy influence of reason and liberty over the face of the earth, is my fervent prayer to heaven.

There was much for Jefferson to do before he could join the administration in New York. Patsy had fallen in love with her second cousin, twenty-one-year-old Thomas Mann Randolph, Jr., the eldest son of Colonel Randolph of Tuckahoe. The courtship went quickly, and the couple was married at Monticello on February 23. Jefferson prepared to leave Virginia secure in the knowledge that his eldest daughter had chosen "a young gentleman of genius, science and honorable mind." Six days after the wedding he set out for New York, with stops in Richmond to arrange his share of payment on his father-in-law's debt and in Philadelphia to visit Benjamin Rush and the eighty-four-year-old Franklin, who was near death.

Autobiography, 1821

He was then on the bed of sickness from which he never rose. My recent return from a country in which he had left so many friends, and the perilous convulsions to which they had been exposed, revived all his anxieties to know what part they had taken, what had been their course, and what their fate. He went over all in succession, with a rapidity and animation almost too much for his strength.

On March 21 Jefferson arrived in New York City, which had been the seat of government for the last five years, and immediately faced an intimidating backlog of work. Congress was in session, Washington had been President for more than a year, and the other department heads—Alexander Hamilton in the Treasury, Henry Knox in the War Department, and Edmund Randolph, the Attorney General—had been functioning for several months. Jefferson's main concern was with the development of a foreign policy that would strengthen the nation's commercial independence and assert United States neutrality in European wars. When a Senate committee met in May to consider an appropriation bill to enable the President to employ representatives abroad, Jefferson was ill with another of his periodic headaches. But he felt it was important to speak to the committee in person. William Maclay, a senator from central Pennsylvania who was hostile to the idea of having diplomatic agents at all, recorded his impressions of the new Secretary whose "scrany Aspect" betrayed his pain.

A crude 1820 silhouette, thought to be of Jefferson, illustrating his "loose shackling Air."

Journal of William Maclay..., May 24th [1790]
Jefferson is a slender Man. Has rather the Air of Stiffness in his Manner. His cloaths seem too small for him. He sits in a lounging Manner on one hip, commonly, and with one of his shoulders elevated much above the other. His face has a scrany Aspect. His whole figure has a loose shackling Air. He had a rambling Vacant look and nothing of that firm collected deportment which I expected would dignify the presence of a Secretary or Minister. I looked for Gravity but a laxity of Manner, seemed shed about him. He spoke almost without ceasing. But even his discourse partook of his personal demeanor. It was loose and rambling and yet he scattered information wherever he went, and some even brilliant Sentiments sparkled from him. The information which he gave us respecting foreign Ministers, &ca. was all high Spiced. He has been long enough abroad to catch the tone of European folly.

The senators were persuaded by Jefferson's apt arguments in support of the bill, and he recovered from his illness at the end of May in time to help solve a legislative crisis that threatened to cripple the new government at its start. In December Alexander Hamilton had submitted to Congress his first *Report on the Public Credit.* It recommended systematic repayment of America's domestic and foreign debts through a system of funding, the conversion of existing certificates of indebtedness into new securities that would be redeemed by opening new loans. This portion of his program was comparatively noncontroversial, but the Secretary also argued that the United States should assume unpaid state debts incurred during the Revolution. Most of the opponents of assumption were from states that had already paid a large proportion of their war debts and saw no reason to be burdened with the obligations of less provident states. But they had a moral argument as well. They insisted that Hamilton's proposals would enrich wealthy speculators who had bought up the certificates from the soldiers and farmers who had originally accepted them in lieu of payment for services or produce.

The stalemate in Congress over funding and assumption had become entangled in yet another issue—the location of the national capital. Southerners, who opposed assumption, supported a temporary move to Philadelphia and the eventual construction of a new capital on the Potomac. For some, their eagerness to leave New York was not only a matter of sectional pride but a desire to remove government from the influence of the "monied" interests. Northerners blocked funding of the public debt unless assumption was included with it. Jefferson was no friend to assumption, but he was primarily concerned that the government not be threatened with disunion. He intended to keep a proper distance from the legislative branch, but some compromise was obviously needed. "My duties preventing me from mingling in these questions," he told George Mason on June 13, "I do not pretend to be very competent to their decision. In general I think it necessary to give as well as take in a government like ours." Some two years later, he jotted down the details of the part he played in working out an agreement.

[1792?]

Going to the President's one day I met Hamilton as I approached the door. His look was sombre, haggard, and dejected beyond description. Even his dress uncouth and neglected. He asked to speak with me. We stood in the street near the door. He opened the subject of the assumption of the state debts, the necessity of it in the general fiscal arrangement and it's indispensible necessity towards a preservation of the union.... That as to his own part, if he had not credit enough to carry such a measure as that, he could be of no use, and was determined to resign. He observed at the same time, that tho' our particular business laid in separate departments, yet the administration and it's success was a common concern, and that we should make common cause in supporting one another. He added his wish that I would interest my friends from the South, who were those most opposed to it. I answered that I had been so long absent from my country that I had lost a familiarity with it's affairs, and being but lately returned had not yet got into the train of them, that the fiscal system being out of my department, I had not yet undertaken to consider and understand it, that the assumption had struck me in an unfavorable light, but still not having considered it sufficiently I had not concerned in it, but that I would revolve what he had urged in my mind.... On considering the situation of things I thought the first step towards some conciliation of views would be to bring Mr. Madison and Colo. Hamilton to a friendly discussion of the subject. I immediately wrote to each to come and dine with me the next day, mentioning that we should be alone, that the object was to find some temperament for the present fever, and that I was persuaded that men of sound heads and honest views needed nothing more than explanation and mutual understanding to enable them to unite in some measures which

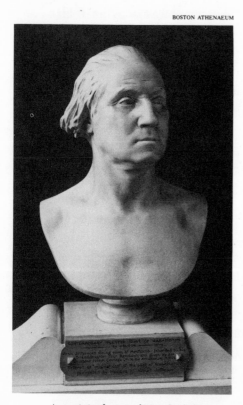

An original cast of Houdon's bust of Washington which Jefferson kept in the dining room at Monticello

A watercolor of the upper end of Broad Street in New York City, looking uptown to Federal Hall

GEORGE-TOWN, *October* 20.

Last Friday arrived here, from Mount-Vernon, the PRESIDENT of the United States, and on Saturday morning, in company with the principal Gentlemen of this town and neighbourhood, set to view the country adjacent to the River Patowmac, in order to fix upon a proper situation for the GRAND COLUMBIAN FEDERAL CITY. The PRESIDENT returned on Saturday evening, and on Sunday morning early set out for the Great Falls and Congogue.

We are informed, that since the arrival of the PRESIDENT in these parts, bets respecting the Seat of Government run high in favour of George-Town; by the return of the PRESIDENT, we hope to have it in our power to lay a circumstantial account of this important matter before the Public.

News item from the Maryland Journal *of October 26, 1790, describing a visit by Washington to "the country adjacent to the River Patowmac" to look over the site of the Federal City*

might enable us to get along. They came. I opened the subject to them, ackuoleged that my situation had not permitted me to understand it sufficiently but encouraged them to consider the thing together. They did so. It ended in Mr. Madison's acquiescence in a proposition that the question should be again brought before the house by way of amendment from the Senate, that tho' he would not vote for it, nor entirely withdraw his opposition, yet he should not be strenuous, but leave it to it's fate. It was observed, I forget by which of them, that as the pill would be a bitter one to the Southern states, something should be done to soothe them; that the removal of the seat of government to the Patowmac was a just measure, and would probably be a popular one with them, and would be a proper one to follow the assumption. It was agreed to speak to Mr. [Alexander] White and Mr. [Richard Bland] Lee, whose districts lay on the Patowmac and to refer to them to consider how far the interests of their particular districts might be a sufficient inducement to them to yield to the assumption. This was done. Lee came into it without hesitation. Mr. White had some qualms, but finally agreed. The measure came down by way of amendment from the Senate and was finally carried by the change of White's and Lee's votes. But the removal to Patowmac could not be carried unless Pennsylvania could be engaged in it. This Hamilton took on himself, and chiefly, as I understood, through the agency of Robert Morris, obtained the vote of that state, on agreeing to an intermediate residence at Philadelphia.

Jefferson's part in the bargain may not have been as central as he believed. The necessary realignment of votes was well under way before his meeting with Hamilton and Madison. But he came to consider the bargain a bad one, not merely for Virginia but for the nation as well, and he later deeply regretted the role he felt he had been "duped" into assuming. As the residence and funding bills moved through Congress, Jefferson was completing one of the most important state papers of his career, the *Report on Weights and Measures.* Two months before he arrived in New York, Congress had requested that the Secretary of State draft a plan "for establishing uniformity in the Currency, Weights and Measures of the United States." Jefferson took to the task with relish. After carefully working out a standard measure of invariable length, he recommended a decimal system of weights and measures similar to the coinage system Congress had adopted at his suggestion in 1785. He favored a thorough reform of the existing hodgepodge of bushels, barrels, firkins, crooms, wine gallons, etc., but he realistically suggested an alternative, less comprehensive plan and recommended a gradual transition.

Report on Weights and Measures [July 4, 1790]
To obtain uniformity in measures, weights and coins, it is necessary to find some measure of invariable length, with which, as a standard, they may be compared. . . .

The motion of the earth round it's axis, tho' not absolutely uniform. and invariable, may be considered as such for every human purpose. It is measured obviously but unequally, by the departure of a given meridian from the sun, and it's return to it, constituting a solar day. Throwing together the inequalities of Solar days, a mean interval, or day, has been found, and divided by very general consent into 86,400 equal parts.

A pendulum, vibrating freely in small and equal arcs, may be so adjusted in it's length as by it's vibrations, to make this division of the earth's motion into 86,400 equal parts called seconds of mean time.

Such a pendulum then becomes itself a measure of determinate length, to which all others may be referred, as to a standard. . . .

[There were "uncertainties," however, with that kind of pendulum, and Jefferson took up the suggestion of Robert Leslie, a Philadelphia watchmaker, of using a "uniform cylindrical rod."]

Let the Standard of measure then be an uniform cylindrical rod of iron, of such length as in lat. 45.° in the level of the ocean, and in a cellar or other place, the temperature of which does not vary thro' the year, shall perform it's vibrations, in small and equal arcs, in one second of mean time.

A standard of invariable length being thus obtained, we may proceed to identify by that the measures, weights, and coins of the U.S. . . .

[Jefferson's alternative plan, which he described first, was to retain existing measures but render them "uniform and invariable, by bringing them to the same invariable standard." The second proposal was more thorough.]

But if it be thought that, either now, or at any future time, the citizens of the U.S. may be induced to undertake a thorough reformation of their whole system of measures, weights and coins, reducing every branch to the same decimal ratio already established in their coins, and thus bringing the calculation of the principal affairs of life within the arithmetic of every man who can multiply and divide plain numbers, greater changes will be necessary.

The Unit of measure is still that which must give law through the whole system: and from whatever unit we set out, the coincidences between the old and new ratios will be rare. All that can be done will be to chuse such an Unit as will produce the most of these. . . .

Measures of length.

Let the Second rod then, as before described, be the Standard of measure; and let it be divided into five equal parts, each of which shall be called a *Foot:* for perhaps it may be better, generally to retain the name of the nearest present measure, where there is one tolerably near. It will be about one quarter of an inch shorter than the present foot.

> Let the foot be divided into 10. inches;
>> The Inch into 10. lines;
>> The line into 10. points;
> Let 10. feet made a decad;
>> 10. decads a rood;
>> 10. roods a furlong;
>> 10. furlongs a mile. . . .

[After a similar delineation of measures of capacity and weights and coins, Jefferson concluded the lengthy report.]

Measures, weights, and coins thus referred to standards, unchangeable in their nature, (as is the length of a rod vibrating seconds, and the weight of a definite mass of rain water) will themselves be unchangeable. These standards too are such as to be accessible to all persons, in all times and places. The measures and weights derived from them fall in so nearly with some of those now in use, as to facilitate their introduction; and being arranged in decimal ratio, they are within the calculation of every one who possesses the first elements of

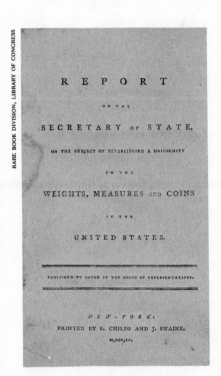

Jefferson's copy, from his library, of Report on Weights and Measures

REPORT

OF THE

SECRETARY OF STATE,

ON THE SUBJECT OF ESTABLISHING A UNIFORMITY

IN THE

WEIGHTS, MEASURES AND COINS

OF THE

UNITED STATES.

PUBLISHED BY ORDER OF THE HOUSE OF REPRESENTATIVES.

NEW-YORK:
PRINTED BY F. CHILDS AND J. SWAINE.
M,DCC,XC.

arithmetic, and of easy comparison, both for foreigners and citizens, with the measures, weights, and coins of other countries.

A gradual introduction would lessen the inconveniences which might attend too sudden a substitution, even of an easier, for a more difficult system. After a given term, for instance, it might begin in the Custom houses, where the merchants would become familiarised to it. After a further term, it might be introduced into all legal proceedings, and merchants, and traders in foreign commodities, might be required to use it in their dealings with one another. After a still further term, all other descriptions of people might recieve it into common use. — Too long a postponement on the other hand, would increase the difficulties of it's reception, with the increase of our population.

To Jefferson's disappointment, Congress and the practical men of Hamiltonian persuasion did not share his farsightedness; they failed to adopt a metric system when it might have been implemented most easily in the United States. Jefferson continued throughout his life, nevertheless, to promote a simple, universal system that could be easily understood by the ordinary person in his daily transactions. The same day the Secretary sent his report to the House, he wrote Edward Rutledge of the resolution of the funding and residence controversies. Simultaneously, a jurisdictional dispute between Britain and Spain over Nootka Sound on the Pacific Coast threatened to develop into a general war and focus the administration's attention on foreign policy.

New York July 4. 1790.
Some questions have lately agitated the mind of Congress more than the friends of union on catholic principles would have wished.... The question of residence you know was always a heating one. A bill has past the Senate for fixing this at Philadelphia ten years, and then at Georgetown: and it is rather probable it will pass the lower house. That question then will be put to sleep for ten years; and this and the funding business being once out of the way, I hope nothing else may be able to call up local principles. If the war between Spain and England takes place, I think France will inevitably be involved in it. In that case I hope the new world will fatten on the follies of the old. If we can but establish the principles of the armed neutrality for ourselves, we must

become the carriers for all parties as far as we can raise vessels.

In an effort to communicate America's intent to remain neutral, Jefferson wrote to a friend in London, Benjamin Vaughan, describing some of his new duties in the area of issuing patents for new inventions. Beneath all the discussion of maple sugar and prevention of worm damage to ships and wharves was a message that the United States would soon cease to be dependent on British manufactures and was already independent of Britain's West Indian sugar plantations. Vaughan grasped the meaning of the letter correctly and immediately forwarded it to the British foreign office. The letter is a typical example of Jefferson's use of private and indirect means to transmit views about public policy.

New York June 27. 1790.

Late difficulties in the sugar trade have excited attention to our sugar trees, and it seems fully believed by judicious persons, that we can not only supply our own demand, but make for exportation. I will send you a sample of it if I can find a conveyance without passing it through the expensive one of the post. What a blessing to substitute a sugar which requires only the labour of children, for that which it is said renders the slavery of the blacks necessary.

An act of Congress authorising the issuing patents for new discoveries has given a spring to invention beyond my conception. Being an instrument in granting the patents, I am acquainted with their discoveries. Many of them indeed are trifling, but there are some of great consequence which have been proved by practice, and others which if they stand the same proof will produce great effect. Yesterday, the man who built the famous bridge from Boston to Charlestown was with me, asking a patent for a pile engine of his own construction. He communicated to me another fact of which he makes no secret, and it is important. He was formerly concerned in shipbuilding, but for 30. years past, has been a bridge builder. He had early in life observed on examining worm eaten ships, that the worms never eat within the seams where the corking chissel enters, and the oil &c. He had observed that the whaling vessels would be eaten to a honeycomb except a little above and below water where the whale is brought into contact with the vessel and lies beating against it till it is cut up. A plank

The timbers of the Charles River Bridge, which opened for public use in June, 1786, had been soaked with codfish oil to preserve them.

lying under water at a mill of his had been obliged to be renewed annually, because eaten up by the worm within the course of the year. At length a plank was accidentally put down which for some purpose had been thoroughly impregnated with oil. It remained seven years without being affected. Hence he took the idea of impregnating the timber of his bridges thoroughly with oil, by heating the timber as deeply as possibly, and doing it well in that state with the liver oil of the codfish. He has practised this for 30. years and there is no instance of the worm attacking his timbers, while those in neighboring places are immediately destroyed....

We are told you are going to war. Peace and profit I hope will be our lot. A high price and sure market for our productions, and no want of carrying business will I hope enable my countrymen to pay off both their private and public debts....

One of Jefferson's goals as Secretary of State was to secure the territorial boundaries of the United States, especially with respect to control of navigation on the Mississippi and access to the seas through New Orleans. This was a matter of paramount importance to the settlers in the West, a group Jefferson was anxious to tie to the Republic. He saw in the Nootka Sound controversy an opportunity for bargaining with the two principals from a position of neutrality. Jefferson conferred with Madison at the President's request and discussed the possibility that France, with whom the United States still had a treaty of amity and commerce, might be called on to aid Spain and that Britain might "attempt the conquest of Louisiana and the Floridas." On July 12 he gave Washington a succinct outline of the dangers if Britain tried to acquire Western territories, of the decisions that had to be confronted, and of the initiatives that were possible.

July 12. 1790.

The dangers to us should Great Britain possess herself of those countries.

She will possess a territory equal to half ours, beyond the Missisipi

She will seduce that half of ours which is on this side the Missisipi by her language, laws, religion, manners, government, commerce, capital.

by the possession of N. Orleans, which draws to it the dependance of all the waters of Misspi

by the markets she can offer them in the gulph of Mexico and elsewhere.

BRITISH MUSEUM

George Beckwith

She will take from the remaining part of our States the markets they now have for their produce by furnishing those markets cheaper with the same articles. . . .

She will have then possessions double the size of ours, as good in soil and climate.

She will encircle us compleatly, by these possessions on our landboard, and her fleets on our sea-board.

Instead of two neighbors balancing each other, we shall have one, with more than the strength of both.

Would the prevention of this be worth a war?

Consider our abilities to take part in a war.

Our operations would be by land only.

How many men should we need to employ? — Their cost?

Our resources of taxation and credit equal to this. . . .

No need to take a part in the war as yet. We may chuse our own time. Delay gives us many chances to avoid it altogether. . . .

Delay enables us to be better prepared:

To obtain from the allies a price for our assistance.

[After making recommendations as to policy toward Spain, Jefferson confronted the question of policy toward Britain. Since the fall of 1789, Hamilton had been in close touch with an unofficial agent of the British government, George Beckwith, who had hurried down from Quebec in July to try to determine what the United States would do if a war developed. Since he was not accredited, he could speak to neither Washington nor Jefferson, but Hamilton reassured him that the United States would maintain its friendly disposition, despite the harder line Jefferson recommended.]

As to England? Say to Beckwith

'that as to a Treaty of commerce, we would prefer amicable, to adversary arrangements, tho the latter would be infallible, and in our own power:

That our ideas are that such a treaty should be founded in perfect reciprocity; and would therefore be it's own price:

That as to an Alliance, we can say nothing till it's object be shewn, and that it is not to be inconsistent with existing engagements:

That in the event of war between Gr. Brit. and Spain

221

we are disposed to be strictly neutral:

That however, we should view with extreme uneasiness any attempts of either power to seize the possessions of the other on our frontier, as we consider our own safety interested in a due balance between our neighbors'....

As a price for American neutrality, Jefferson hoped for concessions from both Britain and Spain. In his instructions to William Carmichael, the United States envoy in Madrid, he emphasized America's natural right to the navigation of the Mississippi, a right Spain should not contravene, he warned, except at the risk of war. He included a long outline of the American position with the letter.

New York August 2d. 1790.

The present appearances of war between our two neighbours, Spain and England, cannot but excite all our attention. The part we are to act is uncertain, and will be difficult. The unsettled state of our dispute with Spain may give a turn to it very different from what we would wish. As it is important that you should be fully apprised of our way of thinking on this subject, I have sketched, in the enclosed paper, general heads of consideration arising from present circumstances.... With this information ... you will be enabled to meet the minister in conversations on the subject of the navigation of the Mississippi to which we wish you to lead his attention immediately. Impress him thoroughly with the necessity of an early and even an immediate settlement of this matter, and of a return to the field of negociation for this purpose: and though it must be done delicately, yet he must be made to understand unequivocally that a resumption of the negociation is not desired on our part, unless he can determine, in the first opening of it, to yield the immediate and full enjoyment of that navigation.... It may be asked what need of negociation, if the navigation is to be ceded at all events? You know that the navigation cannot be practised without a port where the sea and river vessels may meet and exchange loads, and where those employed about them may be safe and unmolested. The right to use a thing comprehends a right to the means necessary to it's use, and without which it would be useless: the fixing on a proper port, and the degree of freedom it is to enjoy in it's operations, will require negociation, and be governed

Impression of official seal of the United States, used by Jefferson

by events. There is danger indeed that even the unavoidable delay of sending a negociator here, may render the mission too late for the preservation of peace: it is impossible to answer for the forbearance of our western citizens. We endeavor to quiet them with the expectation of an attainment of their rights by peaceable means, but should they, in a moment of impatience, hazard others, there is no saying how far we may be led: for neither themselves nor their rights will ever be abandoned by us.

The Secretary directed William Short in Paris to use his influence with the French government to exert pressure on Spain. Since January, 1790, Washington had used Gouverneur Morris, a private citizen from New York, as his personal agent in Britain, and Jefferson wrote to him, outlining his part in the overall strategy. Morris was to communicate to the ministry in London that American neutrality might be guaranteed by Britain's adherence to the Treaty of 1783—especially the provision requiring withdrawal from forts in the Northwest—and by her forbearance from seizing lands on the American frontiers.

New York August 12th. 1790.
You have placed their proposition of exchanging a Minister on proper ground. It must certainly come from them, and come in unequivocal form; with those who respect their own dignity so much, ours must not be counted at nought.... Besides what they are saying to you, they are talking to us through Quebec; but so informally that they may disavow it when they please.... These tamperings prove they view a war as very possible; and some symptoms indicate designs against the Spanish possessions adjoining us. The consequences of their acquiring all the country on our frontier from the St. Croix to the St. Mary's [rivers] are too obvious to you to need developement. You will readily see the dangers which would then environ us. We wish you therefore to intimate to them that we cannot be indifferent to enterprizes of this kind, that we should contemplate a change of neighbours with extreme uneasiness; and that a due balance on our borders is not less desireable to us, than a balance of power in Europe has always appeared to them. We wish to be neutral, and we will be so, *if they will execute the treaty fairly,* and *attempt no conquests adjoining us.* The first condition is just; the second imposes no hardship on them....If the war takes

place, we would really wish to be quieted on these two points, offering in return an honorable neutrality; more than this they are not to expect.

The Nootka Sound affair did not develop into a war. Jefferson's instructions to Morris had no effect, but the negotiations with Spain would eventually bear fruit. As the summer ended, Congress and Cabinet scattered for the fall legislative recess. Just before leaving New York, Jefferson prepared a draft "Agenda" for Washington on the location of the seat of government, a step toward insuring that the other half of the funding bargain would be carried out.

[August 29, 1790]

Proceedings to be had under the Residence act.

A territory not exceeding 10. miles square (or, I presume, 100 square miles in any form) to be located by metes and bounds.

3. commissioners to be appointed.

I suppose them not entitled to any salary....

The Commissioners to purchase or accept 'such quantity of land on the E. side of the river as the President shall deem *proper for the U.S.*' viz. for the federal Capitol, the offices, the President's house and gardens, the town house, Market house, publick walks, hospital....

The expression 'such quantity of land as the President shall deem *proper for the U.S.*' is vague. It may therefore be extended to the acceptance or purchase of land enough for the town, and I have no doubt it is the wish, and perhaps expectation. In that case it will be to be laid out in lots and streets. I should propose these to be at right angles as in Philadelphia, and that no street be narrower than 100. feet, with foot-ways of 15. feet....

The Commissioners should have some taste in Architecture, because they may have to decide between different plans.

They will however be subject to the President's direction in every point.

When the President shall have made up his mind as to the spot for the town, would there be any impropriety in his saying to the neighboring landholders, 'I will fix the town here if you will join and purchase and give the lands.' They may well afford it from the increase of value

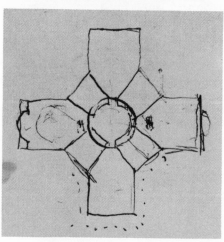

Jefferson's sketches suggesting the Pantheon in Paris as a model for the new Capitol; floor plan shows space for the Senate and House, conferences, vestibule, and rotunda.

Bas-relief of James Madison modeled from life by Ceracchi in 1792, then carved in alabaster at Florence

it will give to their own circumjacent lands.

The lots to be sold out in breadths of 50. feet: their depths to extend to the diagonal of the square.

I doubt much whether the obligation to build the houses at a given distance from the street, contributes to it's beauty. It produces a disgusting monotony. All persons make this complaint against Philadelphia. The contrary practice varies the appearance, and is much more convenient to the inhabitants.

In Paris it is forbidden to build a house beyond a given height, and it is admitted to be a good restriction. It keeps down the price of ground, keeps the houses low and convenient, and the streets light and airy. Fires are much more manageable where houses are low. This however is an object of legislation.

As he left for Virginia with James Madison on September 1, Jefferson had time to reflect and to share impressions with the man who had become the principal "opposition" leader in New York City. The Secretary of State and the congressman from Virginia had begun collaborating on domestic affairs and foreign policy in the new government while Jefferson was still at Monticello, where Madison sent him a copy of Hamilton's *Report on Public Credit*. Their thoughts and conversations, as they visited acquaintances in Philadelphia and surveyed possible sites on the Potomac, must have been disquieting. There was good reason to believe that the compromise on assumption had ended only one cause of division in the Union and had not eliminated basic areas of disagreement. Jefferson's introduction to New York society and to the opinions of members of the First Congress had put him on notice that a new faction was developing, one with "monarchical" leanings. More than forty years later, he wrote of those disturbing discoveries.

Monticello Jan. 8. [18]25.

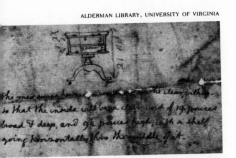

While home at Monticello in 1790, Jefferson made this sketch and noted specifications for a desk.

When I arrived at N. York in 1790, to take a part in the administration, being fresh from the French revolution, while in it's first and pure stage, and consequently somewhat whetted up in my own republican principles, I found a state of things, in the general society of the place, which I could not have supposed possible. Being a stranger there, I was feasted from table to table, at large set dinners, the parties generally from 20. to 30. The revolution I had left, and that we had just gone thro' in the recent change of our own government, being the common topics of conversation, I was astonished to find the general prevalence of monarchical sentiments, insomuch that in maintaining those of republicanism, I had always the whole company on my hands, never scarcely finding among them a single co-advocate in that argument, unless some old member of Congress happened to be present.

The next session of Congress, beginning in December, convinced Jefferson that the "monarchical" interest he had sensed was no phantom and that the leader of that interest was Alexander Hamilton. The conflict between Jefferson and Hamilton reflected basically different views of government. Hamilton distrusted the common man as much as Jefferson venerated his intelligence and sense of responsibility. Hamilton saw America's future as best served by strengthening economic ties with Britain, whereas Jefferson thought the United States was already much too dependent on Britain commercially; he wanted to continue developing commerce with France and promoting trade with other nations. Foreign policy was closely connected to Hamilton's fiscal and domestic plans, a fact that led him to meddle freely outside the concerns of his department. His interference was facilitated by the manner in which foreign policy decisions were made: by collective deliberation in the Cabinet. Hamilton's views as to domestic policy unfolded more completely that same month when he submitted a series of reports that included a proposal for a national bank. The bank would hold the funds of the government but would be controlled by private citizens. Madison fought doggedly against the bank bill in the House after it was approved by the Senate, but it was sent to the President for signing in mid-February.

In the meantime, Jefferson had submitted to the President a report on the failure of Gouverneur Morris's mission to Great Britain. He concluded that Britain would not surrender the forts in the Northwest nor negotiate a treaty of commerce without a treaty of alliance as well. Furthermore, it was still uncertain whether an accredited minister would be sent. Washington delayed reporting dispatches to Congress until February, when, in a terse note Jefferson had drafted, he said he "thought it proper to give you this information, as it might at some time have influence on matters under your consideration."

The matters Jefferson hoped would be under consideration were proposals for discriminatory navigation laws aimed at Great Britain. Jefferson had made such recommendations in a report on the plight of the New England cod and whale fisheries he had submitted the first week in February, in response to a request from the General Court of Massachusetts. The fisheries had been in a decline, primarily as a result of British dominance of the seas and a loss of markets after the Revolution. Jefferson criticized the British

Navigation Act's regulations "for mounting their navigation on the ruin of ours." He proposed counterregulations, recommended measures for establishing new markets and relief from certain taxes, and stressed the importance of reviving the carrying trade.

Report on the Cod and Whale Fisheries
[February 1, 1791]

Alexander Hamilton as Secretary of the Treasury (above) and Thomas Jefferson as Secretary of State (below), both by Charles W. Peale

The representation [of the General Court of Massachusetts] sets forth that, before the late war, about 4,000 Seamen and 24,000 Tons of shipping were annually employed from that State in the Whale Fishery, the produce whereof was about £350,000 lawful money a year.

That, previous to the same period, the Cod Fishery of that State employed 4000 men and 28,000 Ton of Shipping and produced about £250,000 a year.

That these branches of business, annihilated during the war, have been in some degree recovered since: but that they labour under many and heavy embarrassments, which, if not removed, or lessened, will render the Fisheries every year less extensive and important.

That these embarrassments are, heavy duties on their produce abroad, and bounties on that of their competitors: and duties at home on several articles particularly used in the Fisheries.

And it asks that the duties be taken off, that bounties be given to the fishermen, and the national influence be used abroad for obtaining better markets for their produce.

The Cod and Whale Fisheries, carried on by different persons, from different Ports, in different vessels, in different Seas, and seeking different markets, agree in one circumstance, in being as unprofitable to the adventurer, as important to the public....

[Jefferson surveyed the history of the cod fishery and then listed the advantages under which it operated, including the proximity of the great fisheries, the cheapness of the American vessels used, and the "superiority of our mariners in skill, activity, enterprise, sobriety and order." Despite these advantages, there were numerous disadvantages.]

Of the disadvantages opposed to us, those which depend on ourselves are

OBSERVATIONS
ON THE WHALE-FISHERY.

Whale oil enters, as a raw material, into several branches of manufacture, as of wool, leather, soap: it is used also in painting, architecture and navigation. But its great consumption is in lighting houses and cities. For this last purpose however it has a powerful competitor in the vegetable oils. These do well in warm, still weather, but they fix with cold, they extinguish easily with the wind, their crop is precarious, depending on the seasons, and to yield the same light, a larger wick must be used, and greater quantity of oil consumed. Estimating all these articles of difference together, those employed in lighting cities find their account in giving about 25 per cent. more for whale than for vegetable oils. But higher than this the whale oil, in its present form, cannot rise; because it then becomes more advantageous to the city-lighters to use others. This competition then limits its price, higher than which no encouragement can raise it, and becomes, as it were, a law of its nature, but, at this low price; the whale fishery is the poorest business into which a merchant or sailor can enter. If the sailor, instead of wages, has a part of what is taken, he finds that this, one year with another, yields him less than he could have got as wages in any other business. It is attended too with great risk, singular hardships, and long absences from his family. If the voyage is made solely at the expence of the merchant, he finds that, one year with another, it does

A

Jefferson's report to Congress on the New England fisheries continued the research he had begun in Paris, which resulted in Observations on the Whale-Fishery, *printed in 1788.*

Tonnage and Naval duties on the vessels employed in the fishery.

Impost duties on Salt.
on Tea, Rum, Sugar, Molasses
hooks, Lines and Leads.
Duck, Cordage and Cables.
Iron, Hemp and Twine
} used in the fishery....

Of the disadvantages which depend on others are
1. The loss of the Mediterranean markets.
2. Exclusions from the markets of some of our neighbours.
3. High duties in those of others, and
4. Bounties to the individuals in competition with us....

[Jefferson similarly perused the history of the whale fishery, the effects of British bounties and trade restrictions, and the 50 percent decline in the number of American ships involved in the industry from 1771 to 1789. These observations led him to make certain conclusions.]

These details will enable Congress to see with what a competition we have to struggle for the continuance of this fishery, not to say it's increase. Against prohibitory duties in one country, and bounties to the adventurers in both of those which are contending with each other for the same object, ours have no auxiliaries but poverty and rigorous economy. The business, unaided, is a wretched one....

This brings us to the question what relief does the condition of this fishery require?

1. A remission of duties on the Articles used for their calling.

2. A retaliating duty on foreign oils, coming to seek a competition with them in or from our Ports.

3. Free markets abroad.

1. The remission of duties will stand on nearly the same ground with that to the Cod fishermen.

2. The only Nation whose oil is brought hither for competition with our own, makes ours pay a duty of about 82. dollars the Ton in their Ports....

The 3d. and principal object is to find markets for the

vent of oil. . . .

England is the market for the greater part of our Spermaceti oil. They impose on all our oils a duty of £18.5. sterling the Ton, which, as to the common kind, is a prohibition as has been before observed, and as to that of the Spermaceti, gives a preference of theirs over ours to that amount, so as to leave in the end but a scanty benefit to the fisherman, And not long since, by a change of construction, without any change of the law, it was made to exclude our oils from their ports, when carried in our own vessels. On some change of circumstances it was construed back again to the reception of our oils, on paying always however the same duty of £18.5. This serves to shew that the tenure by which we hold the admission of this commodity in their markets, is as precarious as it is hard. Nor can it be announced that there is any disposition on their part to arrange this or any other commercial matter to mutual convenience. The exparte regulations which they have begun for mounting their navigation on the ruins of ours, can only be opposed by counter-regulations on our part. And the loss of seamen, the natural consequence of lost and obstructed markets for our fish and oil, calls in the first place for serious and timely attention. It will be too late when the seaman shall have changed his vocation, or gone over to another interest. . . .

If regulations, exactly the counterpart of those established against us, would be ineffectual, from a difference of circumstances, other regulations equivalent can give no reasonable ground of complaint to any nation. Admitting their right of keeping their markets to themselves, ours cannot be denied of keeping our carrying trade to ourselves. And if there be any thing unfriendly in this, it was in the first example.

The loss of seamen, unnoticed, would be followed by other losses in a long train. If we have no seamen, our ships will be useless, consequently our Ship timber, Iron and hemp: our Ship building will be at an end, ship carpenters go over to other nations, our young men have no call to the Sea, our produce, carried in foreign bottoms, be saddled with war freight and insurance, in times of war. . . . It is easier, as well as better, to stop this train at it's entrance, than when it shall have ruined or banished whole classes of useful and industrious Citizens.

The fisheries report and the disclosure of the intransigent British attitude revealed in Morris's dispatches prompted a navigation bill that was reported out of a House committee headed by Madison. It was delayed by being referred to the Secretary of State with a request for a general report on the state of American commerce, but the Hamiltonians had been thrown on the defensive. Although Hamilton could not oppose the navigation bill openly, he disliked its anti-British stance; much of the Treasury's revenue depended on duties on imported British goods. The split in the national councils between those who sought a rapprochement with England, led by Hamilton, and those who wanted to lessen American commercial dependence on that country, led by Madison and Jefferson, was widening.

Jefferson was less directly involved in consideration of the national bank, but the issue of its constitutionality was troubling Washington. He asked for opinions from his Cabinet, and Jefferson—after listing his legal objections— gave his opinion that the bill was unconstitutional. He concluded with the recommendation of a veto.

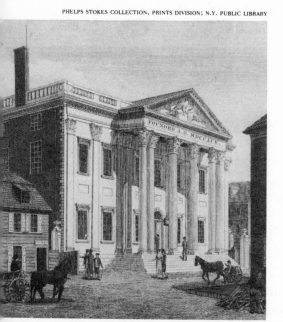

Hamilton won the fight for the bank bill and the first Bank of the United States rose in Philadelphia.

Feb. 15. 1791.

I consider the foundation of the Constitution as laid on this ground that 'all powers not delegated to the U.S. by the Constitution, not prohibited by it to the states, are reserved to the states or to the people' [XIIth. Amendmt.]. To take a single step beyond the boundaries thus specially drawn around the powers of Congress, is to take possession of a boundless feild of power, no longer susceptible of any definition.

The incorporation of a bank, and other powers assumed by this bill have not, in my opinion, been delegated to the U.S. by the Constitution....

It has been much urged that a bank will give great facility, or convenience in the collection of taxes. Suppose this were true: yet the constitution allows only the means which are 'necessary,' not those which are merely 'convenient' for effecting the enumerated powers. If such a latitude of construction be allowed to this phrase as to give any non-enumerated power, it will go to every one, for there is no one which ingenuity may not torture into a *convenience, in some way or other, to some one* of so long a list of enumerated powers. It would swallow up all the delegated powers, and reduce the whole to one phrase as before observed. Therefore it was that the constitution restrained them to the *necessary* means, that is to say, to those means without which the grant of the power would be nugatory....

Pencil sketch, perhaps by Cornelia Jefferson Randolph, a granddaughter, of the lost bust of Jefferson by Ceracchi, modeled from life c. 1791

Can it be thought that the Constitution intended that for a shade or two of *convenience*, more or less, Congress should be authorised to break down the most antient and fundamental laws of the several states, such as those against Mortmain, the laws of alienage, the rules of descent, the acts of distribution, the laws of escheat and forfeiture, the laws of monopoly? Nothing but a necessity invincible by any other means, can justify such a prostration of laws which constitute the pillars of our whole system of jurisprudence. Will Congress be too strait-laced to carry the constitution into honest effect, unless they may pass over the foundation-laws of the state-governments for the slightest convenience to theirs?

The Negative of the President is the shield provided by the constitution to protect against the invasions of the legislature 1. the rights of the Executive 2. of the Judiciary 3. of the states and state legislatures. The present is the case of a right remaining exclusively with the states and is consequently one of those intended by the constitution to be placed under his protection.

It must be added however, that unless the President's mind on a view of every thing which is urged for and against this bill, is tolerably clear that it is unauthorised by the constitution, if the pro and the con hang so even as to balance his judgment, a just respect for the wisdom of the legislature would naturally decide the balance in favour of their opinion. It is chiefly for cases where they are clearly misled by error, ambition, or interest, that the constitution has placed a check in the negative of the President.

Washington evidently found Jefferson's legal and constitutional arguments unconvincing, and he did not respond to the thrust of the Secretary's final implication, that the bill was indeed the product of "error, ambition, and interest." Instead, the President signed it into law on February 23. That defeat made Jefferson realize that he must combat the underlying principles of Hamilton's policies as well as his programs. In April, 1791, the President left Philadelphia for a semiofficial tour of the southern states. In his absence, the Vice President and Cabinet were to "consult & act" on any "serious and important cases" that arose in his absence. The procedure gave rise to the following incident, recalled in a compilation of notes and memorandums Jefferson titled the *Anas*.

Invitation to dinner with engraved
facsimile of Jefferson's signature

Anas, [February 4, 1818]

Some occasion for consultation arising, I invited those gentlemen (and the Attorney genl. as well as I remember) to dine with me in order to confer on the subject. After the cloth was removed, and our question agreed & dismissed, conversation began on other matters and, by some circumstance, was led to the British constitution, on which Mr. Adams observed 'purge that constitution of it's corruption, and give to it's popular branch equality of representation, and it would be the most perfect constitution ever devised by the wit of man.' Hamilton paused and said, 'purge it of it's corruption, and give to it's popular branch equality of representation, & it would become an *impracticable* government: as it stands at present, with all it's supposed defects, it is the most perfect government which ever existed.' And this was assuredly the exact line which separated the political creeds of these two gentlemen. The one was for two hereditary branches and an honest elective one: the other for a hereditary King with a house of lords & commons, corrupted to his will, and standing between him and the people. Hamilton was indeed a singular character. Of acute understanding, disinterested, honest, and honorable in all private transactions, amiable in society, and duly valuing virtue in private life, yet so bewitched & perverted by the British example, as to be under thoro' conviction that corruption was essential to the government of a nation.

In an earlier account of this meeting Jefferson described another incident that revealed even more about the character of the man he was subsequently to refer to as "our Buonaparte." Hamilton had looked around the room of his home and asked whose portraits hung on the wall.

Monticello Jan. 16. [18]11.

Another incident took place on the same occasion which will further delineate Hamilton's political principles. The room being hung around with a collection of the portraits of remarkable men, among them were those of Bacon, Newton & Locke. Hamilton asked me who they were. I told him they were my trinity of the three greatest men the world had ever produced, naming them. He paused for some time: 'The greatest man, said he, that ever lived was Julius Caesar.'

Before Jefferson could escape Philadelphia for a vacation during the legislative recess in the summer, he saw traces of the hated monarchism in a man he considered an "antient" and trusted friend, John Adams. A copy of the English edition of Tom Paine's *The Rights of Man*, a pamphlet written in praise of the French Revolution, was lent to Jefferson with the request that it be forwarded to a Philadelphia printer when the Secretary had finished studying it. Jefferson obliged and sent it to Jonathan B. Smith with a brief covering note which said, in part, that he was pleased the pamphlet was to be reprinted and "that something is at length to be publicly said against the political heresies which have sprung up among us."

This note, unfortunately, was included in the preface to the Philadelphia edition without Jefferson's prior knowledge or permission. No one needed to be told that the "political heresies" referred to were such essays as John Adams's "Discourses on Davila," which had recently been published in the *Gazette of the United States.* Jefferson wrote immediately to the President explaining the circumstances of the publication, but it was more than two months before he could bring himself to write to the Vice President.

Philadelphia July 17. 1791.

I have a dozen times taken up my pen to write to you and as often laid it down again, suspended between opposing considerations. I determine however to write from a conviction that truth, between candid minds, can never do harm....I thought so little of this note that I did not even keep a copy of it: nor ever heard a tittle more of it till, the week following, I was thunderstruck with seeing it come out at the head of the pamphlet. I hoped however it would not attract notice.... Thus were our names thrown on the public stage as public antagonists. That you and I differ in our ideas of the best form of government is well known to us both: but we have differed as friends should do, respecting the purity of each other's motives, and confining our difference of opinion to private conversation. And I can declare with truth in the presence of the almighty that nothing was further from my intention or expectation than to have had either my own or your name brought before the public on this occasion. The friendship and confidence which has so long existed between us required this explanation from me, and I know you too well to fear any misconstruction of the motives of it.

THE following Extract from a note accompanying a copy of this Pamphlet for republication, is so respectable a testimony of its value, that the Printer hopes the distinguished writer will excuse its present appearance. It proceeds from a character equally eminent in the councils of America, and conversant in the affairs of France, from a long and recent residence at the Court of Versailles in the Diplomatic department; and, at the same time that it does justice to the writings of Mr. Paine, it reflects honor on the source from which it flows, by directing the mind to a contemplation of that Republican firmness and Democratic simplicity which endear their possessor to every friend of the " RIGHTS OF MAN."

After some prefatory remarks, the Secretary of State observes:

" I am extremely pleased to find it will be re-printed here, and that " something is at length to be publicly said against the political heresies " which have sprung up among us.

" I have no doubt our citizens will *rally* a second time round the " *standard* of COMMON SENSE."

Extract of the note to Jonathan B. Smith which appeared as a printer's notice in the American edition of The Rights of Man *by Thomas Paine*

The incident embarrassed Jefferson. It not only interrupted his close friendship with the Adamses but also altered his relationship with Washington. With these regrets in mind, Jefferson set out on a "botanizing tour" of the northern states with James Madison on May 17. Their observations and studies would not be confined to botany, however, and their enemies charged then, as their critics still do, that the tour had political motives and that the pair planned their travels through upstate New York and New England with an eye to mobilizing opposition to Hamilton and his policies. The two Virginians journeyed north not so much to talk to the leaders of these areas, whose views they already knew, but to learn whether their constituents agreed with the positions the New England bloc had taken on assumption, the Bank, and commercial retaliation against Britain. Yet Jefferson's reports on the journey were scrupulously confined to nature and scenic beauty. After sailing up the Hudson to Albany and traveling to Lakes George and Champlain, he wrote his daughter Martha of the splendors he had seen.

Public Men, SULLIVAN

A view of "muddy" Lake Champlain

Lake Champlain May 31 [1791]

Lake George is without comparison the most beautiful water I ever saw: formed by a contour of mountains into a bason 35 miles long, and from 2 or 4 miles broad, finely interspersed with islands, its waters limpid as chrystal and the mountain sides covered with rich groves of Thuya, silver fir, white pine, Aspen, and paper birch down to the water edge, here and there precipices of rock to checquer the scene and save it from monotony. An abundance of speckled trout, salmon trout, bass, and other fish, with which it is stored, have added, to our other amusements the sport of taking them. Lake Champlain, tho much larger, is a far less pleasant water. It is muddy, turbulent, and yields little game. After penetrating into it about 25 miles we have been obliged by a head wind and high sea to return, having spent a day and a half in sailing on it....Our journey hitherto has been prosperous and pleasant except as to the weather which has been as sultry hot through the whole as could be found in Carolina or Georgia.... On the whole, I find nothing any where else in point of climate which Virginia need envy to any part of the world. Here they are locked up in ice and snow for six months. Spring and autumn, which make a paradise of our country, are rigorous winter with them, and a Tropical summer breaks on them all at once.

From New York the travelers went to Vermont, which had recently been admitted to the Union, and to areas of Massachusetts and

Connecticut. The leisurely tour was cut short in mid-June when Madison fell ill. Nonetheless, their travels had made Jefferson less a stranger to public opinion in the region. Shortly after their return, Madison finally succeeded in enlisting a new ally—a New York journalist named Philip Freneau—in the fight against Hamilton. For some time, Hamiltonians had been at an advantage in exerting influence through Joseph Fenno's *Gazette of the United States.* Jefferson's main objective in encouraging another newspaper was to see that the one-sided view of European affairs, taken by Fenno from the British press, was counterbalanced with information he could supply from other European sources. Just before leaving for New York in May, Jefferson had written his son-in-law of the sad condition of the Philadelphia press where only Benjamin Franklin Bache's amateurishly produced *General Advertiser* opposed Fenno.

> Philadelphia, May 15. 1791.
> I inclose you Bache's as well as Fenno's papers. You will have percieved that the latter is a paper of pure Toryism, disseminating the doctrines of monarchy, aristocracy, & the exclusion of the influence of the people. We have been trying to get another *weekly or half weekly* paper set up excluding advertisements, so that it might go through the states, & furnish a whig-vehicle of intelligence. We hoped at one time to have persuaded Freneau to set up here, but failed. In the mean time Bache's paper, the principles of which were always republican, improves in it's matter. If we can persuade him to throw all his advertisements on one leaf, by tearing that off, the leaf containing intelligence may be sent without over-charging the post, & be generally taken instead of Fenno's.

Freneau, Madison's friend since college days, had declined an earlier offer of a post in the State Department but in August agreed to come to Philadelphia. He received an appointment as a department translator and also set up shop as proprietor of the new *National Gazette,* which published its first issue late in October. By the time the next session of Congress was underway that winter, this opposition press was gaining flattering recognition. Jefferson did not interfere with Freneau's paper or contribute to its columns. Even if he had felt such an inclination, his increasing official duties left little time for journalism. Britain had, at last, sent a minister, twenty-eight-year-old George Hammond, but Jefferson soon forced him to admit that he had no power to conclude a commercial treaty. Hammond conversed immediately and frequently with Hamilton, whose views toward Britain he found more sympathetic.

France, too, had sent a new minister, Jean Baptiste Ternant. In December, the President submitted reciprocal nominations to the Senate: Thomas Pinckney of South Carolina to London and Gouverneur Morris to Paris. William Short, who had hoped to succeed Jefferson as minister at the French court, would have to content himself with duties as minister at The Hague. Congress was also persuaded to confirm Short and Carmichael in a joint mission to Spain for a renewal of negotiations on the subject of the Mississippi. As a result of an initiative by Jefferson on an indemnification issue and pressure from the French, Spain was willing to negotiate. But Short was delayed from joining Carmichael in Madrid until February, 1793, and by that time the opportunity had temporarily passed.

Jefferson was determined to leave the government at the end of "our first Federal cycle," Washington's first term in office, and his determination grew during the fall session. At that time he began making regular notes of his conversations and activities; "very often...," he wrote, "I made memorandums on loose scraps of paper, taken out of my pocket in the moment, and laid by to be copied fair at leisure, which, however, they hardly ever were." These "memorandums" were later bound in three volumes which became known as the *Anas* and are an invaluable record of these years of public service. Two notes in this series were made in 1791, but regular entries began with a description of conversations with President Washington on February 28 and 29, 1792. Washington, driven by an "irresistible passion" for retirement, confided that recent "symptoms of dissatisfaction" might become dangerous if there were "too great a change in the administration." Jefferson, alarmed by Hamilton's recent *Report on Manufactures*, permitted himself a frank statement of what he felt were the causes of those "symptoms"—the policies of the Treasury Department.

Anas [March 1, 1792]

I told him that in my opinion there was only a single source of these discontents. Tho' they had indeed appear[ed] to spread themselves over the war department also, yet I considered that as an overflowing only from their real channel which would never have taken place, if they had not first been generated in another department, to wit that of the treasury. That a system had there been contrived, for deluging the states with paper-money instead of gold and silver, for withdrawing our citizens from the pursuits of commerce, manufactures, buildings, and other branches of useful industry, to occupy themselves and their capitals in a species of gambling, destructive of morality, and which had introduced it's poison into the government itself. That it was a fact, as certainly known as that he and I were then conversing, that particular members of the legislature,

Gilbert Stuart portrait of José de Jaudenes y Nebot, Spanish diplomat who was sent by his government to negotiate the Mississippi question

Explanatory note to the Anas

while those laws were on the carpet, had feathered their nests with paper, had then voted for the laws, and constantly since lent all the energy of their talents, and instrumentality of their offices to the establishment and enlargement of this system: that they had chained it about our necks for a great length of time; and in order to keep the game in their hands had from time to time aided in making such legislative constructions of the constitution as made it a very different thing from what the people thought they had submitted to: that they had now brought forward a proposition, far beyond every one ever yet advanced, and to which the eyes of many were turned, as the decision which was to let us know whether we live under a limited or an unlimited government. He asked me to what proposition I alluded? I answered, to that in the Report on manufactures....

That winter Jefferson filled scraps of paper with reflections on Hamilton's program, past and present. On March 11 he summarized Hamilton's role in furthering British interests throughout the 1791–92 session and recounted the ploy Hamilton used to prevent him from submitting the report on American trade Congress had requested.

Anas [March 11, 1792]

It was observable that whenever at any of our consultations, anything was proposed as to Great Britain Hamilton has constantly ready something which Mr. Hammond had communicated to him, which suited the subject, and proved the intimacy of their communications; insomuch that I believe he communicated to Hammond all our views and knew from him in return the views of the British court.... At one of our consultations, about the last of December [1791], I mentioned that I wished to give in my report on commerce, in which I could not avoid recommending a commercial retaliation against Great Britain. Hamilton opposed it violently; and among other arguments observed that it was of more importance to us to have the posts [in the Northwest] than to commence a commercial war; that this, and this alone, would free us from the expence of the Indian wars; that it would therefore be the height of imprudence in us while treating for the surrender of the posts to engage in anything which would irritate them; that if we did so, they would naturally say, 'these people mean war, let us therefore hold what we have in our hands.' This argument struck me forcibly, and I said, 'if there is a hope of obtaining the posts, I agree it would be imprudent to risk that hope by a commercial retaliation. I will therefore wait till Mr. Hammond gives me in his assignment of breaches, and if that gives a glimmering of hope that they mean to surrender the posts, I will not give in my report till the next session.' Now, Hammond had received my assignment of breaches on the 15th of December, and about the 22d or 23d had made me an apology for not having been able to send me his counter-assignment of breaches; but in terms which showed I might expect it in a few days. From the moment it escaped my lips in the presence of Hamilton that I would not give in my report till I should see Hammond's counter-complaint, and judge if there were a hope of the posts, Hammond never said a word to me on any occasion as to the time he should be ready.

Example of Jefferson's personal seal with motto: "Rebellion to Tyrants is Obedience to God"

At the end of the legislative session, some of the forward momentum of Hamilton's fiscal program had been stopped. The *Report on Manufactures,* calling for government subsidies and bounties for industrial development, had been ignored by Congress; the House had launched an embarrassing investigation of the Treasury Department; and speculators in bank stock and government securities had triggered a financial panic that confirmed all the warnings issued by Jefferson and his supporters. But after two years of Cabinet struggles, Jefferson no longer enjoyed the close confidence of the President, who often sided with the Federalist position. At sixty, Washington was determined to retire after one term. In 1792 Jefferson believed America could do without his own services, but he knew full well the nation could not survive without Washington. After the President had returned to Virginia in May, Jefferson urged him to reconsider.

Philadelphia May 23. 1792.

When you first mentioned to me your purpose of retiring from the government, tho' I felt all the magnitude of the event, I was in a considerable degree silent. I knew that, to such a mind as yours, persuasion was idle & impertinent: that before forming your decision, you had weighed all the reasons for & against the measure, had made up your mind on full view of them, & that there could be little hope of changing the result. Pursuing my reflections too I knew we were some day to try to walk alone; and if the essay should be made while you should be alive & looking on, we should derive confidence from that circumstance, & resource if it failed. The public mind too was then calm & confident, and therefore in a favorable state for making the experiment. Had no change of circumstances supervened, I should not, with any hope of success, have now ventured to propose to you a change of purpose. But the public mind is no longer so confident and serene; and that from causes in which you are no ways personally mixed....I am perfectly aware of the oppression under which your present office lays your mind, & of the ardor with which you pant for retirement to domestic life. But there is sometimes an eminence of character on which society have such peculiar claims as to controul the predilection of the individual for a particular walk of happiness, & restrain him to that alone arising from the present & future benedictions of mankind. This seems to be your condition, & the law imposed on you by providence in forming your character, & fashioning the events on which it was to operate: and it is to motives like these, & not to personal anxieties of mine or others who have no right to call on you for sacrifices, that I appeal from your former determination & urge a revisal of it, on the ground of change in the aspect of things.

The campaign to persuade Washington to accept a second term was bipartisan: Hamilton pleaded as urgently as Jefferson and Madison did to keep the President in office. By midsummer, Washington had not yet conceded, but he had gone so far as to admit that it would be his duty to remain in office if America was in danger of disunion. The same men who urged him to a second term gave him that evidence. A bitter journalistic battle had developed. Freneau's *National Gazette* attacked government policies, Hamilton, and eventually even Washington; while Hamilton, using a pseudonym, attacked the Secretary of State in a series of letters that appeared in Fenno's *Gazette of the United States* between July and December of 1792. It was obvious to any reader that a serious conflict existed in the Cabinet. At the end of August, Washington wrote to Jefferson and Hamilton urging a conciliation so that the administration might continue. From Jefferson he demanded "liberal allowances, mutual forbearances, and temporizing yieldings on all sides." Stung by what he considered unjustified criticism, Jefferson replied from Monticello on September 9. He surveyed the development of his differences with Hamilton, especially his bitterness over being "duped" into cooperating in the bargain on assumption.

A page from Jefferson's letter to
Washington of September 9, 1792

Monticello Sep. 9. 1792.

When I embarked in the government, it was with a determination to intermeddle not at all with the legislature, and as little as possible with my co-departments. The first and only instance of variance from the former part of my resolution, I was duped into by the Secretary of the treasury and made a tool for forwarding his schemes, not then sufficiently understood by me; and of all the errors of my political life this has occasioned me the deepest regret. . . . That I have utterly, in my private conversations, disapproved of the system of the Secretary of the treasury, I acknolege & avow: and this was not merely a speculative difference. His system flowed from principles adverse to liberty, & was calculated to undermine and demolish the republic, by creating an influence of his department over the members of the legislature. . . . These were no longer the votes then of the representatives of the people, but of deserters from the rights & interests of the people: & it was impossible to consider their decisions, which had nothing in view but to enrich themselves, as the measures of the fair majority, which ought always to be respected. . . .

[Jefferson turned to the Secretary of the Treasury's meddling in foreign policy, an action that was contrary to his own views on the independence of each department.]

To say nothing of other interferences equally known, in the case of the two nations with which we have the most intimate connections, France & England, my system was to give some satisfactory distinctions to the former, of little cost to us, in return for the solid advantages yielded us by them; and to have met the English with some restrictions which might induce them to abate their severities against our commerce. I have always supposed this coincided with your sentiments. Yet the Secretary of the treasury, by his cabals with members of the legislature, & by hightoned declamation on other occasions, has forced down his own system, which was exactly the reverse. He undertook, of his own authority, the conferences with the ministers of those two nations, and was, on every consultation, provided with some report of a conversation with the one or the other of them, adapted to his views. These views, thus made to prevail, their execution fell of course to me. . . . Whose principles of administration best justify, by their purity, conscientious adherence? And which of us has, notwithstanding, stepped farthest into the controul of the department of the other?

[As to charges that Freneau was his official spokesman in the *Gazette*, Jefferson asserted that he had not taken any hand in Freneau's paper, unlike Hamilton who had contributed to Fenno's press. Jefferson reminded Washington of his intention to leave the Cabinet at the end of the first term, and he hinted that in retirement he would not feel obliged to keep silent about his differences with Hamilton.]

When I came into this office, it was with a resolution to retire from it as soon as I could with decency. It pretty early appeared to me that the proper moment would be the first of those epochs at which the constitution seems to have contemplated a periodical change or renewal of the public servants. In this I was confirmed by your resolution respecting the same period; from which however I am happy in hoping you have departed. I look to that period with the longing of a wave-worn mariner who has at length the land in view, & shall count the days & hours which still lie between me & it. . . . I will not suffer my retirement to be clouded by the slanders of a man whose history, from the moment at which history can stoop to notice him, is a tissue of machinations against the liberty of the country which has not only recieved and given him bread, but heaped it's honors on his head.

The Senate Journal's *record of the unanimous reelection of George Washington to a second term*

Pressure on Washington continued that fall. Jefferson visited the President at Mount Vernon to urge him to stay in office. Letters from other friends and advisers argued the same course, and by the end of October, Washington's colleagues knew that he would accept another term. His promised "valedictory" at the opening of Congress was not delivered, and he and Adams were easy victors in the November elections. But Jefferson would not be dissuaded from leaving. In a letter to Thomas Pinckney in London Jefferson reported an event that would make his retirement easier and that he wanted to make well known in England: Republican victories in the recent elections for the Third Congress.

Philadelphia Dec. 3. 1792.
The elections for Congress have produced a decided majority in favor of the republican interest.... I think we may consider the tide of this government as now at the fullest, and that it will from the commencement of the next session of Congress retire and subside into the true principles of the Constitution.

But disturbing news from France soon shook Jefferson's determination to retire. He had always felt that America and France stood in a special relationship to each other, their wartime alliance deepened by France's turn from despotism to constitutional government. That friendship would become harder to maintain, however, in 1793. With the new year, Americans learned of the alarming train of events in France since September—a reign of terror against aristocrats and royalist sympathizers, followed by the abolition of the monarchy and the institution of a republican government under the National Convention. William Short had been disgusted by the excesses of the Jacobins, or radical French republicans, and Jefferson knew that Hamilton and his followers would be even more eager to attack that movement. His letter to Short in January reflected the defense of French policies Jefferson would soon have to offer at home.

Philadelphia Jan 3. 1793.
The tone of your letters had for some time given me pain, on account of the extreme warmth with which they censured the proceedings of the Jacobins of France. I considered that sect as the same with the Republican patriots, & the Feuillants as the Monarchical patriots, well known in the early part of the revolution, & but little distant in their views, both having in object the establishment of a free constitution, & differing only on the question whether their chief Executive should be hereditary or not. The Jacobins (as since called) yeilded to the Feuillants & tried the experiment of retaining their hereditary Executive. The experiment failed completely, and would have brought on the re-establishment of despotism had it been pursued. The Jacobins saw this, and that the expunging that officer was of absolute necessity. And the Nation was with them in opinion, for however they might have been formerly for the constitution framed by the first assembly, they were come over from their hope in it, and were now generally Jacobins. In the struggle which was necessary, many guilty persons fell without the forms of

A French anti-Jacobin cartoon

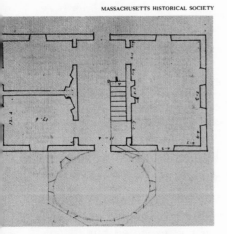

*Floor plan of the house Jefferson
rented in the summer of 1793 on
the banks of the Schuylkill River*

trial, and with them some innocent. These I deplore as much as any body, & shall deplore some of them to the day of my death. But I deplore them as I should have done had they fallen in battle. It was necessary to use the arm of the people, a machine not quite so blind as balls and bombs, but blind to a certain degree. A few of their cordial friends met at their hands the fate of enemies. But time and truth will rescue & embalm their memories, while their posterity will be enjoying that very liberty for which they would never have hesitated to offer up their lives. The liberty of the whole earth was depending on the issue of the contest, and was ever such a prize won with so little innocent blood? My own affections have been deeply wounded by some of the martyrs to this cause, but rather than it should have failed, I would have seen half the earth desolated. Were there but an Adam & an Eve left in every country, & left free, it would be better than as it now is.

France stood in even greater need of a friend in the Cabinet as the year progressed, and Jefferson notified Washington, to the President's relief, of his willingness to stay on a while longer. On January 21 Louis XVI was guillotined. Eleven days later France was at war with Britain, Holland, and Spain. Shortly after Congress adjourned, Jefferson reported to James Madison on the public reaction in Philadelphia and the response Congress might make to interference by the three powers with American trade to France.

> [Philadelphia] March. [24,] 1793.
> I should hope that Congress instead of a denunciation of war, would instantly exclude from our ports all the manufactures, produce, vessels & subjects of the nations committing this aggression, during the continuance of the aggression & till full satisfaction made for it. This would work well in many ways, safely in all, & introduce between nations another umpire than arms. It would relieve us too from the risks & the horrors of cutting throats. The death of the king of France has not produced as open condemnations from the Monocrats as I expected. I dined the other day in a company where the subject was discussed.... It is certain that the ladies of this city, of the first circle are all open-mouthed against the murderers of a sovereign, and they generally speak those sentiments which the more cautious husband smothers.

243

The bloody progress of the French Revolution gave Hamilton an opportunity to press for what Jefferson perceived had long been his goal: a destruction of the Franco-American alliance of 1778. This became clear in April when official reports of the hostilities in Europe brought Washington back from Mount Vernon for emergency sessions with the Cabinet. All agreed that America should remain neutral, though Jefferson was dissatisfied with the timing and form of the Proclamation of Neutrality issued on April 22. But there was little agreement on how that neutrality could be maintained. Under the treaties of 1778, France might call on the United States to guarantee the safety of the French West Indies. Ternant the last royal minister, was due to be succeeded by Edmond Charles Genêt, the first republican envoy, and the Cabinet was asked to consider the implications of his mission: would the United States be bound by the treaty with Louis XVI to aid the republican government that had executed him? Could Genêt be given an unqualified reception without an implicit recognition of the treaty obligations? Hamilton answered both questions in the negative. In an opinion submitted April 28, Jefferson answered firmly in favor of fulfilling the treaty obligations (if France demanded it) and in favor of granting Genêt a full and cordial reception.

[Philadelphia,] Apr. 28. 1793.

I consider the people who constitute a society or nation as the source of all authority in that nation, as free to transact their common concerns by any agents they think proper, to change these agents individually, or the organisation of them in form or function whenever they please: that all the acts done by those agents under the authority of the nation, are the acts of the nation, are obligatory on them, & enure to their use, & can in no wise be annulled or affected by any change in the form of the government, or of the persons administering it. Consequently the Treaties between the U.S. and France, were not treaties between the U S & Louis Capet, but between the two nations of America & France, and the nations remaining in existence, tho' both of them have since changed their forms of government, the treaties are not annulled by these changes. . . .

Badge of the French Revolution

Washington, quite sensibly, left the question of treaty obligations in abeyance. He decided, also, to receive Genêt with appropriate dignity and warmth. When the young French diplomat arrived in Philadelphia on May 16, local citizens greeted him enthusiastically. Jefferson's enthusiasm faded quickly, however. The ambitious, irresponsible young "Citizen" had violated American neutrality by commissioning privateers for the

French service at Charleston, South Carolina, and other towns before he even arrived in Philadelphia. As the privateers brought their prizes into American ports, the Cabinet was overwhelmed by the protests of the British minister. Jefferson's comment to Monroe of June 28 was a carefully modulated understatement: "I do not augur well of the mode of conduct of the new French minister; I fear he will enlarge the circle of those disaffected to his country." Genêt ignored the protests of the Cabinet and continued to use coastal towns as bases for French naval raids on the British. In July matters came to a head. The *Little Sarah*, captured by the French and renamed the *Petit Democrat*, was fitted out as a privateer in Philadelphia. The ship was at anchor near Mud Island in the Delaware River when Jefferson met with Genêt on Sunday, July 7, to investigate reports that the brig would be sent to sea before Washington could return to the capital. The next day, the three Cabinet members still in Philadelphia —Jefferson, Hamilton, and Knox—met to consider Pennsylvania Governor Thomas Mifflin's request for advice. The minutes of their conference carried an account of Jefferson's position.

Governor Thomas Mifflin

[Cabinet meeting, Philadelphia, July 8, 1793]

...that a conversation has been had between the Secretary of State and the Minister Plenipotentiary of France, in which conversation the Minister refused to give any explicit assurance that the brigantine would continue until the arrival of the President, and his decision in the case, but made declarations respecting her not being ready to sail within the time of the expected return of the President, from which the Secretary of State infers with confidence, that she will not sail till the President will have an opportunity of considering and determining the case; that in the course of the conversation, the Minister declared that the additional guns which had been taken in by the Little Sarah were French property, but the Governor of Pennsylvania declared that he has good ground to believe that two of her cannon were purchased here of citizens of Philadelphia....

The Secretary of the Treasury and the Secretary of War are of opinion, that it is expedient that immediate measures should be taken provisionally for establishing a battery on Mud Island, under cover of a party of militia, with direction that if the brig Sarah should attempt to depart before the pleasure of the President shall be known concerning her, military coercion be employed to arrest and prevent her progress.

The Secretary of State dissents from this opinion.

Before Washington arrived on the morning of July 11, the *Petit Democrat* had moved downriver out of reach of any guns that might be set on Mud Island. Despite the President's explicit orders to keep the privateer in the Delaware, Genêt then sent it out to sea. This action damaged the French cause, Jefferson reported sadly to Monroe.

> Philadelphia July 14. 1793.
> I fear the disgust of France is inevitable. We shall be to blame in part. But the new minister much more so. His conduct is indefensible by the most furious Jacobin. I only wish our countrymen may distinguish between him & his nation, and if the case should ever be laid before them, may not suffer their affection to the nation to be diminished. H[amilton] sensible of the advantage they have got, is urging a full appeal by the Government to the people. Such an explosion would manifestly endanger a dissolution of the friendship between the two nations, & ought therefore to be deprecated by every friend to our liberty.

His assessment of the damage to the Republican cause and to friendship with France was not exaggerated. By his actions, Genêt had discredited himself and played into Federalist hands. Hamilton successfully proposed a system of enforcement of the Proclamation of Neutrality by customs officers of the Treasury Department and Jefferson suffered another foreign policy defeat. By the end of July, he was again convinced that he should leave the proximity of a "circle which I know to bear me peculiar hatred." He submitted a letter of resignation to the President that revealed his discouragement.

> Philadelphia, July 31, 1793.
> When you did me the honor of appointing me to the office I now hold, I engaged in it without a view of continuing any length of time, & I pretty early concluded on the close of the first four years of our republic as a proper period for withdrawing; which I had the honor of communicating to you. When the period however arrived, circumstances had arisen, which, in the opinion of some of my friends, rendered it proper to postpone my purpose for awhile. These circumstances have now ceased in such a degree as to leave me free to think again of a day on which I may withdraw, without it's exciting disadvantageous opinions or conjectures of any kind. The close of the present quarter seems to be a convenient period.... At the close, therefore, of the ensuing month

of September, I shall beg leave to retire to scenes of greater tranquility, from those which I am every day more & more convinced that neither my talents, tone of mind, nor time of life fit me. I have thought it my duty to mention the matter thus early, that there may be time for the arrival of a successor, from any part of the union, from which you may think proper to call one. That you may find one more able to lighten the burthen of your labors, I most sincerely wish; for no man living more sincerely wishes that your administration could be rendered as pleasant to yourself, as it is useful & necessary to our country, nor feels for you a more rational or cordial attachment & respect than, Dear Sir, your most obedient & most humble servant.

At Washington's request, Jefferson consented to remain in office until the end of the year, a continuation that allowed him to finish one item at the heart of his program: the report on American trade Congress had requested almost three years earlier. This document, which bore the imposing title of *Report on the Privileges and Restrictions on the Commerce of the United States in Foreign Countries,* was submitted on December 16. It has been unfairly neglected in the history of great state papers of the Federal period, although it brilliantly outlined the continuing thread of Jefferson's policies: retaliation by a navigation act against Great Britain and full reciprocity with any nation ready to engage in amicable commercial relations. Opening with detailed tables of American tonnage, imports, and exports, Jefferson proceeded to ask, concerning restrictions on American ships and goods in foreign ports, "in what way they may best be removed, modified or counteracted." He conceded that the "most eligible" method was "by friendly arrangements with the several nations with whom these restrictions exist" but pointed out that this would not always be possible. America's problems lay not with nations willing to negotiate equitable trade treaties, but with the powers that continued to bar free commerce.

Report on Commerce
[Philadelphia, December 16, 1793]
But should any nation, contrary to our wishes, suppose it may better find it's advantage by continuing it's system of prohibitions, duties and regulations, it behoves us to protect our citizens, their commerce and navigation, by counter prohibitions, duties and regulations, also. Free commerce and navigation are not to be given in exchange for restrictions and vexations; nor are they likely to produce a relaxation of them.

Our navigation involves still higher considerations. As a branch of industry, it is valuable, but as a resource of defence essential.

It's value, as a branch of industry, is enhanced by the dependence of so many other branches on it. In times of general peace it multiplies competitors for employment in transportation, and so keeps that at it's proper level; and in times of war, that is to say, when those nations who may be our principal carriers, shall be at war with each other, if we have not within ourselves the means of transportation, our produce must be exported in belligerent vessels, at the increased expence of war-freight and insurance, and the articles which will not bear that must perish on our hands.

But it is as a resource for defence that our navigation will admit neither negligence nor forbearance. The position and circumstances of the United States leave them nothing to fear on their land-board, and nothing to desire beyond their present rights. But on their sea-board, they are open to injury, and they have there, too, a commerce which must be protected. This can only be done by possessing a respectable body of citizen-seamen, and of artists and establishments in readiness for ship-building.

Were the Ocean, which is the common property of all, open to the industry of all, so that every person and vessel should be free to take employment wherever it could be found, the United States would certainly not set the example of appropriating to themselves, exclusively, any portion of the common stock of occupation.... But if particular nations grasp at undue shares, and, more especially, if they seize on the means of the United States, to convert them into aliment for their own strength, and withdraw them entirely from the support of those to whom they belong, defensive and protecting measures become necessary on the part of the nation whose marine resources are thus invaded....

[Jefferson outlined several plans for commercial retaliation against those who hesitated to open their ports to American vessels and goods. He conceded that schedules of discriminatory duties and other measures might produce "some inconvenience," but that would be nothing compared to eventual benefits for the United States.]

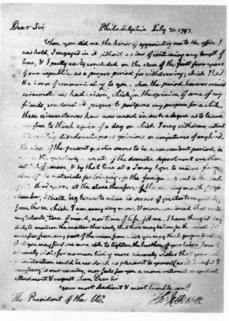

*Jefferson's letter of July 31
asking to be relieved of office*

The SECRETARY *of* STATE, *to whom was referred by the* HOUSE *of* REPRESENTATIVES, *the* REPORT *of a* COMMITTEE *on the written* MESSAGE *of the* PRESIDENT *of the* UNITED STATES, *of the 14th of February, 1791, with instruction to report to Congress the nature and extent of the* PRIVILEGES *and* RESTRICTIONS *of the* COMMERCIAL INTERCOURSE *of the United States with Foreign Nations, and the measures which he should think proper to be adopted, for the improvement of the Commerce and Navigation of the same, has had the same under consideration, and thereupon makes the following*

REPORT:

THE countries with which the UNITED STATES have their chief commercial intercourse, are, SPAIN, PORTUGAL, FRANCE, GREAT-BRITAIN, the UNITED NETHERLANDS, DENMARK, and SWEDEN, and their American possessions: and the articles of export which constitute the basis of that commerce, with their respective amounts, are—

	Dollars.
Bread-stuff, that is to say, bread-grains, meals, and bread, to the annual amount of	7,649,887
Tobacco	4,349,567
Rice	1,753,796
Wood	1,263,534
Salted fish	941,696
Pot and pearl-ash	839,093
Salted meats	599,130
Indigo	537,379
Horses and mules	339,753
Whale oil	252,591
Flax-feed	236,072
Tar, pitch and turpentine	217,177
Live provisions	137,743
Ships	
Foreign goods	620,274

First page of Report on Commerce

It is true we must expect some inconvenience in practice from the establishment of discriminating duties. But in this, as in so many other cases, we are left to chuse between two evils. These inconveniences are nothing, when weighed against the loss of wealth and loss of force, which will follow our perseverance in the plan of indiscrimination. When once it shall be perceived that we are either in the system or in the habit of giving equal advantages to those who extinguish our commerce and navigation by duties and prohibitions, as to those who treat both with liberality and justice, liberality and justice will be converted by all into duties and prohibitions. It is not to the moderation and justice of others we are to trust for fair and equal access to market with our productions, or for our due share in the transportation of them; but to our own means of independence, and the firm will to use them.... In our case one distinction alone will suffice: that is to say, between nations who favor our productions and navigation, and those who do not favor them. One set of moderate duties, say the present duties, for the first, and a fixed advance on these as to some articles and prohibitions as to others, for the last.

Like so many of the reports Jefferson had drafted as Secretary of State, this one, too, was virtually ignored and once again his attempts to promote a foreign policy based on commercial reciprocity were thwarted. As he prepared to leave Philadelphia in January, 1794, Jefferson was justifiably disheartened by his four years in the Cabinet. On all major aspects of his official policies, both domestic and foreign, the Hamiltonian forces had triumphed. Only the negotiations with Spain were successful, resulting in Pinckney's Treaty of 1795 guaranteeing free navigation of the Mississippi. The battles had been bitter and Jefferson felt that he was powerless to reverse the drift away from republican principles.

Beyond the sense of frustration and repudiation he felt, however, were some grounds for optimism: Hamilton's influence was waning; a cloud of distrust hung over the Treasury Department; and Jefferson's estimation in the eyes of the people had risen as his stock in the administration declined. A man of integrity, honor, and devotion to the public interest would not long be allowed the diversions and pleasures of retirement.

Chapter 9

Retirement and Recall

When Jefferson returned to Monticello on January 16, 1794, he viewed his withdrawal from national politics as a much-needed chance to enjoy family life, to catch up with his reading, and to superintend his land and home which he had long been forced to neglect. He immediately plunged into the life of a Piedmont farmer, and during the next three years he never ventured more than seven miles from his mountaintop. Two weeks after his arrival home, Jefferson received an invitation to visit General Horatio Gates at Rose Hill, but he declined, preferring to give full attention to his domestic pursuits.

> Monticello Feb. 3. 1794.
> [T]he length of my tether is now fixed . . . from Monticello to Richmond. My private business can never call me elsewhere, and certainly politics will not, which I have ever hated both in theory & practice. I thought myself conscientiously called from those studies which were my delight by the political crisis of my country. . . . In storms like those all hands must be aloft. But calm is now restored, & I leave the bark with joy to those who love the sea. I am but a landsman, forced from my element by accident, regaining it with transport, and wishing to recollect nothing of what I have seen, but my friendships.

Nevertheless, Jefferson seems to have experienced a brief period of irksome readjustment during his first months at Monticello. Occasionally he seemed to vacillate between reveling in his freedom from official duties and chafing at his isolation from the outside world. The first mood is apparent from a remark in a letter to Edmund Randolph on February 3: "I think it is Montaigne who has said that ignorance is the softest pillow on which a man can rest his head. I am sure it is true as to every thing political, and shall endeavor to estrange myself to every thing of that character." But twelve days later, he confessed concern to Madison for Virginia's ignorance of current political events.

Notes Jefferson made in 1791 on sugar maples and a variety of fruit trees to be planted at Monticello

Monticello, Feb. 15, 1794.

We are here in a state of great quiet, having no public news to agitate us. I have never seen a Philadelphia paper since I left that place, nor learnt anything of later date except some successes of the French the account of which seemed to have come by our vessel from Havre....I could not have supposed, when at Philadelphia, that so little of what was passing there could be known even at Kentuckey, as is the case here. Judging from this of the rest of the Union, it is evident to me that the people are not in a condition either to approve or disapprove of their government, nor consequently to influence it.

By mid-March, when he wrote to James Monroe, Jefferson betrayed distinct irritation with the dearth of news in Albemarle County, due in part to a smallpox epidemic.

Monticello Mar. 11, 1794.

The small pox at Richmond has cut off the communication by post to or through that place. I should have thought it [the postmaster's] duty to have removed his office a little way out of town, that the communication might not have been interrupted. Instead of that it is said the inhabitants of the country are to be prosecuted because they thought it better to refuse a passage to his postriders than take the smallpox from them. Straggling travellers who have ventured into Richmd. now and then leave a newspaper with Colo. Bell....I have never received a letter from Philadelphia since I left it except a line or two once from E[dmund] R[andolph].

In April, the post office in Richmond reopened and Jefferson could at last keep abreast of maneuvers in Congress. Madison's navigation bill, benefiting from public reaction to renewed British interference with American shipping, had come close to passage. Madison had delayed pressing the matter in April, he wrote Jefferson, because even

251

harsher anti-British resolutions were on the floor. But Federalists managed to counteract cries for retaliation against Britain by proposing a special envoy to negotiate Anglo-American differences in London. Rumors that Hamilton himself might be given the appointment appalled Jefferson; the whole scheme was evidence of the control the Treasury Secretary had asserted over foreign policy since Jefferson's resignation. On April 24 he wrote Monroe, one of Virginia's two senators, describing the anti-British sentiment he had found in the state and offering his personal opinion of the proposed mission.

Monticello Apr. 24. [17]94

The spirit of war has grown much stronger, in this part of the country, as I can judge of myself, and in other parts along the mountains from N.E. to S.W. as I have had opportunities of learning by enquiry. Some few very quiet people, not suffering themselves to be inflamed as others are by the kicks & cuffs Gr. Britain has been giving us, express a wish to remain in peace. But the mass of thinking men seem to be of opinion that we have borne so much as to invite eternal insults in future should not a very spirited conduct be now assumed. For myself, I wish for peace, if it can be preserved, salva fide et honore. I learn...that a special mission to England is meditated, & H. the missionary. A more degrading measure could not have been proposed: and why is Pinckney to be recalled? For it is impossible he should remain there after such a testimony that he is not confided in. I suppose they think him not thorough paced enough: I suspect too the mission, besides the object of placing the aristocracy of this country under the patronage of that government, has in view that of withdrawing H. from the disgrace & the public execrations which sooner or later must fall on the man who...has alienated for ever all our ordinary & easy resources, & will oblige us hereafter to extraordinary ones for every little contingency out of the common line....

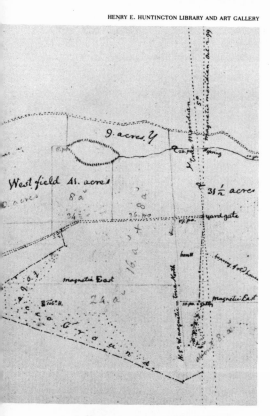

Jefferson's survey of his fields at Shadwell shows ground set aside for tobacco, a crop he did not like but depended on for cash income.

With the resumption of the mail and the reopening of communications to the world outside Albemarle County, Jefferson seemed more content as a farmer; he could regulate the degree of his solitude at Monticello. As the spring planting season began, he initiated his plans for scientific crop rotation on his acres. John Adams wrote congratulating him "on the charming opening of the Spring" and added that he heartily wished

"I was enjoying of it as you are upon a Plantation, out of the hearing of the Din of Politicks." Jefferson responded that his ardor as a farmer had made him neglect even the love of study that had hitherto marked his life.

> Monticello Apr. 25. 1794.
>
> The difference of my present and past situation is such as to leave me nothing to regret but that my retirement has been postponed four years too long. The principles on which I calculate the value of life are entirely in favor of my present course. I return to farming with an ardour which I scarcely knew in my youth, and which has got the better entirely of my love of study. Instead of writing 10. or 12. letters a day, which I have been in the habit of doing as a thing of course, I put off answering my letters now, farmer-like, till a rainy day, & then find it sometimes postponed by other necessary occupations.

The next month brought a letter from the President. Washington commiserated with Jefferson on their mutual problems as farm-owners, then revealed that foreign policy was continuing along the same lines that had led to Jefferson to resign. "We are going on in the old way 'Slow'," he wrote. "I hope events will justify me in adding 'and sure' that the proverb may be fulfilled—'Slow and Sure'." As he remarked to John Adams that spring, Jefferson had "seen enough of one war never to wish to see another." But he had seen enough, too, of subservience to Britain. His reply to Washington opened with an enthusiastic explanation of his plans to restore his fields and closed with a reaffirmation of the political opinions he had held from the beginning.

> Monticello May 14. 1794.
>
> I find on a more minute examination of my lands, than the short visits heretofore made to them permitted, that a 10. years abandonment of them to the unprincipled ravages of overseers, has brought on a degree of degradation far beyond what I had expected. As this obliges me to adopt a milder course of cropping, so I find that they have enabled me to do it by having opened a great deal of lands during my absence. I have therefore determined on a division of my farms into 6. fields to be put under this rotation: 1st. year, wheat; 2d. corn, potatoes, peas; 3d. rye or wheat, according to circumstances; 4th. & 5th. clover where the fields will bring it, & buckwheat dressings where they will not; 6th. folding, and buckwheat dressings. But it will take me

from 3. to 6. years to get this plan underway.... Time, patience & perseverance must be the remedy; and the maxim of your letter 'slow & sure' is not less a good one in agriculture than in politics. I sincerely wish it may extricate us from the event of a war, if this can be done saving our faith and our rights. My opinion of the British government is that nothing will force them to do justice but the loud voice of their people, & that this can never be excited but by distressing their commerce.

Jefferson's attitude toward his political enemies during his early retirement was probably similar to his feelings about the "invading tyrants" who threatened the French republic: "I am still warm whenever I think of these scoundrels, tho I do it as seldom as I can." After Congress recessed in the summer, Jefferson lived contentedly without bulletins from his friends of affairs at Philadelphia. At the end of the summer, he received a request from Edmund Randolph, his successor in the State Department, to go to Spain as a special envoy. Negotiations over navigation of the Mississippi had broken down, and Washington was alarmed by talk of secession in the West. Jefferson firmly declined the appointment.

Monticello Sep. 7. [17]94.
No circumstances my dear Sir will ever more tempt me to engage in any thing public. I thought myself perfectly fixed in this determination when I left Philadelphia, but every day & hour since has added to it's inflexibility.

The curtness of Jefferson's answer was prompted partly by the fact that the offer had been channeled through Randolph, like any routine matter, rather than coming from the President. This discourtesy was compounded by an enclosure asking Jefferson to forward a duplicate invitation to Washington's second choice—Jefferson's time-honored enemy, Patrick Henry. Jefferson sent the note to Henry, who also turned down the mission, and then resumed his domestic duties, more certain than ever that he had chosen well in returning to Monticello.

With Jefferson no longer providing an antidote to Hamilton's policies, the administration veered farther from the neutral, above-politics course Washington had originally charted. Fresh evidence of this drift came in the President's reaction to the Whisky Rebellion in the late summer and fall of 1794. Small farmers in the backcountry of western Pennsylvania protested Hamilton's excise tax on their only cash product. Having sent an expedition accompanied by Hamilton to quell the "rebels," Washington, in his annual address to Congress, blamed the rebellion on the influence of "certain self-created societies." This was a reference to the new pro-French, Republican-dominated Democratic Societies which had sprung up in various states. Jefferson vented his private indignation at the speech's unfounded charges in a letter to Madison.

Monticello Dec. 28. [17]94.

The denunciation of the democratic societies is one of the extraordinary acts of boldness of which we have seen so many from the faction of Monocrats. It is wonderful indeed that the President should have permitted himself to be the organ of such an attack on the freedom of discussion, the freedom of writing, printing & publishing. It must be a matter of rare curiosity to get at the modifications of these rights proposed by them, and to see what line their ingenuity would draw between democratical societies, whose avowed object is the nourishment of the republican principles of our constitution, and the society of the Cincinnati [the organization of Revolutionary War officers of which Hamilton was a member], a self-created one, carving out for itself hereditary distinctions, lowering over our constitution eternally, meeting together in all parts of the Union periodically, with closed doors . . . corresponding secretly & regularly, & of which society the very persons denouncing the democrats are themselves the fathers, founders or high officers.

[Washington's justification of the expedition against the perpetrators of the Whisky Rebellion also inspired Jefferson's acid sarcasm.]

I expected to have seen some justification of arming one part of the society against another, of declaring a civil war the moment before the meeting of that body which has the sole right of declaring war, of being so patient of the kicks & scoffs of our enemies, & rising at a feather against our friends, of adding a million to the public debt & deriding us with recommendations to pay it if we can &c., &c. But the part of the speech which was to be taken as a justification of the armament reminded me of parson Saunders' demonstration why minus into minus make plus. After a parcel of shreds of stuff from Aesop's fables, & Tom Thumb, he jumps all at once into his Ergo, minus multiplied into minus makes

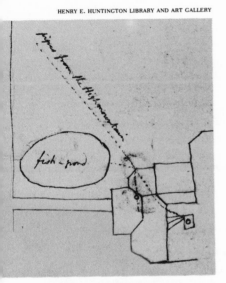

Jefferson's sketch for a fish pond and water supply at Monticello

An exciseman, lured by his "evil genius," carries off two kegs of whiskey in detail from a cartoon about the Whisky Rebellion.

James Madison married the widow Dolley Payne Todd on September 15, 1794; this miniature of her was made from a 1789 drawing.

plus. Just so the 15,000 men enter after the fables in the speech....

[Jefferson closed by encouraging Madison in his fight for Republican measures.]

The changes in your house I see are going on for the better, and even the Augean herd over your heads are slowly purging off their impurities. Hold on then, my dear friend, that we may not ship-wreck in the mean while. I do not see in the minds of those with whom I converse a greater affliction than the fear of your retirement; but this must not be, unless to a more splendid & a more efficacious post. There I should rejoice to see you: I hope I may say, I shall rejoice to see you. I have long had much in my mind to say to you on that subject. But double delicacies have kept me silent.

Throughout the winter, Jefferson expanded on the "more splendid" post Madison should seek—that of Washington's successor. Jefferson himself was content to remain at home, delighting in his lively grandchildren, four-year-old Anne and three-year-old Thomas Jefferson Randolph. When their parents left the toddlers at Monticello that winter, while they prepared their Varina plantation for occupancy, Jefferson sent his daughter reports on the children's antics.

Monticello Jan. 22. [17]95

Th. J. to his dear M. J.

...Jefferson is very robust. His hands are constantly like lumps of ice, yet he will not warm them. He has not worn his shoes an hour this winter. If put on him, he takes them off immediately & uses one to carry his nuts &c. in. Within these two days we have put both him & Anne into mockaseens, which being made of soft leather, fitting well & lacing up, they have never been able to take them off. So that I believe we may consider that as the only effectual shoe which can be made for them. They are inseparable in their sports. Anne's temper begins to develope itself advantageously. His tempests give her opportunities of shewing & exercising a placid disposition: and there is no doubt but that a little time will abate of his impatience as it has done hers. I called her in to ask what I should write for her to yourself & her papa. She says I must tell you that she loves you, & that you must come home. In both these sentiments we all join her.

With the end of that bitter winter ("so much the better for our wheat, and for the destruction of the weavil," Jefferson remarked) came the spring planting. As the master of plantations and uncleared lands scattered across central and western Virginia, Jefferson presided over more than ten thousand acres worked by two hundred slaves. He wrote William Branch Giles, the stalwart Republican congressman, of his new pursuits.

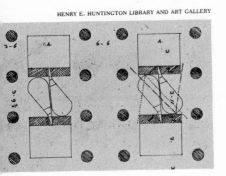

Monticello Apr. 27. 1795.

If you visit me as a farmer, it must be as a condisciple: for I am but a learner; an eager one indeed but yet desperate, being too old now to learn a new art. However I am as much delighted & occupied with it as if I was the greatest adept. I shall talk with you about it from morning till night, and put you on very short allowance as to political aliment. Now and then a pious ejaculation for the French & Dutch republicans, returning with due dispatch to clover, potatoes, wheat, &c.

It should not be imagined that Jefferson approached the management of Monticello and his other lands as a "gentleman farmer." His family's income came from these acres, and agriculture was, quite simply, the source of his livelihood. His years of public service had forced him to leave his business in the hands of overseers who had farmed out the soil. A careful program of crop rotation could eventually restore the land, but he seized every opportunity to gain additional income until the soil was once again completely productive. In the spring of 1795 he wrote optimistically to Jean Nicolas Demeunier, a French scholar, of a new enterprise on his plantation.

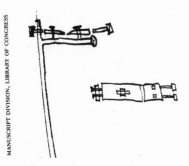

Jefferson's plan for a nailery (top), which he built in 1794, and the design of a nail-cutting machine used at Monticello (above)

Monticello. Virginia Apr. 29. [17]95

...I found my farms so much deranged, that I saw evidently they would be a burthen to me instead of a support till I could regenerate them; and consequently that it was necessary for me to find some other resource in the mean time. I thought for a while of taking up the manufacture of pot-ash, which requires but small advances of money. I concluded at length however to begin a manufacture of nails, which needs little or no capital, & I now employ a dozen little boys from 10. to 16. years of age, overlooking all the details of their business myself and drawing from it a profit on which I can get along

257

till I can put my farms into a course of yielding profit. My new trade of nailmaking is to me in this country what an additional title of nobility, or the ensigns of a new order are in Europe.

Theories Jefferson had sketched out years before were put to practical application. A request from the American Philosophical Society, the group of scientists and promoters of useful knowledge organized by Benjamin Franklin, evoked a modest description from Jefferson of his design for a moldboard plow "of least resistance," which he had conceived during his travels abroad.

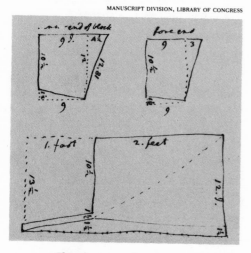

Sketches reproduced in the American Philosophical Society's Transactions *of Jefferson's design for moldboard*

Monticello July 3. 1796.

You wish me to present to the Philosophical society the result of my philosophical researches since my retirement. But my good Sir I have made researches into nothing but what is connected with agriculture. In this way I have a little matter to communicate, and will do it ere long. It is the form of a Mouldboard *of least resistance.* I had some years ago concieved the principles of it, and I explained them to Mr. [David] Rittenhouse [the president of the society]. I have since reduced the thing to practice and have reason to believe the theory fully confirmed. I only wish for one of those instruments used in England for measuring the force exerted in the draughts of different ploughs &c. that I might compare the resistance of my mould board with that of others. But these instruments are not to be had here.

It was perhaps the happiest of the three summers of his retirement. Jefferson's slave Isaac remembered the master as a "straight up man" who was always to be heard "singing when ridin or walking. Hardly see him anywhar out doors but what he was a-singing," Isaac recounted. Jefferson enjoyed the company of his daughters and grandchildren; his nail manufacturing seemed promising and his plans to remodel his home were almost ready for execution. He was indeed, for those few months, a content and ardent farmer.

The summer ended on a less pleasant note. John Jay, who had been appointed the special envoy to London, returned with a treaty that triggered a national crisis when its terms were made public. Although the treaty had been concluded in London in November, 1794, it did not reach America until Congress had adjourned in the spring of 1795. The President called the Senate back into special session in June, and despite some provisions that alarmed even the Federalists, the treaty scraped through to ratification at the end of the month. Public opposition was so great that Washington hesitated to sign it, and Jefferson viewed the outcome of Jay's negotiations with undisguised disgust. He described the agreement's apparent sacrifice of American rights and prerogatives to Monroe, who had become the United States Minister to France.

NEW-YORK HISTORICAL SOCIETY

Monticello. Sep. 6, [17]95.

Mr. Jay's treaty has at length been made public. So general a burst of dissatisfaction never before appeared against any transaction. Those who understand the particular articles of it, condemn these articles. Those who do not understand them minutely, condemn it generally as wearing a hostile face to France. This last is the most numerous class, comprehending the whole body of the people, who have taken a greater interest in this transaction than they were ever known to do in any other. It has in my opinion completely demolished the monarchial party here.... *Adams* holds his tongue with an address above his character. We do not know whether the President has signed it or not. If he has it is much believed the H. of representatives will oppose it as constitutionally void, and thus bring on an embarrassing & critical state in our government.

A Federalist cartoon, c. 1795, of Washington repelling an invasion by French "cannibals" and Jefferson, at far right, trying to "Stop de wheels of de gouvernement"

The matter was not settled even when the President signed the treaty—after considerable pressure from Hamilton. Trying to rally public support, Hamilton had begun publishing in July a series of essays signed "Camillus" in the New York press. Near the end of September Jefferson urged Madison, the only Republican he felt could effectively oppose Hamilton, to reply.

Monticello Sep. 21. [17]95.

Hamilton is really a colossus to the antirepublican party. Without numbers, he is an host within himself. They have got themselves into a defile, where they might be finished; but too much security on the Republican part, will give time to his talents & indefatigableness to extricate them. We have had only midling performances to oppose to him. In truth, when he comes forward, there is nobody but yourself who can meet him. His adversaries having begun the attack, he has the advantage of answering them, & remains unanswered himself.... For god's sake take up your pen, and give a fundamental reply to Curtius & Camillus.

259

Many of the treaty's provisions required expenditures, and the Republican opposition, led by Madison, continued in the House which had sole power to originate appropriations. Madison hardly needed Jefferson's reminder on strategy in November.

A page dated January 1, 1796, in Jefferson's notebook of plans for remodeling Monticello calculates amounts of stone and brick needed.

[Monticello,] Nov. 26. [17]95.

. . . as the articles which stipulate what requires the consent of the three branches of the legislature, must be referred to the H. of R. for their concurrence, so they, being free agents, may approve or reject them, either by a vote declaring that, or by refusing to pass acts. I should think the former mode the most safe and honorable. The people in this part of the country continue very firmly disposed against the treaty. . . . I observe an expression in Randolph's printed secret [a pamphlet published by Edmund Randolph] intimating that the President, tho' an honest man himself, may be circumvented by snares and artifices, and is in fact surrounded by men who wish to clothe the Executive with more than constitutional powers. This when public, will make great impression. It is not only a truth, but a truth levelled to every capacity and will justify to themselves the most zealous votaries, for ceasing to repose the unlimited confidence they have done in the measures which have been pursued.

A few days later Jefferson wrote in a similar vein to Edward Rutledge of South Carolina, who was active in his state's politics. The letters show Jefferson's desire to continue his enjoyment of retirement and his simultaneous encouragement of friends to remain active in politics. The President, searching for men who would accept the vacant posts of Secretary of State, Secretary of War, and Attorney General, was in dire need of competent advisers.

Monticello Nov. 30. [17]95.

He [Rutledge's son] found me in a retirement I doat on, living like an Antediluvian patriarch among my children & grand children, and tilling my soil. . . . You hope I have not abandoned entirely the service of our country. After a five & twenty years continual employment in it, I trust it will be thought I have fulfilled my tour, like a punctual soldier, and may claim my discharge. But I am glad of the sentiment from you my friend, because it gives a hope you will practice what you preach, and come forward in aid of the public vessel. I will not admit your old excuse, that you are in public service tho' at home. The campaigns which are fought in a man's own house are not to be counted. The present situation of the President, unable to get the offices filled, really calls with uncommon obligation on those whom nature has fitted for them.

Jefferson's support of others who were serving the nation was a consistent thread in his correspondence that winter while he added another item to his own program of busy rustication: the remodeling of Monticello. The modest but handsome house, which had seemed appropriate for a Virginia planter in the 1770s, would not do for the sophisticated traveler who returned to Albemarle in 1794. As early as 1792, Jefferson had decided to incorporate the original structure into a larger mansion that would show to advantage his European furniture and art and would accommodate his growing library and constant train of guests. Throughout 1794 and 1795 bricks and stone were collected on the mountaintop, but actual demolition of the old wings and construction of the new did not begin until 1796. In March Jefferson jovially invited William Branch Giles to visit.

> Monticello Mar. 19. 1796.
>
> I have begun the demolitions of my house, and hope to get through it's re-edification in the course of this summer. But do not let this discourage you from calling on us if you wander this way in the summer. We shall have the eye of a brick-kiln to poke you into, or an Octagon to air you in.

The Duke de La Rochefoucauld-Liancourt, who visited Monticello later that year, described the progress of reconstruction.

> Travels through the United States
> of North America, 1799
>
> The house stands on the summit of the mountain, and the taste and arts of Europe have been consulted in the formation of its plan. Mr. Jefferson had commenced its construction before the American revolution; since that epocha his life has been constantly engaged in public affairs, and he has not been able to complete the execution of the whole extent of the project which it seems he had at first conceived.... Mr. Jefferson ... is now employed in repairing the damage occasioned by this interruption, and still more by his absence; he continues his original plan, and even improves on it, by giving to

Duke de La Rochefoucauld-Liancourt

261

According to his slave Isaac, Jefferson spent forty years at work on Monticello; the 1803 rendering above by Robert Mills is the west elevation of the final version.

his buildings more elevation and extent. He intends that they should consist only of one story, crowned with balustrades; and a dome is to be constructed in the center of the structure. The apartments will be large and convenient; the decoration, both outside and inside, simple, yet regular and elegant. Monticello, according to its first plan, was infinitely superior to all other houses in America, in point of taste and convenience; but at that time Mr. Jefferson had studied taste and the fine arts in books only. His travels in Europe have supplied him with models; he has appropriated them to his design; and his new plan, the execution of which is already much advanced, will be accomplished before the end of next year, and then his house will certainly deserve to be ranked with the most pleasant mansions in France and England.

From the top of the "little mountain," Jefferson's perspective on what he called the balance in American government among the "three branches of the legislature" was a dim one that winter. The Senate was firmly in Federalist hands; the House, despite Republican gains in 1794, was still largely unsympathetic to Jefferson and Madison's goals; and the President, the "third branch," continued to depart from his earlier nonpartisan course. Jefferson still admired Washington but remarked that he "errs as other men do, but errs with integrity." Perhaps encouraged by Vice President Adams's uncharacteristic silence in the Jay Treaty controversy, Jefferson sent his old friend this exhortation to keep America free of the corrupting influence of the British example of government.

Monticello Feb. 28. [17]96.
This I hope will be the age of experiments in government, and that their basis will be founded on principles of honesty, not of mere force. We have seen no instance of this since the days of the Roman republic, nor do we read of any before that. Either force or corruption has been the principle of every modern government, unless the Dutch perhaps be excepted, & I am not well enough informed to except them absolutely. If ever the morals of a people could be made the basis of their own government, it is our case; and he who could propose to govern such a people by the corruption of their legislature, before he could have one night of quiet sleep, must convince himself that the human soul as well as body is mortal....I am sure, from the honesty of your heart,

you join me in detestation of the corruption of the English government, and that no man on earth is more incapable than yourself of seeing that copied among us, willingly. I have been among those who have feared the design to introduce it here, & it has been a strong reason with me for wishing there was an ocean of fire between that island and us.

Oceans of fire, alas, would not spring up at Jefferson's bidding, and he relied on James Madison to protect America from British domination by persuading the House to withhold appropriations for the Jay Treaty. Madison's chances of success seemed good, and Jefferson reminded him at the end of March that his Virginia constituents looked on him as "their last hope" in breaking the chain of conspiracy between the Hamiltonians and Britain.

[Monticello,] Mar. 27. [17]96.
If you decide in favor of your right to refuse cooperation in any case of treaty, I should wonder on what occasion it is to be used, if not on one where the rights, the interest, the honor & faith of our nation are so grossly sacrificed, where a faction has entered into a conspiracy with the enemies of their country to chain down the legislature at the feet of both; where the whole mass of your constituents have condemned this work in the most unequivocal manner, and are looking to you as their last hope to save them from the effects of the avarice & corruption of the first agent, the revolutionary machinations of others, and the incomprehensible acquiescence of the only honest man who has assented to it. I wish that his honesty and his political errors may not furnish a second occasion to exclaim, 'curse on his virtues, the've undone his country.'

In March, it was not known how much longer that "honest man"—Washington—would continue in office. It seemed unlikely that he would accept a third term, but no other candidates could be announced until the President gave his decision to retire. Jefferson continued to urge Madison to seek the Presidency. His slight, bookish friend had developed into a brilliant leader in the rough world of congressional politics, and Jefferson had every reason to believe Madison would be best suited to lead their fledgling Republican party in the executive branch. The President's errors, honest though they might be, were becoming more dangerous, and his successor would have to be able to deal with the corruption Jefferson saw in American politics. In this mood he wrote to Philip Mazzei, a former neighbor in Virginia, who had returned to Italy.

Monticello Apr. 24. 1796.

The aspect of our politics has wonderfully changed since you left us. In place of that noble love of liberty & republican government which carried us triumphantly thro' the war, an Anglican, monarchical & aristocratical party has sprung up, whose avowed object is to draw over us the substance, as they have already done the forms, of the British government. The main body of our citizens however remain true to their republican principles. The whole landed interest is republican; and so is a great mass of talents. Against us are the Executive, the Judiciary, two out of three branches of the legislature, all the officers of the government, all who want to be officers, all timid men who prefer the calm of despotism to the boisterous sea of liberty, British merchants, & Americans trading on British capitals, speculators & holders in the banks & public funds, a contrivance invented for the purposes of corruption, & for assimilating us, in all things, to the rotten as well as the sound parts of the British model. It would give you a fever were I to name to you the Apostates who have gone over to these heresies; men who were Samsons in the field and Solomons in the council, but who have had their heads shorn by the harlot England. In short, we are likely to preserve the liberty we have obtained only by unremitting labors & perils.

Philip Mazzei, a Florentine who had settled near Monticello in 1773 and cultivated vineyards

More than a year later, the Mazzei letter would be published in the American press and Federalists would denounce Jefferson, based on his reference to "Samsons and Solomons," as an enemy of Washington. Jefferson certainly felt that Washington had been led astray, but the allusion was to members of the Cincinnati, he later declared. Although its language was not intended for publication, the letter stated the same opinions Jefferson had communicated to Washington in September, 1792.

Jefferson soon had more reason to despair of the President's ability to face the "unremitting labors and perils" America now demanded from her patriots. Republicans failed to win the fight against the treaty when Federalists raised the phantom fear of war with Great Britain if the provisions were not funded. Some Republicans argued as strongly that implementation would mean a rupture with France, but Washington seemed unable to accept the sincerity of the opposition. At the same time, the President confided that he would not accept another term. His decision was not public knowledge, but political leaders, Federalist and Republican alike, spent May and June fashioning "tickets" for the 1796 election.

Jefferson's name, of course, was prominently mentioned in his own party, and his possible candidacy must have been known to Washington. In this strained atmosphere, Jefferson saw a copy of the Philadelphia *Aurora* that contained thirteen queries the President had presented to the Cabinet in April, 1793, concerning America's policy of neutrality in the war between France and Great Britain. Jefferson discerned the fine hand of the former Treasury Secretary trying to implicate him in the leak and hastened to assure Washington that he had not been responsible for its publication.

Monticello, June 19, 1796.

I cannot be satisfied as to my own part till I relieve my mind by declaring, and I attest everything sacred & honorable to the declaration, that it has got there neither thro' me nor the paper confided to me. This has never been from under my own lock & key, or out of my own hands. No mortal ever knew from me that these questions had been proposed. Perhaps I ought to except one person who possesses all my confidence as he has possessed yours. I do not remember indeed that I communicated it even to him. But as I was in the habit of unlimited trust & counsel with him, it is possible I may have read it to him. No more: for the quire of which it makes a part was never in any hand but my own, nor was a word ever copied or taken down from it, by any body. I take on myself, without fear, any divulgation on his part. We both know him incapable of it. From myself then or my paper this publication has never been derived. I have formerly mentioned to you that, from a very early period of my life, I had laid it down as a rule of conduct never to write a word for the public papers. From this I have never departed in a single instance: & on a late occasion when all the world seemed to be writing, besides a rigid adherence to my own rule, I can say with truth that not a line for the press was ever communicated to me by any other. . . .

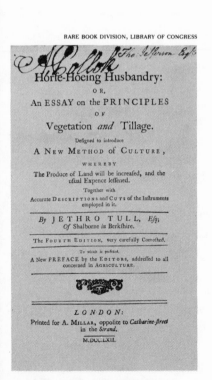

Jefferson's library included a book that revolutionized English agriculture, Jethro Tull's famous Horse-Hoeing Husbandry.

[Jefferson categorized the imputation as typical of attacks on his loyalty by such men as Henry Lee of Virginia.]

I learn that this last [Lee] has thought it worth his while to try to sow tares between you & me, by representing me as still engaged in the bustle of politics, & in turbulence & intrigue against the government. I never believed for a moment that this could make any impression on you, or that your knolege of me would not overweigh the slander of an intriguer, dirtily employed in sifting the conversations of my table, where alone he could hear of me, and seeking to atone for his sins against you by sins against another who had never done him any other injury than that of declining his confidences. Political conversations I really dislike, & therefore avoid where I can without affectation. But when urged by others, I have never concieved that having been in public life requires me to bely my sentiments, nor even to conceal them. When I am led by conversation to express them, I do it with the same independance here which I have practised everywhere, and which is inseparable from my nature....

I put away this disgusting dish of old fragments, & talk to you of my peas & clover.

Washington, in reply, assured Jefferson that he had not suspected him of the leak, but he conceded that he had heard reports that Jefferson and his followers had described him as "a person under a dangerous influence." "My answer invariably has been," Washington wrote, "that I had never discovered any thing in the conduct of Mr. Jefferson to raise suspicions, in my mind, of his insincerity...." After this statement, however, Washington angrily turned to the subject of the Republican press. He implied that if Jefferson had not connived at or inspired the scurrilous attacks on his character, he had at least not exercised his influence to condemn them, something Jefferson would not have done given his previously stated views on the role of a free press.

Jefferson found the tone of the letter and the implication of character assassination so wounding that he made a tacit decision to end their twenty-year correspondence. Since there was nothing in Washington's letter that demanded an immediate reply, Jefferson simply did not answer it, thus closing an association that had begun in the Virginia House of Burgesses in 1769. In later years, Jefferson was generous in praising the Washington he had known and respected in the first two decades of their friendship. His sketch of the President's personality, given in response to a request for information in 1814, is a classic and perceptive study.

Monticello Jan. 2. [18]14.

His mind was great and powerful, without being of the very first order; his penetration strong, tho' not so acute as that of a Newton, Bacon or Locke; and as far as he saw, no judgment was ever sounder. It was slow in operation, being little aided by invention or imagination, but sure in conclusion. . . . He was incapable of fear, meeting personal dangers with the calmest unconcern. Perhaps the strongest feature in his character was prudence, never acting until every circumstance, every consideration was maturely weighed; refraining if he saw a doubt, but, when once decided, going through with his purpose, whatever obstacles opposed. His integrity was most pure, his justice the most inflexible I have ever known, no motives of interest or consanguinity, of friendship or hatred, being able to bias his decision. He was indeed, in every sense of the words, a wise, a good, & a great man. His temper was naturally irritable and high toned; but reflection & resolution had obtained a firm and habitual ascendancy over it. If ever however it broke it's bonds he was most tremendous in his wrath. . . . His heart was not warm in it's affections; but he exactly calculated every man's value, and gave him a solid esteem proportioned to it. . . .

. . . I am satisfied the great body of republicans thinks of him as I do. We were indeed dissatisfied with him on his ratification of the British treaty. But this was short lived. We knew his honesty, the wiles with which he was encompassed, and that age had already begun to relax the firmness of his purposes: and I am convinced he is more deeply seated in the love and gratitude of the republicans, than in the Pharisaical homage of the Federal monarchists. For he was no monarchist from preference of his judgment. The soundness of that gave him correct views of the rights of man, and his severe justice devoted him to them. He has often declared to me that he considered our new constitution as an experiment on the practicability of republican government, and with what dose of liberty man could be trusted for his own good: that he was determined the experiment should have a fair trial, and would lose the last drop of his blood in support of it.

Portrait of Washington as Patriæ Pater *by Rembrandt Peale*

Although Jefferson himself would never have phrased the matter so harshly, Washington had outlived his usefulness to the Republic. An old man, in failing health, the President was surrounded by a

Cabinet of second-rate men who were unable to advise him well. The publication of Washington's Farewell Address in early September finally made it possible for other candidates to declare themselves. John Adams became the Federalist choice; Jefferson had hoped that Madison would be the Republican candidate, but he had just married and would not even stand for re-election to the House. Madison, with a shrewder sense of practical politics, knew that Jefferson would lend far more prestige to their party's ticket, but he had all he could do to keep Jefferson from discouraging his would-be supporters. At the end of September, Madison confided to Monroe: "I have not seen Jefferson and have thought it best to present him no opportunity of protesting to his friends against being embarked in the contest."

An unwilling candidate, Jefferson waited patiently to learn his fate after the November elections. The cumbersome system of voting meant that the victor would not be definitely known for several weeks, but by early December, Jefferson had accurately analyzed the polls. He told Madison of the strategy to be followed should a tie vote in the Electoral College threaten Adams's majority in the popular vote.

> Monticello Dec. 17. [17]96.
>
> It begins to appear possible that there may be an equal division where I had supposed the republican vote would have been considerably minor. It seems also possible that the Representatives [who would decide the issue if the electoral votes were tied] may be divided. This is a difficulty from which the constitution has provided no issue. It is both my duty & inclination therefore to relieve the embarrasment should it happen: and in that case I pray you and authorize you fully to sollicit on my behalf that Mr. Adams may be preferred. He has always been my senior from the commencement of our public life, and the expression of the public will being equal, this circumstance ought to give him the preference.... Let those come to the helm who think they can steer clear of the difficulties. I have no confidence in myself for the undertaking.

Knowing Adams well, Jefferson was aware that it was not enough simply to inform his fellow Republicans of his willingness to accept second place, which would make him Vice President. Three days after Christmas, he drafted a letter to Adams.

> Monticello Dec. 28. 1796
> The public & the public papers have been much occupied lately in placing us in a point of opposition to each other. I trust with confidence that less of it has been felt by

First page of the Farewell Address

ourselves personally. In the retired canton where I am, I learn little of what is passing. Pamphlets I see never; papers but a few; and the fewer the happier. Our latest intelligence from Philadelphia at present is of the 16th. inst. But tho' at that date your election to the first magistracy seems not to have been known as a fact, yet with me it has never been doubted.... I have never one single moment expected a different issue; tho' I know I shall not be believed, yet it is not the less true that I have never wished it. My neighbors, as my compurgators, could aver that fact, because they see my occupations & my attachment to them. Indeed it is possible that you may be cheated of your succession by a trick worthy the subtlety of your arch-friend [Hamilton, who had supported the Federalist vice-presidential candidate, Thomas Pinckney, against Adams] of New York, who has been able to make of your real friends tools to defeat their & your just wishes. Most probably he will be disappointed as to you; & my inclinations place me out of his reach. I leave to others the sublime delights of riding in the storm, better pleased with sound sleep & a warm birth below, with the society of neighbors, friends & fellow laborers of the earth, than of spies & sycophants. No one then will congratulate you with purer disinterestedness than myself.

Even as he completed the letter, Jefferson had doubts about its propriety. Instead of sending it directly to Adams, he enclosed it with a covering note to Madison, asking him to read it and to return it "if anything should render the delivery of it ineligible in your opinion." He assured Madison that neither his ambitions nor his vanity had been disappointed by the outcome of the elections, in which he had received 68 electoral votes to Adams's 71 and Pinckney's 59.

[Monticello,] Jan. 1. [17]97.
I know the difficulty of obtaining belief to one's declarations of a disinclination to honors, and that it is greatest with those who still remain in the world. But no arguments were wanting to reconcile me to a relinquishment of the first office or acquiescence under the second. As to the first it was impossible that a more solid unwillingness settled on full calculation, could have existed in any man's mind, short of the degree of absolute refusal.... As to the second, it is the only office in the

269

world about which I am unable to decide in my own mind whether I had rather have it or not have it. Pride does not enter into the estimate; for I think with the Romans that the General of to-day should be a soldier tomorrow if necessary. I can particularly have no feelings which would revolt at a secondary position to mr. Adams. I am his junior in life, was his junior in Congress, his junior in the diplomatic line, his junior lately in the civil government.

Madison prudently chose to return the enclosure to its author at Monticello, fearing it might be misinterpreted. "You know the temper of Mr. A. better than I do," he tactfully told Jefferson, "but I have always conceived it to be rather a ticklish one." Even before Jefferson learned of Madison's decision, he heard news that made personal assurances of loyalty to the President-elect seem unnecessary. He wrote happily to Madison in Philadelphia on January 22.

[Monticello,] Jan. 22. [17]97.
My letters inform me that Mr. A speaks of me with great friendship, and with satisfaction in the prospect of administering the government in concurrence with me. I am glad of the first information, because tho' I saw that our antient friendship was affected by a little leaven produced partly by his constitution, partly by the contrivance of others, yet I never felt a diminution of confidence in his integrity, and retained a solid affection for him. His principles of government I knew to be changed, but conscientiously changed.

To be sure Adams did not mistake his intentions, Jefferson wrote several New Englanders of his pleasure in serving as Vice President under his old colleague. He had done all that he could to reassure the President-elect that he would have a faithful and cooperative aide in the administration. The need for a new regime became more obvious daily. French reaction to Jay's Treaty had been as bitter as the most "Jacobin" of American Republicans had predicted, and Washington clearly could not meet the crisis. On January 4, Jefferson wrote his friend Archibald Stuart that it would be futile to petition the President concerning the danger of war with France.

Monticello, Jan 4, 1797.
Such is the popularity of the President that the people will support him in whatever he will do, or will not do,

without appealing to their own reason or to anything but their feelings toward him. His mind has been so long used to unlimited applause that it could not brook contradiction, or even advice offered unasked. To advice, when asked, he is very open. I have long thought therefore it was best for the republican interest to soothe him by flattery where they could approve his measures, & to be silent where they disapprove, that they may not render him desperate as to their affections, & entirely indifferent to their wishes; in short to lie on their oars while he remains at the helm, and let the bark drift as his will and a superintending providence shall direct.... It seems he is earnest that the war should be avoided, & to have the credit of leaving us in full peace. I think then it is best to leave him to his own movements, & not to risk the ruffling them by what he might deem an improper interference with the constituted authorities.... As to the President elect, there is reason to believe that he (Mr. Adams I mean) is detached from Hamilton, & there is a possibility he may swerve from his politics in a greater or less degree. Should the British faction attempt to urge him to the war by addresses of support with life & fortune, as may happen, it would then be adviseable to counteract their endeavors by dissuasive addresses.

John Adams, in an engraving by Amos Doolittle which appeared in The Connecticut Magazine

Jefferson returned to public life because the electorate compelled it, but he was reassured in doing so by the independence of mind that characterized the President he would serve. Adams was his own man, not a tool of Hamilton, and whatever the New Englander's peculiarities of temperament and pro-British leanings, Jefferson pointed out to Edward Rutledge that "he is perhaps the only sure barrier against Hamilton's getting in." The nature of the office he would hold also appealed to Jefferson. He believed that the Vice Presidency was solely a legislative position, confined to presiding over the Senate, and that it should be conducted within the strict limits laid down by the Constitution. He had warned Madison in his letter of January 22 to expect nothing more of him.

[Monticello,] Jan. 22. [17]97.
As to my participating in the administration, if by that he [Adams] meant the executive cabinet, both duty & inclination will shut that door to me. I cannot have a wish to see the scenes of 93. revived as to myself, & to descend daily into the arena like a gladiator to suffer

martyrdom in every conflict. As to duty, the constitution will know me only as the member of a legislative body: and it's principle is that of a separation of legislative executive & judiciary functions.

Indeed, although Jefferson was flattered and pleased by the Republican showing in the polls, he seemed relieved that they had not won. He had informed Edward Rutledge in December that he had no illusions about the glories of the Presidency.

Monticello Dec. 27. 1796.

I know well that no man will ever bring out of that office the reputation which carries him into it. The honey moon would be as short in that case as in any other, & it's moments of extasy would be ransomed by years of torment & hatred. I shall highly value indeed the share which I may have had in the late vote, as an evidence of the share I hold in the esteem of my countrymen. But in this point of view a few votes more or less will be little sensible, and in every other the minor will be preferred by me to the major vote.

Silhouette of Jefferson distributed at Peale's Museum, Philadelphia

The office of Vice President seemed ideal for Jefferson. He looked forward to attending meetings of the American Philosophical Society in Philadelphia but expected to spend much of his time at home. He commented to Benjamin Rush in late January, "I have no wish to meddle again in public affairs.... If I am to act however, a more tranquil & unoffending station could not have been found for me.... It will give me philosophical evenings in the winter, & rural days in the summer."

And so, on February 20, Jefferson left Monticello for Philadelphia to take his oath of office. He would miss the spring planting, but as he rode north to give his personal support to Adams, he was convinced that the sacrifice would be minor and temporary. He left his peaceful little mountain, with its unfinished mansion and his growing brood of grandchildren, planning to be away only a few weeks of the year for the next four years. "I would not have wished to leave it at all," Jefferson confessed. "However, if I am to be called from it, the shortest absences and most tranquil station suit me best." The absences, however, would not be short, nor would the station be tranquil.

Chapter 10

Second Vice President

When Jefferson left Monticello to serve as Vice President to John Adams, he regarded his comrade from Massachusetts as a man who might reunite the nation, now divided between British and French partisans, and liberate politics and the economy from the legacy of Hamilton's influence. If Jefferson, by his mere presence in the administration, could persuade Southerners and Westerners of the merits of Adams's regime, he would feel that he had played as active and useful a role as any Vice President should properly assume. But this modest goal for his Vice Presidency was to fail, not from any lack of sincerity on his part but because others refused to accept him at his word. On his arrival in Philadelphia, most Federalists and even some Republicans considered him a party leader, a role he had not yet consciously adopted. If anyone deserved the title in 1797 it was James Madison who had marshaled the Republican interest in the House since 1789 and turned it into a disciplined legislative force while courting support among state officeholders and coordinating propaganda programs to broaden the party's support. Jefferson, however, had long been the symbol of Republican strength, and with Madison's retirement he was to become the dominant Republican.

Before leaving Monticello, Jefferson wrote to George Wythe, under whose tutelage he had made a thorough study of English parliamentary history and law, asking for any notes the scholar still had pertaining to rules of order the Vice President would be enforcing in the Senate. Although Wythe was unable to help him, Jefferson eventually compiled a manual of parliamentary procedure which was long used by both houses of Congress.

Monticello Jan. 22. [17]97

It seems probable that I shall be called on to preside in a legislative chamber. It is now so long since I have acted in the legislative line that I am entirely rusty in the Parliamentary rules of procedure. I know they have been more studied and are better known by you than by any man in America, perhaps by any man living. I am in hopes that while enquiring into the subject you made notes on it. If any such remain in your hands, however informal, in books or in scraps of paper, and you will be so good as to trust me with them a little while, they shall be most faithfully returned.

Even the timing of his trip to Philadelphia reflected Jefferson's desire to become a modest, secondary member of the new administration. He told Madison he did not think it was necessary for him to go that far to take the oath of office, but he had decided that "respect to the public" demanded the inconvenience.

LIBRARY OF CONGRESS

Congress Hall (with cupola), where Jefferson presided over the Senate

[Monticello,] Jan. 30. [17]97. I have turned to the constitution & laws, and find nothing to warrant the opinion that I might not have been qualified here or wherever else I could meet with a Senator, every member of that body being authorised to administer the oath, without being confined to time or place, & consequently to make a record of it, and to deposit it with the records of the Senate. However, I shall come on on the principle which had first determined me, respect to the public. I hope I shall be made a part of no ceremony whatever. I shall escape into the city as covertly as possible.

Jefferson's arrival in Philadelphia was not quite as "covert" as he had hoped: an artillery salute and a banner proclaiming "Jefferson the Friend of the People" greeted him as he alighted from the stagecoach. But his inaugural address to the Senate maintained the modest tone he felt was in keeping with the nature of the office. The message opened with an apology for any errors of procedure he might commit and closed with a tribute to the man he succeeded.

[March 4, 1797] Entering on the duties of the office to which I am called, I feel it incumbent on me to apologize to this honorable House for the insufficient manner in which I fear they may be discharged. At an earlier period of my life, and through some considerable portion of it, I have been a member of legislative bodies, and not altogether inattentive to the forms of their proceedings; but much time has elapsed since that; other duties have occupied my

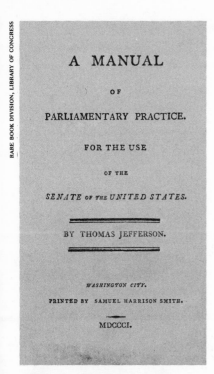

A MANUAL

OF

PARLIAMENTARY PRACTICE.

FOR THE USE

OF THE

SENATE OF THE UNITED STATES.

BY THOMAS JEFFERSON.

WASHINGTON CITY.

PRINTED BY SAMUEL HARRISON SMITH.

MDCCCI.

Jefferson's personal copy of his Manual of Parliamentary Practice, *which he completed in 1800; it was printed in Washington in 1801.*

mind, and in a great degree it has lost its familiarity with this subject. I fear that the House will have but too frequent occasion to perceive the truth of this acknowledgment. If a diligent attention, however, will enable me to fulfil the functions now assigned me, I may promise that diligence and attention shall be sedulously employed....

I might here proceed, and with the greatest truth, to declare my zealous attachment to the constitution of the United States, that I consider the union of these States as the first of blessings, and as the first of duties, the preservation of that constitution which secures it; but I suppose these declarations not pertinent to the occasion of entering into an office whose primary business is merely to preside over the forms of this House, and no one more sincerely prays that no accident may call me to the higher and more important functions which the constitution eventually devolves on this office. These have been justly confided to the eminent character which has preceded me here, whose talents and integrity have been known and revered by me through a long course of years, have been the foundation of a cordial and uninterrupted friendship between us, and I devoutly pray he may be long preserved for the government, the happiness, and prosperity of our common country.

Jefferson and the senators then adjourned to the House chamber where that "eminent character" took the presidential oath resplendent in sash and sword. Jefferson recorded no reaction to the new President's remarkable costume; he may have concentrated more on Adams's speech, which was conciliatory, reaffirming his faith in the Constitution and in republican institutions. Adams even spoke of his personal esteem for the French, who were then governed by the three-man Directory. Before leaving Virginia, Jefferson had learned that Charles C. Pinckney, Monroe's successor as minister in Paris, had been denied an official reception. The pro-British policies that dominated Washington's second term had brought their inevitable result. As he remarked to Madison, Jefferson expected Adams to be saddled with the diplomatic errors of his predecessor.

[Monticello,] Jan. 8. [17]97.

The President [Washington] is fortunate to get off just as the bubble is bursting, leaving others to hold the bag. Yet, as his departure will mark the moment when the difficulties begin to work, you will see, that they will be ascribed to the new administration, and that he will have his usual good fortune of reaping credit from the good acts of others, and leaving to them that of his errors.

As soon as Jefferson arrived in Philadelphia, he had been approached by Adams with a plan to establish a rapprochement with France: the creation of a special bipartisan commission, drawing its members from different regions, to be sent to Paris to negotiate French grievances. He recorded the progress of the plan before and after Inauguration Day.

Anas

Mar. 2. 1797. I arrived at Phila. to qualify as V. P., and called instantly on Mr. Adams who lodged at Francis's in 4th. street. The next morning he returned my visit at Mr. Madison's, where I lodged. He found me alone in my room, and, shutting the door himself, he said he was glad to find me alone for that he wished a free conversation with me. He entered immediately on an explanation of the situation of our affairs with France, & the danger of rupture with that nation, a rupture which would convulse the attachments of this country. That he was impressed with the necessity of an immediate mission to the Directory; that it would have been the first wish of his heart to have got me to go there, but that he supposed it was out of the question, as it did not seem justifiable for him to send away the person destined to take his place in case of accident to himself, nor decent to remove from competition one who was a rival in the public favor. That he had therefore concluded to send a mission which by it's dignity should satisfy France, & by it's selection from the three great divisions of the Continent should satisfy all parts of the US. In short that he had determind to join [Elbridge] Gerry and Madison to Pinckney, and he wished me to consult Mr. Madison for him. I told him that as to myself I concurred in the opinion of the impropriety of my leaving the post assigned me, and that my inclinations moreover would never permit me to cross the Atlantic again: that I would as he desired consult Mr. Madison, but I feared it was desperate.... He said that if Mr. Madison should refuse, he would still appoint him, and leave the responsibility on him.— I consulted Mr. Madison who declined as I expected. I think it was on Monday the 6th. of March, Mr. Adams

These contemporary views by William Birch of Market Street from the County Market (above) and Second Street from the corner of Second and Market (opposite) were not far from Adams's and Jefferson's usual lodgings at Francis's Hotel.

and myself met at dinner at General Washington's, and we happened in the evening to rise from table and come away together. As soon as we got into the street I told him the event of my negociation with Mr. Madison. He immediately said that on consultation some objections to that nomination had been raised which he had not contemplated, and was going on with excuses which evidently embarrassed him, when we came to 5th. street where our road separated, his being down Market street, mine off along 5th. and we took leave.... The opinion I formed at the time on this transaction was that Mr. A. in the first moments of the enthusiasm of the occasion (his inauguration,) forgot party sentiments, and as he never acted on any system, but was always governed by the feeling of the moment, he thought for a moment to steer impartially between the parties; that Monday the 6th. of Mar. being the first time he had met his cabinet, on expressing ideas of this kind he had been at once diverted from them, and returned to his former party views.

Adams's puzzling about-face on Madison's appointment could be traced to his Cabinet—all holdovers from Washington's second-rate council who were still strongly influenced by Hamilton. In this case the former Secretary of the Treasury urged that Madison be included on the commission for the sake of national unity, but Jefferson guessed correctly that the Cabinet had advised Adams against it. Adams's conciliatory attitude and his differences of opinion with some of his fellow party members presaged the split between moderate and High Federalists that would develop during his term.

A few days after the inauguration, Jefferson and Adams left Philadelphia for their homes in Virginia and Massachusetts. They returned in May for a special session of Congress called to consider the international situation. By then, Jefferson was less sanguine about the possibility of harmonious relations with the President. Two days before the Senate met, he wrote of his concern to Elbridge Gerry, the moderate Massachusetts Republican who was being considered for the mission to France.

Philadelphia May 13. 1797.

You express apprehensions that stratagems will be used to produce a misunderstanding between the President and myself. Tho' not a word having this tendency has ever been hazarded to me by any one, yet I consider as a certainty that nothing will be left untried

Elbridge Gerry

to alienate him from me. These machinations will proceed from the Hamiltonians by whom he is surrounded, and who are only a little less hostile to him than to me. It cannot but damp the pleasure of cordiality when we suspect that it is suspected. I cannot help fearing that it is impossible for Mr. Adams to believe that the state of my mind is what it really is; that he may think I view him as an obstacle in my way. I have no supernatural power to impress truth on the mind of another, nor he any to discover that the estimate which he may form on a just view of the human mind as generally constituted, may not be just in it's application to a special constitution. This may be a source of private uneasiness to us. I honestly confess that it is so to me at this time. But neither of us are capable of letting it have effect on our public duties. Those who may endeavor to separate us, are probably excited by the fear that I might have influence on the executive councils. But when they shall know that I consider my office as constitutionally confined to legislative functions, and that I could not take any part whatever in executive consultations, even were it proposed, their fears may perhaps subside, & their object be found not worth a machination.

During the special legislative session, Jefferson took no part in executive policy conferences spurred by the French rejection of Charles C. Pinckney. The discussion of the commission to France in March was the last time Adams "ever consulted me as to any measures of government," Jefferson later noted. The Federalists in Congress seemed driven by a war fever, which he described to Thomas Pinckney.

Philadelphia May 29. 1797.
When I contemplate the spirit which is driving us on here, & that beyond the water which will view us but as a mouthful the more, I have little hope of peace. I anticipate the burning of our seaports, havoc of our frontiers, household insurgency, with a long train of et ceteras, which it is enough for a man to have met once in his life....War is not the best engine for us to resort to. Nature has given us one in our *commerce* which, if properly managed, will be a better instrument for obliging the interested nations of Europe to treat us with justice. If the commercial regulations had been adopted which

our legislature were at one time proposing, we should at this moment have been standing on such an eminence of safety & respect as ages can never recover.

A dams's program of increased military preparedness at home and a joint commission to Paris was adopted in May and June. Jefferson considered the plan for defense needlessly expensive, and he hardly approved of the Virginian named to the commission instead of Madison — young John Marshall, his Federalist kinsman. But Elbridge Gerry, who was sympathetic to France, would be the New England representative, and Jefferson sent him a warm letter of congratulations, urging him to seize the chance to fight for both interest and honor.

> Philadelphia June 21. [17]97.
>
> Peace is undoubtedly at present the first object of our nation. Interest & honor are also national considerations. But interest, duly weighed, is in favor of peace even at the expence of spoliations past & future; & honor cannot now be an object. The insults & injuries committed on us by both the belligerent parties from the beginning of 1793. to this day, & still continuing by both, cannot now be wiped off by engaging in war with one of them. As there is great reason to expect this is the last campaign in Europe, it would certainly be better for us to rub thro this year as we have done through the four preceding ones, and hope that on the restoration of peace we may be able to establish some plan for our foreign connections more likely to secure our peace, interest & honor in future. Our countrymen have divided themselves by such strong affections to the French & the English, that nothing will secure us internally but a divorce from both nations. And this must be the object of every real American, and it's attainment is practicable without much self-denial. But for this, peace is necessary. Be assured of this, my dear Sir, that if we engage in a war during our present passions & our present weakness in some quarters, that our union runs the greatest risk of not coming out of that war in the shape in which it enters it.

Silhouette of John Marshall as an older man, by William H. Brown

P olitical factionalism reached new heights that summer in Philadelphia. Jefferson described the atmosphere to Edward Rutledge, a colleague in the old Continental Congress.

Philadelphia June 24. [17]97.
You & I have formerly seen warm debates and high political passions. But gentlemen of different politics would
then speak to each other, & separate the business of
the senate from that of society. It is not so now. Men
who have been intimate all their lives cross the streets
to avoid meeting, & turn their heads another way,
lest they should be obliged to touch their hat.

In a letter more than six months later, Jefferson explained to John Wise of Virginia what he thought were the differences
between the first two major political parties to develop in America.

Philadelphia February 12. 1798.
It is now well understood that two political Sects have
arisen within the U.S. the one believing that the executive is the branch of our government which the most
needs support; the other that like the analogous branch
in the English Government, it is already too strong
for the republican parts of the constitution; and therefore in equivocal cases they incline to the legislative
powers: the former of these are called federalists, sometimes aristocrats or monocrats, and sometimes tories,
after the corresponding sect in the English Government
of exactly the same definition: the latter are stiled republicans, whigs, jacobins, anarchists, disorganizers
&c. these terms are in familiar use with most persons...
both parties claim to be federalists and republicans, and
I believe with truth as to the great mass of them....

John Wayles Eppes by St. Mémin

As June drew to a close, Jefferson waited impatiently
for the Senate adjournment that would allow him to "exchange the roar &
tumult of bulls & bears, for the prattle of my grand-children & senile rest."
Family life at Monticello was becoming even more idyllic, for young Mary
had fallen in love with her cousin, John Wayles Eppes. Jefferson wrote
lightheartedly of the engagement to his older daughter, Martha Randolph.

Philadelphia June 8. 1797.
I now see our fireside formed into a groupe, no one member of which has a fibre in their composition which can
ever produce any jarring or jealousies among us. No
irregular passions, no dangerous bias, which may render problematical the future fortunes and happiness of
our descendants.

Even at Monticello, Jefferson could not escape reminders of the political animosities he had left behind. His enemies skillfully used and misused his own words to hound him. A garbled version of his letter to Philip Mazzei, with its reference to the "Samsons" and "Solomons" who had succumbed to British influence, had been published in a New York newspaper. Federalists labeled the letter an attack on Washington. That implication was a distortion, but, as Jefferson explained to Madison in August, there seemed no way to defend himself without making the situation even worse.

Monticello, Aug 3, [17]97.
I first met with it [the published Mazzei letter] at Bladensburgh, and for a moment concieved I must take the field of the public papers. I could not disavow it wholly, because the greatest part was mine in substance tho' not in form. I could not avow it as it stood because the form was not mine, and in one place the substance very materially falsified. This then would render explanations necessary. Nay, it would render proofs of the whole necessary, & draw me at length into a publication of all (even the secret) transactions of the administration while I was of it; and embroil me personally with every member of the Executive, with the Judiciary, and with others still. I soon decided in my own mind to be entirely silent.... Now it would be impossible for me to explain this publicly without bringing on a personal difference between Genl. Washington & myself, which nothing before the publication of this letter has ever done. It would embroil me also with all those with whom his character is still popular, that is to say, nine tenths of the people of the U S. And what good would be obtained by my avowing the letter with the necessary explanations? Very little indeed in my opinion to counterbalance a good deal of harm.

In a Federalist cartoon entitled "The Providential Detection," an American eagle prevents Jefferson, with the letter to Mazzei in his hand, from burning the Constitution on an "Altar to Gallic Despotism."

When Jefferson left Monticello in December for the second session of the Fifth Congress, he did so with none of the optimism he had felt on his journey to the inauguration. Adams seemed to be under the control of his High Federalist advisors, and Jefferson was increasingly forced to assume the leadership of the opposition. Isolated, almost ostracized by Federalists in and out of Congress that winter, Jefferson's evenings were almost entirely "philosophical," his social life confined to close friends and political associates and members of the American Philosophical Society of which he was then president. He went out of his way to avoid social occasions that might be politically embarrassing, and in Federalist Philadelphia, that meant such polite evasions as "attention to Health" in declining an invitation to a ball.

A membership certificate in the American Philosophical Society signed by Jefferson, as president, for architect Benjamin Latrobe

[Philadelphia,] Feb. 23. [17]98.

Th: Jefferson presents his respects to Mr. [Thomas] Willing, and other gentlemen managers of the ball of this evening. He hopes his non-attendance will not be misconstrued. He has not been at a ball these twenty years, nor for a long time permitted himself to go to any entertainments of the evening, from motives of attention to health. On these grounds he excused to Genl. Washington then living in the city his not going to his birthnight; to Mrs. Washington her evenings; to Mr. Adams his soirées; and to all and sundry who have been so good as to invite him to tea and card parties. Tho desirous to go to them it is an indulgence which his age and habits will he hopes obtain and continue to him. He has always testified his homage to the occasion by his subscription to it.

Adams's coolness was becoming even more marked. Another of Jefferson's letters to a friend, its criticism of the administration misquoted and exaggerated, had been reported to the President in the fall. "It will be a motive," Adams commented to his informant, "in addition to many others, for me to be upon my guard. It is evidence of a mind, soured, yet seeking for popularity, and eaten to a honeycomb with ambition, yet weak, confused, uninformed, and ignorant." Thus Adams dismissed the integrity and intelligence of a man he had known and trusted for more than twenty years. Franklin had once said that Adams was "always an honest man, often a wise one, but sometimes and in some things absolutely out of his senses." And so he must have seemed to Jefferson, who filled the *Anas* that winter with notes on the President's remarks. Jefferson recorded Adams's blunt comments on popular government after a dinner conversation in February, 1798.

Anas

Feb. 15. 98.... That as to trusting to a popular assembly for the preservn of our liberties it was the merest chimœra imaginable. They never had any rule of decision but their own will. That he would as lieve be again in the hands of our old committees of safety who made the law & executed it at the same time. That it had been observed by some writer (I forget whom he named) that anarchy did more mischief in one night than tyranny in a age.... The point in which he views our Senate, as the Colossus of the constitution serves as a key to the politics of the Senate, who are two thirds of them in his sentiments, and accounts for the bold line of conduct they pursue.

Barred from Cabinet conferences, Jefferson was not privy to all the information that influenced Adams's conduct of foreign policy. In March, news arrived that required no inside knowledge for evaluation: France planned to seize neutral ships carrying British goods, and Gerry, Pinckney, and Marshall had been denied recognition. Instead, Talleyrand, the Minister of Foreign Affairs, had referred the diplomats to three agents, designated in their dispatches as X, Y, and Z. The commissioners were told, diplomatically but clearly that they might win recognition and hope to begin negotiations with the Directory if America provided a sizable bribe for the Directory and a large loan to France, the terms of repayment to be almost indefinite. Just as clearly, if less diplomatically, the commissioners had replied: "No; no; not a sixpence." Jefferson indicated to Edmund Pendleton that the only possible Republican response that spring was to try to buy time.

Philadelphia Apr. 2. [17]98.
The only source of anxiety therefore is to avoid war for the present moment. If we can defeat the measures leading to that during this session, so as to gain this summer, time will be given as well for the tide of the public mind to make itself felt, as for the operations of France to have their effect in England as well as here. If on the contrary war is forced on, the tory interest continues dominant, and to them alone must be left, as they alone desire to ride on the whirlwind & direct the storm. The present period therefore of two or three weeks is the most eventful ever known since that of 1775. and will decide whether the principles established by that contest are to prevail or give way to those they subverted.

Talleyrand

Jefferson anticipated, correctly, that time was on the Republicans' side. Writing in May, he foresaw that the expense of internal defence would be an important "sedative" for the war fever.

Philadelphia, May 9, [17]98.
At this moment all the passions are boiling over, and one who keeps himself cool and clear of the contagion, is

283

so far below the point of ordinary conversation, that he finds himself insulated in every society. However, the fever will not last. War, land tax & stamp act, are sedatives which must clam it's ardor. They will bring on reflection, and that, with information, is all which our countrymen need, to bring themselves and their affairs to rights. They are essentially republican. They retain unadulterated the principles of 75. and those who are conscious of no change in themselves, have nothing to fear in the long run.

The Adams administration reached its height of popularity that spring and summer, but Federalists did not succeed in forcing America into war or even press for particularly effective defense measures. Rather, they provided for a makeshift army of "provisional" troops, to be commanded by George Washington from his retreat at Mount Vernon. While settling for a quasi war with France, they launched a full-scale campaign against Republicans at home with a series of statutes known as the Alien and Sedition Acts. When Jefferson first heard of the bills, he believed that the mass of the people would not be swayed by them. In discussing them with Madison, he still expected taxes to be the Republicans' best issue.

An Act

To suspend the commercial intercourse between the United States and France, and the dependencies thereof.

BE it enacted by the Senate and House of Representatives of the United States of America in Congress assembled, That no ship or vessel, owned, hired, or employed, wholly or in part, by any person resident within the United States, and which shall depart therefrom after the first day of July next, shall be allowed to proceed directly, or from any intermediate port or place, to any port or place within the territory of the French Republic, or the dependencies thereof, or to any place in the West-Indies, or elsewhere, under the acknowledged government of France, or shall be employed in any traffic or commerce with or for any person resident within the jurisdiction, or under the authority of the French Republic. And if any ship or vessel, in any voyage thereafter commencing, and before her return within the United States, shall be voluntarily carried, or suffered to proceed to any French port or place as aforesaid, or shall be employed as aforesaid, contrary to the intent hereof, every such ship or vessel together with her cargo shall be forfeited, and shall accrue, the one half to the use of the United States, and the other half to the use of any person or persons, citizens of the United States, who shall inform and prosecute for the same; and shall be liable to be seized, prosecuted and condemned in any circuit or district court of the United States which shall be holden within or for the district where the seizure shall be made.

Detail from printed act of Congress to suspend commercial intercourse with France after July 1, 1798

Philadelphia, April 26, 1798.

One of the war party, in a fit of unguarded passion, declared some time ago they would pass a citizen bill, an alien bill, & a sedition bill. Accordingly, some days ago, [Joshua] Coit laid a motion on the table of the H. of R. for modifying the citizen law.... Yesterday mr. [James] Hillhouse laid on the table of the Senate a motion for giving power to send away suspected aliens.... There is now only wanting, to accomplish the whole declaration beforementioned, a sedition bill which we shall certainly soon see proposed. The object of that is the suppression of the whig presses.... The popular movement in the eastern states is checked as we expected: and war addresses are showering in from New Jersey & the great trading towns. However, we still trust that a nearer view of war & a land tax will oblige the great mass of the people to attend.

The temper of Congress at the end of the session had gone from immoderate to hysterical. Jefferson prayed for an adjournment. "To separate Congress now," he wrote Madison on June 21, "will be withdrawing the fire from under a boiling pot." Congress did not "separate" until July, several weeks after Jefferson left Philadelphia, but he was familiar with the contents of the acts that had been passed. The Alien Enemies Act was the least offensive: it provided for the deportation of aliens from a country with which the United States was at war. The Naturalization Act extended the residence requirements for naturalization. The Alien Friends Act was especially disturbing: it granted almost unlimited power to the President to imprison or deport aliens he deemed dangerous. But the Sedition Act, which became law on July 4, ten days after Jefferson's return to Monticello, was even worse and, because it affected the rights of American citizens, was of much greater value as a political issue. This statute provided fines and imprisonment for those who conspired to prevent the execution of federal laws and for those who published "any false, scandalous and malicious writing" that criticized the President, Congress, or government.

At Monticello, away from the madness of Philadelphia for the summer, Jefferson calmly considered what the Republican reaction should be. He was confident that the essentially republican spirit of the people would re-assert itself, but he was worried by rumors of disunion and even threats of secession that were circulating. On June 4, Jefferson wrote firmly to John Taylor of Caroline County, Virginia, who had suggested that the time had come for his state and North Carolina to consider withdrawing from the Union in order to escape the domination of New England Federa-alists. It was not personal or party interests but patriotism that prompted Jefferson to draft an outspoken repudiation of such a move.

Philadelphia June 4 [17]98

...in every free and deliberating society, there must from the nature of man be opposite parties, and violent dissensions and discords; and one of these for the most part must prevail over the other for a longer or shorter time. Perhaps this party division is necessary to induce each to watch and debate to the people the proceedings of the other. But if on a temporary superiority of the one party, the other is to resort to a scission of the union, no federal government can ever exist. If to rid ourselves of the present rule of Massachusets and Connecticut, we break the union, will the evil stop there? Suppose the N. England States alone cut off, will our natures be changed? Are we not men still to the South of that, and with all the passions of men? Immediately, we shall see a Pennsylvania and a Virginia party arise in the residuary confederacy, and the public mind will be dis-tracted with the same party spirit. . . . If we reduce our Union to Virginia and N. Carolina, immediately the conflict will be established between the representatives of these two states, and they will end by breaking into their simple units. Seeing therefore that an association of men who will not quarrel with one another is a thing which never yet existed, from the greatest confederacy of nations down to a town meeting or a vestry, seeing that we must have somebody to quarrel with, I had rather keep our New England associates for that purpose, than to see our bickerings transferred to others.... A little patience, and we shall see the reign of witches pass over, their spells dissolve, and the people recovering their true sight, restore their government to it's true principles. It is true that in the meantime we are suffering deeply in spirit, and incurring the horrors of a war, and long oppressions of enormous public debt. But who can say what would be the evils of a scission and when and where they would end?... If the game runs sometimes against us at home, we must have patience, till luck turns, and then we shall have an opportunity of winning back the *principles* we have lost. For this is a game where principles are the stake.

The passage of the Alien and Sedition Acts gave secessionists even better arguments than the war preparations had: not only were New England merchants ready to force the rest of the nation into a ruinous war to defend their economic interests but the Federalists had used the issue of national security to muffle dissent. The Adams administration seemed to be the enemy of the commercial and diplomatic interests of the South and West and the enemy of the civil liberties of any who differed with its policy as well. In an August letter to Samuel Smith, a Maryland Republican leader, Jefferson weighed his desire to publicize his own sentiments and his lifelong determination "never to put a sentence into any newspaper."

Monticello Aug. 22. [17]98.
I know my own principles to be pure, & therefore am not ashamed of them. On the contrary I wish them known, & therefore willingly express them to every one. They are the same I have acted on from the year 75. to this day, and are the same, I am sure, with those of the great body of the American people. I only wish the real principles of those who censure mine were also known. But, warring against those of the people, the delusion of the people is necessary to the dominant party....

...At a very early period of my life, I determined

Wilson Cary Nicholas

never to put a sentence into any newspaper. I have religiously adhered to the resolution through my life, and have great reason to be contented with it. Were I to undertake to answer the calumnies of the newspapers, it would be more than all my own time, & that of 20. aids could effect. For while I should be answering one, twenty new ones would be invented. I have thought it better to trust to the justice of my countrymen, that they would judge me by what they *see* of my conduct on the stage where they have placed me, & what they knew of me *before* the epoch since which a particular party has supposed it might answer some view of theirs to vilify me in the public eye.

Even had Jefferson been willing to take up his pen, as the Vice President he could submit nothing over his own name. The alternative action he chose was the preparation of resolutions to be introduced in a state legislature. Resolves were drafted sometime in September and then dispatched to Wilson Cary Nicholas, a Virginia Republican, who persuaded Jefferson they would gain a sympathetic hearing in Kentucky. Nicholas passed the draft on to John Breckinridge, a former Albemarle County resident who was on his way to Kentucky, after Jefferson had received "a solemn assurance, which I strictly required, that it should not be known from what quarter they came."

This promise was the more necessary because of the tone of the resolutions and the controversial concept of state and federal relations they espoused. In an effort to save the Union, Jefferson outlined a philosophical argument that would later be used by the very secessionists he hoped to quiet: the doctrine that states might nullify federal laws they deemed unconstitutional. The resolutions opened with Jefferson's contention (stated in his opinion on the Bank in 1791) that the implied powers of the federal government could not include any of the powers reserved to the "states respectively, or to the people" and that the Federalist statutes of June and July, 1798, clearly infringed on those rights. They closed with a proposal for a committee of correspondence that would communicate these views to other state legislatures with certain assurances.

[November, 1798]

... to assure them that this commonwealth continues in the same esteem of their friendship and union which it has manifested from that moment at which a common danger first suggested a common union: that it considers union ... to be friendly to the peace, happiness, and prosperity of all the states: that faithful to that com-

287

*Resolutions, in Jefferson's hand,
on the Alien and Sedition Acts*

pact, according to the plain intent and meaning in which it was understood and acceded to by the several parties, it is sincerely anxious for it's preservation: that it does also believe, that to take from the States all the powers of self-government and transfer them to a general and consolidated government, without regard to the special delegations and reservations solemnly agreed to in that compact, is not for the peace, happiness, or prosperity of these States; and that therefore this commonwealth is determined...to submit to undelegated, and consequently unlimited powers in no man, or body of men on earth: that in cases of an abuse of the delegated powers, the members of the general government, being chosen by the people, a change by the people would be the constitutional remedy; but, where powers are assumed which have not been delegated, a nullification of the act is the rightful remedy: that every State has a natural right in cases not within the compact...to nullify of their own authority all assumptions of power by others within their limits....

[It was with "its co-States" alone that the legislature should properly communicate, since the states were "solely authorized to judge" the constitutionality of federal acts, "congress being not a party, but merely the creature of the compact." Then Jefferson pointed out the consequences of allowing the statutes in question to stand unchallenged.]

...that the General government may place any act they think proper on the list of crimes, and punish it themselves whether enumerated or not enumerated by the constitution as cognisable by them; that they may transfer it's cognisance to the President, or any other person, who may himself be the accuser, counsel, judge and jury, whose *suspicions* may be the evidence, his *order* the sentence, his officer the executioner, and his breast the sole record of the transaction: that a very numerous and valuable description of the inhabitants of these states being, by this precedent, reduced, as Outlaws, to the absolute dominion of one man, and the barrier of the constitution thus swept away for us all, no rampart now remains against the passions and the powers of a majority in Congress, to protect from a like exportation, or other more grievous punishment the minority of the same body...who may venture to reclaim the constitutional rights and liberties of the States and people, or who for other causes, good or bad, may be obnoxious to the views, or marked by the suspicions of the President, or be thought dangerous to his or their elections, or other interests public or personal: that the friendless alien has indeed been selected as the safest subject of a first experiment; but the citizen will soon follow, or rather, has already followed; for already has a Sedition act marked him as it's prey....

["Unless arrested," the Federalist program would drive America "into revolution and blood," and democracy would suffer throughout the world.]

It would be a dangerous delusion were a confidence in the men of our choice to silence our fears for the safety of our rights: that confidence is everywhere the parent of despotism—free government is founded in jealousy, and not in confidence; it is jealousy and not confidence which prescribes limited constitutions, to bind down those whom we are obliged to trust with power: that our Constitution has accordingly fixed the limits to which, and no further, our confidence may go; and let the honest advocate of confidence read the Alien and Sedition acts, and say if the Constitution has not been wise in fixing limits to the government it created, and whether we should be wise in destroying those limits. Let him say what the government is, if it be not a tyranny, which the men of our choice have conferred on our President, and the President of our choice has assented to....In questions of power, then, let no more be heard of confidence in man, but bind him down from mischief by the chains of the Constitution.

Jefferson's response had been prompted by his conviction that the Alien and Sedition Acts were part of a concerted plan to change the form of American government. A few weeks after dispatching the resolutions to Nicholas, he predicted a "federalist reign of terror" to Senator Stevens Thomson Mason of Virginia.

Monticello Oct. 11. [17]98.

For my own part I consider those laws as merely an experiment on the American mind to see how far it will bear an avowed violation of the constitution. If this goes down, we shall immediately see attempted another act of Congress, declaring that the President shall continue in office during life, reserving to another occasion the transfer of the succession to his heirs, and the establishment of the Senate for life.... That these things are in contemplation, I have no doubt, nor can I be confident of their failure, after the dupery of which our countrymen have shewn themselves susceptible.

The Kentucky Resolutions of 1798 were adopted by that state's legislature in November with the mention of nullification deleted. Together with the more moderate resolves Madison drafted and steered through the Virginia legislature in December, they went far toward curing Americans of their "dupery." On returning to Philadelphia in December, Jefferson found other promising signs that the climate of public opinion and the tide of political events were becoming more favorable to the Republicans. Letters from Europe indicated that the Directory sincerely wished to negotiate. In mid-January, Jefferson sent Madison that news and suggested that the time was ripe for him to publish his personal notes of the debates in the Federal Convention of 1787.

> Philadelphia, Jan. 16. [17] 99.
>
> In a society of members between whom & yourself is great mutual esteem & respect, a most anxious desire is expressed that you would publish your debates of the Convention. That these measures of the army, navy & direct tax will bring about a revulsion of public sentiment is thought certain, & that the constitution will then recieve a different explanation. Could those debates be ready to appear critically, their effect would be decisive. I beg of you to turn this subject in your mind. The arguments against it will be personal; those in favor of it moral; and something is required from you as a set-off against the sin of your retirement.... I pray you always to examine the seals of mine to you, & the strength of the impression. The suspicions against the government on this subject are strong.

Jefferson's admonition to Madison to examine the seals of his letters for signs of tampering betrayed the tense mood during the brief congressional session. In reopening his correspondence with Elbridge

Gerry, Jefferson was even more cautious. He concluded the letter with instructions that Gerry destroy "at least the 2d & 3d leaves." Written to a man who was politically loyal to Adams but unsympathetic to the principles of the High Federalists, Jefferson's statement of Republican policy was almost a party platform.

Philada. Jan. 26. 1799.

I do then with sincere zeal wish an inviolable preservation of our present federal constitution, according to the true sense in which it was adopted by the states, that in which it was advocated by it's friends, & not that which it's enemies apprehended, who therefore became it's enemies: and I am opposed to the monarchising it's features by the forms of it's administration, with a view to conciliate a first transition to a President & Senate for life, & from that to a hereditary tenure of these offices, & thus to worm out the elective principle. I am for preserving to the states the powers not yielded by them to the Union, & to the legislature of the Union it's constitutional share in the division of powers: and I am not for transferring all the powers of the states to the general government, & all those of that government to the Executive Branch. I am for a government rigorously frugal & simple, applying all the possible savings of the public revenue to the discharge of the national debt: and not for a multiplication of officers & salaries merely to make partizans, & for increasing, by every device, the public debt, on the principle of it's being a public blessing. I am for relying, for internal defence, on our militia solely till actual invasion, and for such a naval force only as may protect our coasts and harbours from such depredations as we have experienced: and not for a standing army in time of peace which may overawe the public sentiment; nor for a navy which by it's own expences and the eternal wars in which it will implicate us, will grind us with public burthens, & sink us under them. I am for free commerce with all nations, political connection with none, & little or no diplomatic establishment: and I am not for linking ourselves by new treaties with the quarrels of Europe; entering that field of slaughter to preserve their balance, or joining in the confederacy of kings to war against the principles of liberty. I am for freedom of religion, & against all maneuvres to bring about a legal ascendancy of one sect over another: for freedom of the press, & against

Engraving after a lost portrait by the Polish patriot Thaddeus Kosciusko, who depicted the Vice President with a crown of laurel

291

all violations of the constitution to silence by force & not by reason the complaints or criticisms, just or unjust, of our citizens against the conduct of their agents. And I am for encouraging the progress of science in all it's branches; and not for raising a hue and cry against the sacred name of philosophy, for awing the human mind by stories of rawhead & bloody bones, to a distrust of its own vision & to repose implicitly on that of others; to go backwards instead of forwards to look for improvement, to believe that government, religion, morality, & every other science were in the highest perfection in ages of the darkest ignorance, and that nothing can ever be devised more perfect than what was established by our forefathers. To these I will add, that I was a sincere wellwisher to the success of the French revolution, and still wish it may end in the establishment of a free & wellordered republic: but I have not been insensible under the atrocious depredations they have committed on our commerce. The first object of my heart is my own country. In that is embarked my family, my fortune, & my own existence. I have not one farthing of interest, nor one fibre of attachment out of it, nor a single motive of preference of any one nation to another, but in proportion as they are more or less friendly to us.

Engraving from Century *magazine of chair, bench, and table Jefferson put together for more comfortable letter-writing as he grew older*

Gerry did not acknowledge this letter, but if Jefferson was indeed seeking recruits for the Republicans, he found many others that winter and spring. Adams, surprising Federalists and Republicans alike, had abruptly announced that he would resume negotiations with the French as soon as the United States received assurances that new envoys would be received courteously. After returning to Monticello in March, Jefferson prepared an optimistic political summary for Thomas Lomax, a Tidewater Virginian.

Monticello Mar. 12. 1799.

The spirit of 1776. is not dead. It has only been slumbering. The body of the American people is substantially republican. But their virtuous feelings have been played on by some fact with more fiction. They have been the dupes of artful maneuvres, & made for a moment to be willing instruments in forging chains for themselves. But time & truth have dissipated the delusion, & opened their eyes. They see now that France has sincerely wished peace, & their seducers have wished

war, as well for the loaves & fishes which arise out of
war expences, as for the chance of changing the constitution, while the people should have time to contemplate nothing but the levies of men and money.
Pennsylvania, Jersey & N York are coming majestically
round to the true principles....Those three States
will be solidly embodied in sentiment with the six
Southern & Western ones.

While awaiting French assurances of good faith,
Jefferson outlined to Madison a Republican program for developing public
discussion during the summer. Because of his position and his own love of
privacy, Jefferson was unwilling to become a public spokesman, but he
encouraged others to write for the newspapers.

[Philadelphia,] Feb. 5. [17]99.
The public sentiment being now on the creen [careen],
and many heavy circumstances about to fall into the
republican scale, we are sensible that this summer is
the season for systematic energies & sacrifices. The
engine is the press. Every man must lay his purse & his
pen under contribution. As to the former it is possible
I may be obliged to assume something for you. As to
the latter, let me pray & beseech you to set apart a
certain portion of every post-day to write what may
be proper for the public. Send it to me while here, &
when I go away I will let you know to whom you may
send so that your name shall be sacredly secret.

After March 1 Jefferson spent most of the year at
Monticello, and as the spring and summer wore on, he carefully refrained
from making any contributions of his own to the political war he had initiated. But he was always ready to act as host or to arrange meetings for
Republicans who might wish to confer on public affairs. In August he
wrote Wilson Cary Nicholas of the agenda he had planned for him and
Madison with the Kentucky and Virginia legislatures.

Monticello, Aug. 26, [17]99.
I am deeply impressed with the importance of Virginia
& Kentuckey pursuing the same track at the ensuing
sessions of their legislatures. Your going thither furnishes
a valuable opportunity of effecting it, and as mr. Madison will be at our assembly as well as yourself, I thought
it important to procure a meeting between you. I there-

fore wrote to propose to him to ride to this place on Saturday or Sunday next supposing that both he and yourself might perhaps have some matter of business at our court which might render it less inconvenient for you to be here together on Sunday. I...hope and strongly urge your favoring us with a visit at the time proposed. Mrs. Madison, who was the bearer of my letter, assured me I might count on mr. M.'s being here. Not that I mentioned to her the object of my request, or that I should propose the same to you; because I presume the less said of such a meeting the better. I shall take care that Monroe shall dine with us.

Jefferson's role as party leader and coordinator of strategy was recognized by his enemies as well as his friends. He had planned to visit Madison at his home in Orange County en route to Philadelphia for the congressional session. Sadly, he wrote Madison that James Monroe had persuaded him such a meeting would be unwise.

George Washington BY WOODROW WILSON, 1897

James Madison's home, Montpelier

Monticello Nov. 22. [17] 99.

Colo. Monroe dined with us yesterday, and on my asking his commands for you, he entered into the subject of the visit and dissuaded it entirely, founding the motives on the espionage of the little wretch in Charlottesville [the postmaster] who would make it a subject of some political slander, and perhaps of some political injury. I have yeilded to his representations, and therefore shall not have the pleasure of seeing you till my return from Philadelphia. I regret it sincerely, not only on motives of affection but of affairs. Some late circumstances change considerably the aspect of our situation and must affect the line of conduct to be observed. I regret it the more too, because from the commencement of the ensuing session, I shall trust the post offices with nothing confidential, persuaded that during the ensuing twelve-month they will lend their inquisitorial aid to furnish matter for new slanders. I shall send you as usual printed communications, without saying anything confidential on them. You will of course understand the cause.

The "ensuing twelve-month" would be a critical period, since 1800 was an election year. The Federalists had begun quarreling among themselves and would never regain their strength of the year before. Jefferson clearly would be the Republican candidate. His fears of interference with his mail, however, meant that he had more leisure than usual that winter in Philadelphia. Madison did not receive the usual detailed, time-consuming descriptions of congressional politics, and Jefferson had time to consider such nonpolitical projects as the creation of a "broad & liberal & modern" university for Virginia. In that endeavor he sought the expert advice of Joseph Priestley, the British Unitarian clergyman-scientist who had emigrated to Pennsylvania.

Philadelphia Jan. 18. 1800.

We have in that state a college (Wm. & Mary) just well enough endowed to draw out the miserable existence to which a miserable constitution has doomed it. It is moreover eccentric in it's position, exposed to bilious diseases as all the lower country is, & therefore abandoned by the public care, as that part of the country itself is in a considerable degree by it's inhabitants. We wish to establish in the upper & healthier country, & more centrally for the state an University on a plan so broad & liberal & *modern,* as to be worth patronising with the public support, and be a temptation to the youth of other states to come, and drink of the cup of knolege & fraternize with us. The first step is to obtain a good plan; that is a judicious selection of the sciences, & a practicable grouping of some of them together, & ramifying of others, so as to adapt the professorships to our uses, & our means. In an institution meant chiefly for use, some branches of science, formerly esteemed, may be now omitted, so may others now valued in Europe, but useless to us for ages to come.... Now there is no one to whom this subject is so familiar as yourself.... To you therefore we address our sollicitations. And to lessen to you as much as possible the ambiguities of our object, I will venture even to sketch the sciences which seem useful & practicable for us, as they occur to me while holding my pen. Botany. Chemistry. Zoology. Anatomy. Surgery. Medecine. Natl. Philosophy. Agriculture. Mathematics. Astronomy. Geology. Geography. Politics. Commerce. History. Ethics. Law. Arts. Fine arts. This list is imperfect because I make it hastily, and because I am unequal to the subject. It is evident that some of these articles are too much for one professor & must therefore be ramified; others may be ascribed in groups to a single professor. This is the difficult part of

Joseph Priestley by Ellen Sharples

the work, & requires a head perfectly knowing the extent of each branch, & the limits within which it may be circumscribed; so as to bring the whole within the powers of the fewest professors possible, & consequently within the degree of expence practicable for us.

On the rare occasions when a confidential means of communication was available, Jefferson did what he could to supervise the campaign, or what passed for a campaign in 1800. Learning that two trusted friends planned to ride to Virginia, Jefferson wrote Governor James Monroe of Republican prospects in other regions as described to him by Aaron Burr ("113" in his code). The brilliant and flamboyant New York congressman had reported on the Federalist-Republican balance in that state's bicameral legislature. New York was one of several states in which the legislature appointed presidential electors.

[Philadelphia,] Jan. 12. 1800.

I have had today a conversation with 113, who has taken a flying trip here from N. Y. He says, they have really now a majority in the H. of R. but for want of some skilful person to rally around, they are disjointed, & will lose every question. In the Senate there is a majority of 8. or 9. against us. But in the new election which is to come on in April, three or 4. in the Senate will be changed in our favor; & in the H. of R. the county elections will still be better than the last: but still all will depend on the City election, which is of 12. members. At present there would be no doubt of our carrying our ticket there; nor does there seem to be time for any events arising to change that disposition. There is therefore the best prospect possible of a great & decided majority on a joint vote of the two houses. They are so confident of this that the Republican party there will not consent to elect either by districts or a general ticket. They chuse to do it by their legislature. I am told the Republicans of N. J. are equally confident, & equally anxious against an election either by districts or a general ticket. . . . Perhaps it will be thought I ought in delicacy to be silent on this subject. But you, who know me, know that my private gratifications would be most indulged by that issue which should leave me most at home. If anything supersedes this propensity, it is merely the desire to see this government brought back to it's republican principles.

At the end of the Senate session in May Jefferson was free to communicate in person with his trusted lieutenants in Virginia, and he carried news that made the outcome of the fall elections almost a foregone conclusion. Aaron Burr had done his work well in New York City where the April polls gave Republicans control of the state legislature. New York's support would probably insure a Republican victory in November. In a later letter to Benjamin Rush, Jefferson recalled a painful meeting with John Adams shortly after word of those results reached Philadelphia.

Aaron Burr by Gilbert Stuart, 1794

Monticello Jan. 16. 1811.

On the day on which we learned in Philadelphia the vote of the city of New York, which it was well known would decide the vote of the state, and that again the vote of the Union, I called on Mr. Adams on some official business. He was very sensibly affected, and accosted me with these words: 'Well, I understand that you are to beat me in this contest, and I will only say that I will be as faithful a subject as any you will have.' 'Mr. Adams, said I, this is no personal contest between you & me. Two systems of principles on the subject of government divide our fellow-citizens into two parties. With one of these you concur, and I with the other. As we have been longer on the public stage than most of those now living, our names happen to be more generally known. One of these parties therefore has put your name at it's head, the other mine. Were we both to die to-day, tomorrow two other names would be in the place of ours, without any change in the motion of the machine. It's motion is from its principle, not from you or myself.' 'I believe you are right, said he, that we are but passive instruments, and should not suffer this matter to affect our personal dispositions.'

In large part as a reward for his role in winning New York, Burr was chosen as Jefferson's running mate at a caucus of congressional Republicans. Perhaps because Adams's partisans knew they had little chance of victory, they launched an extremely vicious campaign in the press. The President's decision to send envoys to France at the end of 1799 had destroyed any war issue the Federalists might have hoped to use and had infuriated Alexander Hamilton, the Inspector General of the provisional troops which were now disbanded. Hamilton had mobilized strong opposition to Adams within his own party, and Federalist journalists had little to offer on their own behalf but slanders on Jefferson. That year he was accused of every sin from Jacobinism to atheism. He ignored most of these calumnies but could not resist replying to one Uriah McGregory of Connecticut, who had inquired concerning reports that Jefferson had defrauded a poverty-stricken widow and her children. Although Jefferson cautioned the unknown McGregory to keep his reply secret, he must have expected and hoped that it would be publicized.

Monticello Aug. 13. 1800.

From the moment that a portion of my fellow citizens looked towards me with a view to one of their highest offices, the floodgates of calumny have been opened upon me; not where I am personally known, where their slanders would be instantly judged and suppressed from a general sense of their falsehood; but in the remote parts of the union, where the means of detection are not at hand, and the trouble of an enquiry is greater than would suit the hearers to undertake. I know that I might have filled the courts of the United States with actions for these slanders, & have ruined perhaps many persons who are not innocent. But this would be no equivalent to the loss of character. I leave them therefore to the reproof of their own consciences. If these do not condemn them, there will yet come a day when the false witness will meet a judge who has not slept over his slanders.

With trusted personal friends, Jefferson could be more frank about his anger at attacks on his character. Sermons preached from some pulpits concerning his religious views prompted Jefferson to send Benjamin Rush a personal defense that evolved into a stirring statement of his views on freedom of conscience versus religious bigotry.

Monticello Sep. 23. 1800.

I promised you a letter on Christianity, which I have not forgotten. On the contrary it is because I have reflected on it, that I find much more time necessary for it than I can at present dispose of. I have a view of the subject which ought to displease neither the rational Christian or Deist; & would reconcile many to a character they have too hastily rejected. I do not know however that it would reconcile the genus irritabile vatum, who are all in arms against me. Their hostility is on too interesting ground to be softened. The delusions into which the XYZ plot shewed it possible to push the people, the successful experiment made under the prevalence of that delusion, on the clause of the constitution which while it secured the freedom of the press, covered also the freedom of religion, had given to the clergy a very favorite hope of obtaining an establishment of a particular form of Christianity, thro' the US. And as every sect believes it's own form the true one, every one perhaps hoped for it's own: but especially the Episcopalians & Congregationalists. The returning good sense of our country threatens abortion to their hopes, & they believe that any portion of power confided to me will be exerted in opposition to their schemes. And they believe truly. For I have sworn upon the altar of god eternal hostility against every form of tyranny over the mind of man.

At the end of November, Jefferson left Monticello for the last time as Vice President. He would await final news of the election at Washington, the new capital city on the Potomac. By mid-December, his and Burr's victory in the state votes for electors was confirmed. But Federalists in Congress were not ready to admit defeat. Under the cumbersome system for choosing a President each elector was granted two votes, but the Constitution did not stipulate that these could be cast separately for President and Vice President. If each Republican elector cast votes for Jefferson and Burr, the two would be tied and the final decision would rest in a vote by the House of Representatives. To allow for this, the Republicans planned to withhold a few votes from Burr. Jefferson presented the problem to the vice-presidential candidate, tactfully combining a discussion of a possible tie vote with a gracious compliment to Burr's abilities.

Public Men, SULLIVAN

The city of Washington in 1800

Aaron Burr's daughter, Theodosia, was engaged to Joseph Alston of South Carolina who supported his prospective father-in-law against Jefferson in the House vote.

Washington Dec. 15. 1800.

Although we have not official information of the votes for President & Vice President...yet the state of the votes is given on such evidence, as satisfies both parties that the two Republican candidates stand highest....we know enough to be certain that what it is surmised will be withheld will still leave you 4. or 5. votes at least above Mr. A. However it was badly managed not to have arranged with certainty what seems to have been left to hazard. It was the more material because I understand several of the highflying federalists have expressed their hope that the two republican tickets may be equal, & their determination in that case to prevent a choice by the H. of R. (which they are strong enough to do) and let the government devolve on a President of the Senate. Decency required that I should be so entirely passive during the late contest that I never once asked whether arrangements had been made to prevent so many from dropping votes intentionally as might frustrate half the republican wish; nor did I doubt till lately that such had been made.

While I must congratulate you, my dear Sir, on the issue of this contest, because it is more honourable and doubtless more grateful to you than any station within the competence of the chief magistrate, yet for myself, and for the substantial service of the public, I feel most sensibly the loss we sustain of your aid in our new administration. It leaves a chasm in my arrangements, which cannot be adequately filled up.

The tie Jefferson had feared occurred in the Electoral College: Jefferson and Burr received 73 votes each; Adams and Thomas Pinckney were given 65 and 64 votes, respectively. High Federalists then tried to play the Republican victors against one another in the House vote, which was to be by state delegations, each having only one vote. Luckily for the Republicans, Alexander Hamilton was an even more bitter foe of Burr than of Jefferson, and he urged friends in Congress to accept Jefferson. Senator Gouverneur Morris of New York led a move to gain some preliminary promises from Jefferson as a price for Federalist support. In the midst of this bitter scene—the balloting stretched over a period of six days—Jefferson consulted with Adams. In retelling the incident a dozen years later in the letter to Rush, he recaptured his surprise and pain at the President's reaction.

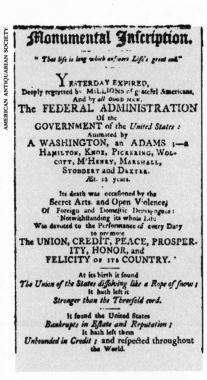

The Columbian Centinel *of Boston lamented Jefferson's election and the expiration of an "animated" government under the Federalists.*

Monticello Jan. 16. 1811.

When the election between Burr and myself was kept in suspence by the federalists, and they were meditating to place the President of the Senate at the head of the government, I called on Mr. Adams with a view to have this desperate measure prevented by his negative. He grew warm in an instant, and said with a vehemence he had not used towards me before, 'Sir, the event of the election is within your own power. You have only to say you will do justice to the public creditors, maintain the navy, and not disturb those holding offices, and the government will instantly be put into your hands. We know it is the wish of the people it should be so.'— 'Mr. Adams, said I, I know not what part of my conduct, in either public or private life, can have authorised a doubt of my fidelity to the public engagements. I say however I will not come into the government by capitulation. I will not enter on it but in perfect freedom to follow the dictates of my own judgment'.... 'Then, said he, things must take their course.' I turned the conversation to something else, and soon took my leave.

Jefferson held firm. He made no promises to the Federalists, and at last, on the thirty-sixth ballot, the House gave him a majority; Federalists in Vermont and Maryland abstained from voting, throwing their states' two votes to Jefferson. The President-elect described the situation to Madison, closing his report on the House vote with a hopeful prediction.

Washington Feb. 18. 1801.

The minority in the H. of R. after seeing the impossibility of electing B. the certainty that a legislative usurpation would be resisted by arms, and a recourse to a Convention to reorganise and amend the government, held a consultation on this dilemma, whether it would be better for them to come over in a body and go with the tide of the times, or by a negative conduct suffer the election to be made by a bare majority, keeping their body entire & unbroken, to act in phalanx on such ground of opposition as circumstances shall offer? We knew their determination on this question only by their vote of yesterday.... There were 10. states for one candidate, 4. for another, & 2. blanks. We consider this therefore as a declaration of war, on the part of this band. But their conduct appears to have brought over to us the whole body of the Federalists, who being alarmed with the danger of a dissolution of the government, had been made most anxiously to wish the very administration they had opposed. . . . They see too their quondam leaders separated fairly from them & themselves aggregated under other banners. . . . This circumstance, with the unbounded confidence which will attach to the new ministry as soon as known, will start us on high ground.

On this optimistic note Jefferson ended his term as Vice President. On February 25, eight days after the deadlock was broken, he sent a message to Thomas Lomax.

Washington Feb. 25. 1801.
The suspension of public opinion from the 11th. to the 17th. the alarm into which it threw all the patriotic part of the federalists, the danger of the dissolution of our union, and unknown consequences of that, brought over the great body of them to wish with anxiety & sollicitude for a choice to which they had before been strenuously opposed. In this state of mind they separated from their Congressional leaders, and came over to us; and the manner in which the last ballot was given, has drawn a fixed line of separation between them and their leaders. . . . I am persuaded that week of ill-judged conduct here, has strengthened us more than years of prudent and conciliatory administration could have done. If we can once more get social intercourse restored to it's pristine harmony, I shall believe we have not lived in vain. And that it may, by rallying them to true republican principles, which few of them had thrown off, I sanguinely hope.

As Jefferson contemplated his duties as Chief Executive, he offered few of the plaintive requests that he be left in domestic retirement with which he had met earlier moves to keep him in public life. He could no longer aim to secure "true republican principles" by urging others to fight tyranny while he withdrew to Monticello. As Madison had recognized in 1796 when he had been urged to seek the Presidency, only Jefferson himself could command the broad public support necessary to counter the policies established during the Federalist era. In 1801 Jefferson accepted that verdict as well.

A Picture Portfolio

Foremost Republican

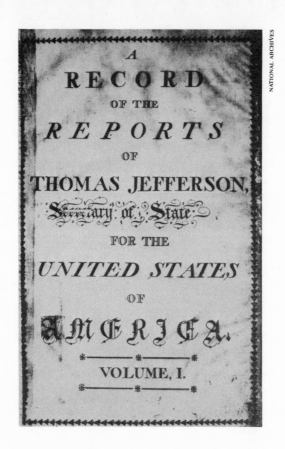

A
RECORD
OF THE
REPORTS
OF
THOMAS JEFFERSON,
Secretary of State
FOR THE
UNITED STATES
OF
AMERICA.
* —— * —— *
VOLUME, I.
* —— * —— *

FIRST SECRETARY OF STATE

In 1789 Jefferson returned home from France for what he expected to be a short leave; instead, he found that George Washington, the nation's first President, had named him to the top-ranking position in his Cabinet—Secretary of State. Although reluctant to quit his post in Paris, Jefferson deferred to Washington's desire: "You are to marshal us as may best be for the public good.... My chief comfort will be to work under your eye." He first met Alexander Hamilton, the brilliant thirty-three-year-old Secretary of the Treasury and his next in rank, at a dinner at the President's House in New York City shortly after he reported for duty in March, 1790. Although the mural at right, painted at a later date by Constantino Brumidi for the Capitol, shows Washington in peaceful consultation with Jefferson and Hamilton, from the outset the two Secretaries were, in Jefferson's words, "pitted like cocks." Jefferson, a republican, a realist, and a nationalist, considered Hamilton an elitist with monarchical leanings, a romantic, and a sectionalist. They often joined in bitter battles, and a torn Washington wrote to Jefferson: "I regret, deeply regret, the difference in opinions which have arisen and divided you and another principal officer of the Government...I have a great, a sincere esteem for you both." As head of the infant Department of State, Jefferson was concerned with matters that ranged from granting patents and devising a uniform system of weights and measures to securing markets for American goods and establishing an untrammeled right of access to the sea via the Mississippi River. He kept a careful record, in handsome folios, of all his reports to Congress; the title page of the first volume is reproduced above.

BY BRUMIDI; ARCHITECT OF THE CAPITOL, WASHINGTON, D.C.

POLITICAL PROGRESSION

The seat of government was moved to Philadelphia in 1790. The Department of State occupied the building at far left, shown with the house in which Jefferson had drafted the Declaration of Independence. In 1793 he rented a charming house on the Schuylkill River (above), but retired at the end of that year. Three years later he became Vice President under his once good friend John Adams (above, right), and in 1800 the tables turned as the victory flag (right) proclaimed: "T. Jefferson President . . . John Adams no more."

307

"FOR JEFFERSON AND LIBERTY"

Jefferson's narrow election was seen by him later as a second American Revolution —"as real a revolution in the principles of government as that of 1776 was in form." He appointed a strong Cabinet, chief among them his close friend James Madison (below, left) as Secretary of State, and declared at the end of his term that he would select the same men if he had to choose again. Madison and his wife Dolley (below, right) lived with Jefferson in the President's House, seen in the center distance in an 1800 view of Washington (above), until they could find their own lodgings. The new President (right in an 1805 portrait by Rembrandt Peale) was honored with a patriotic song: "Rejoice! Columbia's Sons, rejoice! To Tyrants never bend your knee, but join with Heart and Soul and Voice for Jefferson and Liberty."

of kings to govern him? let history — answer this question.

Let us then with courage and confidence pursue our principles of federal republicanism or republic.d federalism

kindly separated by nature & a wide ocean from the ~~exterminating~~ havoc of one quarter of the globe; too high minded to

endure the degradations of the others, possessing a chosen country with room enough for our descendants to the

enjoying the most favorable temperatures of climate, entertaining

thousandth generation, a due sense of our equal right to the use of our own faculties ~~for our own purposes~~

not from birth but

to the acquisitions of our own industry, to ~~the~~ honour & confidence from our fellow citizens resulting ~~from~~ our

own good actions, enlightened by a benign religion, professed indeed and practised in various forms,

yet all of them inculcating honesty, truth, temperance, gratitude & the love of man, acknoleging & adoring an

overruling providence which, by all it's dispensations proves that it delights in the happiness of man here,

and his greater happiness hereafter; with all these blessings, what more is necessary to make us a happy

which shall restrain men from injuring one another, shall leave them other-

still one thing more, fellow citizens

& a prosperous people? a wise & frugal government, ~~wise~~ free to regulate their own pursuits of ~~industry or improvement~~,

of labour

and shall not take from the mouth the bread it has earned. this is the sum of good government, and this is necessary to close the circle of our felicities.

About to enter, fellow citizens, on the exercise of duties which comprehend every thing dear & valuable to you,

it is proper you should ~~understand~~ what I deem the essential principles of our government, and consequently those which are

to ~~give~~ shape to it's administration. I will compress them within the shortest compass they will bear, stating only

the general principle without it's limitations.

equal and exact justice to all men of whatever state or persuasion, religious or political.

and honest friendship

peace & commerce, with all nations, alliance with none.

~~that hospitality to fugitives from oppression, which the savages of the wilderness extended to our fathers ...~~

the most competent administrations of our domestic concerns, and

the support of the state governments in their constitutional rights, as our surest bulwarks against antirepublican tendencies.

government / at home, and safety abroad.

the preservation of the ~~general~~ as the sheet anchor of our peace ~~and administration of it's government on the principles of those who advocated it's adoption, not of those who opposed it.~~

free & frequent elections by the people in person & the more frequent within the limits of their convenience, and the more extensive the right of suffrage, the more ~~nearly~~ the perfectly within the definition of a genuine republic:

absolute acquiescence in the decisions of the majority, the vital principle of republics, from which is no appeal but to force, the vital principle and the parent of despotism.

economy in public expence, that labour may enjoy it's earnings:

a well disciplined militia, our best reliance in peace, & for the first moments of war, till regulars may relieve them:

the honest paiment of debts:

encouragement of agriculture, and of commerce as it's handmaid:

~~[illegible]~~:

the diffusion of ~~information~~, & arraignment of all abuses at the bar of the public reason:

freedom of religion: freedom of the press:

freedom of person, under the never ceasing protection of the Hab. corp.

and trial by juries impartially selected.

FORMIDABLE OPPONENTS

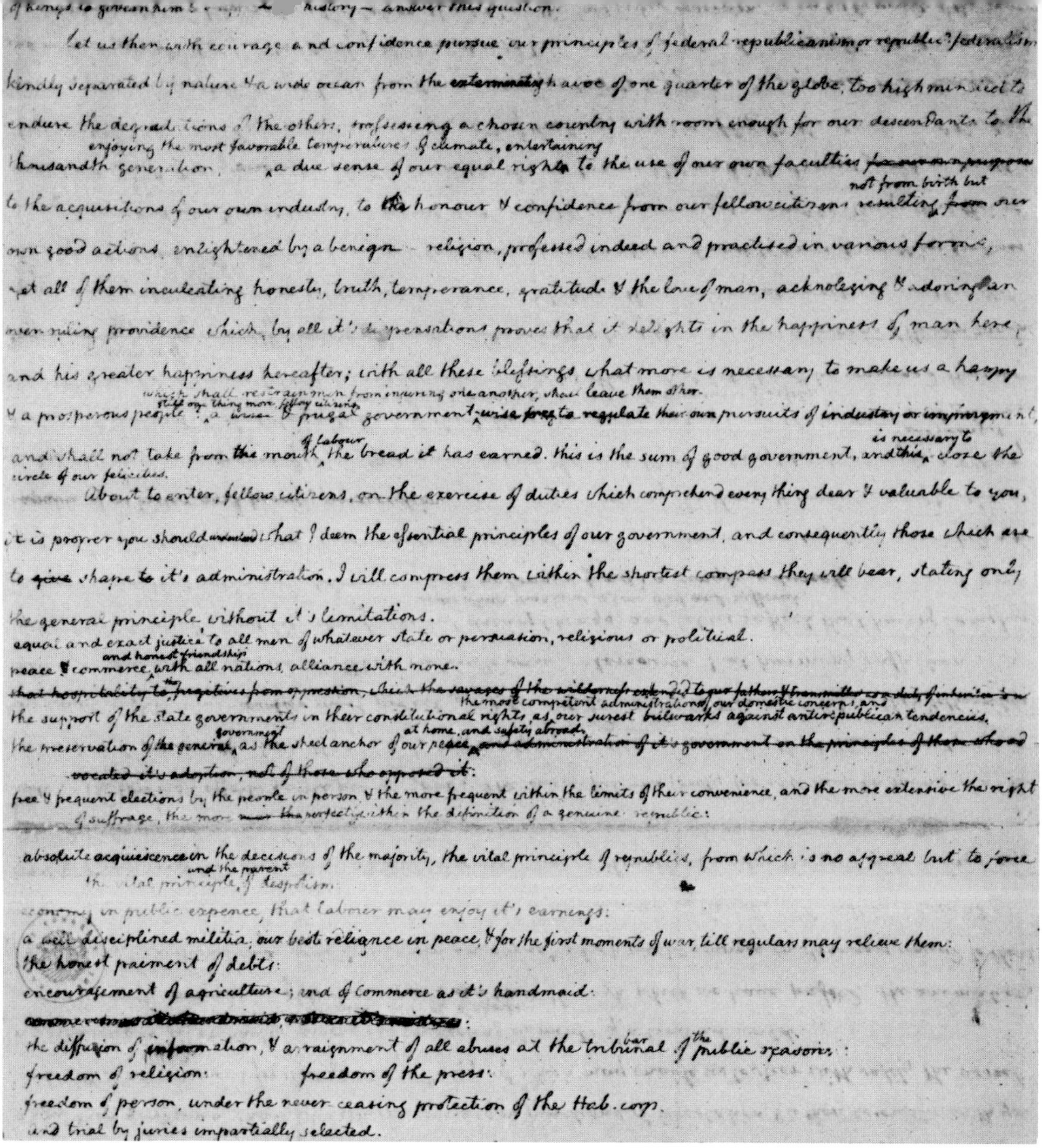

Jefferson was sworn in with Vice President Aaron Burr (right) by the Federalist Chief Justice John Marshall (right, above). In different ways these two men were to plague his Presidency. Jefferson's inaugural speech (part of which appears above) sought to bind up wounds from the bitter campaign: "We are all republicans: we are all federalists." He was incensed, however, to discover that John Adams had worked feverishly the night before appointing to the judiciary men who were his "most ardent political enemies." One of these "midnight judges," William Marbury, deprived of his commission by the new administration, brought his case to the Supreme Court. Marshall backed away from a direct confrontation with the executive in the *Marbury* v. *Madison* decision (reported in the *Aurora,* far right), but he established the right of the federal courts to annul an act of Congress. Marshall was pitted against Jefferson again in 1807 when Burr was charged with treason for attempting to raise troops to separate the West from the Union. Although Jefferson sought a conviction, Marshall presided over a trial that ended in acquittal.

AURORA

SURGO UT PROSIM.

PHILADELPHIA:

FRIDAY, FEBRUARY 4, 1803.

FROM WASHINGTON.

JANUARY 31, 1803.

"This day a debate took place of about four hours, in the senate, upon an application made by Mr. *Marbury* of this place, one of the *midnight appointments* of Mr. Adams, as justice of the peace, for a copy of such part of the executive record of the senate, as related to his nomination and approval by that body. In this debate all the orators on both sides spoke: we have not time to give the detailed debate, but the question was lost 13 to 15.

This business is connected with the celebrated *Mondamus* affair of last year; Marbury being the person *used* by the *tories* to blow up this bubble.

The petition of the *dislocated* judges which was lately before the house of representatives, has been also before the senate. A committee consisting of all on one side was appointed to gratify them, e. g. *James Ross, Gouverneur Morris* and *Jonathan Dayton* :—it will be readily conceived that they have made a *thundering* report, and that it is up to the hub, and calculated to rescue the people from their worst enemies! it is the order of the day for Wednesday next; and the report goes that the New-York *Gouverneur* and our would be *Gouverneur* Ross and the would-be governor and clerk in chancery of Jersey, Ogden, are all to make a *great noise* on that day—they mean to shew themselves before the 4th of March and as the thief said at Tyburn, to die hard—die all, die nobly, die like demi gods.

The house of representatives sat with closed doors this day, on what business is not to be ascertained. It was reported that it was on a motion intended to go to the expulsion of *Rutledge*; this is not however, so certain as that the public mind is much irritated at the length of time he has been suffered to sit in the house after the proofs have been brought so completely home to him. There are other circumstances concerning this man's *arts of* a similar nature that have been brought to light within a few days, and which shall be published very speedily if no steps are taken by the house of representatives to purify congress. Some of the members have shewn a very honorable sense of their own dignity, a very large number of the members declared their determination not to remain in the house should he be called to the chair in committee. This has had its due effect so far. There are others who do not appear to feel the same respect for themselves nor for the character of the government of the country which the forgeries were intended to dishonor."

TRIPOLITAN SHAKEDOWN

Jefferson had long been disturbed by the humiliating practice of paying a yearly, and sizable, tribute to the Barbary States for safe passage of ships in the Mediterranean. In 1801, when the Pasha of Tripoli tried to raise the ante, the President responded in characteristic fashion by sending a squadron to blockade the Tripoli coast. The *Philadelphia*, built in 1799 (right), was captured; but Lt. Stephen Decatur and seventeen volunteers slipped into the harbor at night and set fire to her (far right). During an attack on Tripoli in 1804 (opposite, above), he led his crew aboard a Tripolitan gunboat (above) and shot the captain.

312

THE LOUISIANA PURCHASE

Even before Jefferson had brought the Tripolitan War to a successful conclusion in 1805, he scored one of the greatest diplomatic victories in American history. Since 1763 Spain had owned the Louisiana Territory, 828,000 square miles of virgin land west of the Mississippi, including the strategic port of New Orleans. In the spring of 1802, Jefferson discovered that Spain had secretly ceded the vast expanse to a powerful France under the ambitious Napoleon Bonaparte. Immediately he wrote the American minister in France, Robert R. Livingston: "There is on the globe one single spot, the possessor of which is our natural and habitual enemy. It is New Orleans." He dispatched able James Monroe to bolster Livingston in negotiations (above) with François de Barbé-Marbois, the French Finance Minister, to buy New Orleans and West Florida. Unexpectedly, Napoleon offered them not only New Orleans but the entire Louisiana Territory. Astonished, they accepted and for less than three cents an acre doubled the size of the United States. Jefferson was wildly acclaimed as the American flag was raised over New Orleans on December 20, 1803 (pictured in a later painting at right). In 1809 a national song (left) was published in honor of the event.

PATHFINDERS FOR AMERICA

Jefferson had long been intrigued by the uncharted lands to the west. He had urged Congress to finance a mission "even to the Western Ocean," and one was preparing to depart as the momentous news arrived from Paris of the Louisiana Purchase. Meriwether Lewis and William Clark led the expedition to map the Missouri River and are seen above after they had reached its headwaters and were proceeding west on horseback. They sent Jefferson the painted buffalo hide (right, above) depicting a Mandan Indian attack. On November 7, 1805, their diary records: "Ocian in View! O! the joy!" A detail from Clark's remarkable map (right) delineates Cape Disappointment on the estuary of the Columbia River.

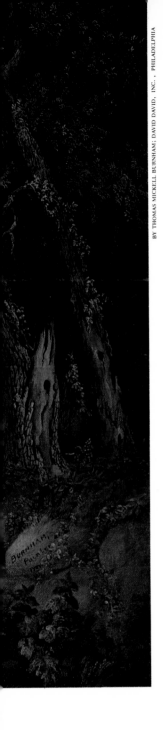

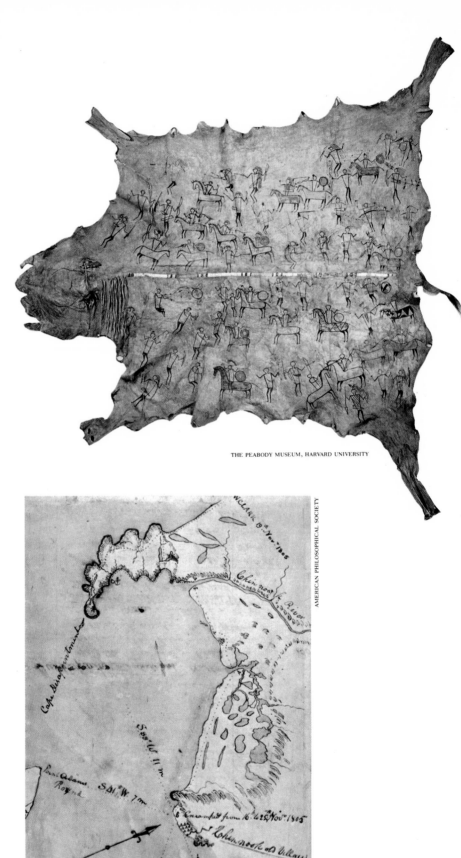

317

In response to hostile acts of Britain, Congress passed the Embargo Act in 1807. This

cartoon shows Jefferson trying to calm the opposition, especially from New England.

THE GLORIOUS FOURTH

As President, the author of the Declaration of Independence
characteristically discouraged suggestions to celebrate his
own birthday in favor of that of his country—the Fourth of
July. He must have approved the 1819 Philadelphia celebration (above), for he had held similar galas on the White House
lawn. When asked in 1826 to help mark the fiftieth anniversary
of the Declaration of Independence, he was mortally ill. But
his carefully drafted letter of June 24 expressing his regrets
(right) was a masterpiece containing the unmistakable sentiments that had shaped his life. Fittingly, he breathed his last
on that very "Glorious Fourth."

320

Respected Sir   Monticello June 24. 26

       The kind invitation I recieve from you on the part of
the citizens of the city of Washington, to be present with them at
their celebration of the 50th anniversary of American independance;
as one of the surviving signers of an instrument, pregnant with our own,
and the fate of the world, is most flattering to myself, and heightened
by the honorable accompaniment proposed for the comfort of such a
journey. it adds sensibly to the sufferings of sickness, to be deprived by it
of a personal participation in the rejoicings of that day. but acquiescence
is a duty, under circumstances not placed among those we are permitted
to controul. I should indeed, with peculiar delight, have met and
exchanged there, congratulations personally, with the small band,
the remnant of that host of worthies, who joined with us, on that
day, in the bold and doubtful election we were to make, for our country,
between submission, or the sword; and to have enjoyed with them the
consolatory fact that our fellow citizens, after half a century of experience
and prosperity, continue to approve the choice we made. may it be to
the world what I believe it will be, (to some parts sooner, to others later,
but finally to all,) the Signal of arousing men to burst the chains, under
which monkish ignorance and superstition had persuaded them to bind
themselves, and to assume the blessings & security of self government. that
form which we have substituted restores the free right to the unbounded exercise
of reason and freedom of opinion. all eyes are opened, or opening to the
rights of man. the general spread of the light of science has already
laid open to every view the palpable truth that the mass of mankind has not been
born, with saddles on their backs, nor a favored few booted and spurred, ready to
ride them legitimately, by the grace of god. these are grounds of hope for others. for
selves let the annual return of this day, for ever refresh our recollections of these n
and an undiminished devotion to them.

form

321

Chapter 11

Third President

A just and solid republican government maintained here," Jefferson wrote shortly after his inauguration in 1801, "will be a standing monument and example for the aim and imitation of the people of other countries; . . . they will see from our example that a free government is of all others the most energetic." This was the credo of his first administration, a belief that he could and must vindicate republican principles in practice as vigorously as he had presented them in theory during the years of Federalist rule.

Many of his theories already seemed to have been borne out in fact. For years he had disagreed with the European philosophers' argument that a republic could survive "only in a small territory." Pointing out the support he and his party had received from the expanding West, Jefferson remarked, "The reverse is the truth. Had our territory been even a third only of what it is, we were gone. But while frenzy & delusion like an epidimic, gained certain parts, the residue remained sound & untouched, and held on till their brethren could recover from the temporary delusion." Similarly, the refusal of Federalist congressmen to heed their leaders and rob him of his election after the tie in the Electoral College confirmed his faith in the sense of justice of men in all parties. "The order and good sense displayed . . . in the momentous crisis which lately arose," he wrote Joseph Priestley, "really bespeak a strength of character in our nation which augers well for the duration of our republic, and I am much better satisfied now of it's stability than I was before it was tried."

Jefferson's views on the methods of insuring that stability were well known. Americans expected modifications of the Hamiltonian system of finance; economies in government, including a reduction of military forces; and a more balanced consideration of the interests of the South and West against the demands of the Northeast. They knew, too, that there would be a different tone and style in government and that Jefferson would not tolerate any "monarchical" trappings. But beyond this, there was much concern over just what a Jeffersonian government might mean. To disprove his Federalist critics and to win over congressmen and restless voters, Jefferson had to persuade his fellow citizens that they were truly one people with a potential for greatness. The Union, torn by the bitter debates of "Jacobins" and "Anglomen," Federalists and Republicans, must be restored. This theme of reunification was at the heart of Jefferson's inaugural message on March 4.

March 4. 1801

Let us then, fellow citizens, unite with one heart & one mind; let us restore to social intercourse that harmony & affection, without which Liberty, & even Life itself, are but dreary things.

And let us reflect that having banished from our land that religious intolerance under which mankind so long bled & suffered, we have yet gained little if we countenance a political intolerance, as despotic, as wicked & capable of as bitter & bloody persecution....

But every difference of opinion, is not a difference of principle. We have called, by different names, brethren of the same principle. We are all republicans: we are all federalists....

[Jefferson next answered his critics' charge that a republican government "cannot be strong" by citing America's natural resources and traditions of liberty, which he said could make the country the "strongest government on earth." He then listed the principles on which his republican administration would be based.]

With all these blessings, what more is necessary to make us a happy and a prosperous people? Still one thing more, fellow citizens a wise & frugal government, which shall restrain men from injuring one another, shall leave them otherwise free to regulate their own pursuits of industry & improvement, and shall not take from the mouth of labour the bread it has earned.

This is the sum of good government, & this is necessary to close the circle of our felicities.

About to enter, fellow citizens, on the exercise of duties which comprehend everything dear & valuable to you, it is proper that you should understand what I deem the essential principles of our government and consequently those which ought to shape it's administration....

Equal & exact justice to all men, of whatever state

Jefferson presidential medal, 1801

of persuasion, religious or political:

Peace, commerce, & honest friendship with all nations, entangling alliances with none:

The support of the State governments in all their rights, as the most competent administrations for our domestic concerns, and the surest bulwarks against anti republican tendencies:

The preservation of the general government, in it's whole constitutional vigor, as the sheet anchor of our peace at home, & safety abroad.

A jealous care of the right of election by the people, a mild and safe corrective of abuses, which are lopped by the sword of revolution, where peaceable remedies are unprovided.

Absolute acquiescence in the decisions of the Majority the vital principle of republics, from which is no appeal but to force, the vital principle & immediate parent of despotism.

A well disciplined militia, our best reliance in peace, & for the first moments of war, till regulars may relieve them: The Supremacy of the Civil over the Military authority:

Economy in public expense, that labor may be lightly burdened:

The honest paiment of our debts and sacred preservation of the public faith:

Encouragement of Agriculture, & of Commerce as it's handmaid:

The diffusion of information, & arraignment of all abuses at the bar of the public reason:

Freedom of Religion, freedom of the press, & freedom of Person under the protection of the Habeas corpus: And trial by juries, impartially selected.

This 1801 cartoon illustrates the Federalist fear that Jefferson and friends such as "Mad Tom" Paine would pull down the government.

Jefferson saw his election as an opportunity to continue the Revolution, to reaffirm its goals, and to return America to the course envisioned by himself and other revolutionaries in 1776. One of the most touching letters of his Presidency went to Samuel Adams, the Boston leader who was spending his old age in obscurity, a victim of Federalist abuse. Jefferson wrote that his inaugural address was a tribute to Adams and to all like him who had seen the Revolution distorted by Federalist administrations.

Washington Mar. 29. 1801.

I addressed a letter to you, my very dear and antient

324

Public Men, SULLIVAN

Samuel Adams of Massachusetts

friend, on the 4th of March: not indeed to you by name, but through the medium of some of my fellow citizens, whom occasion called on me to address.

In meditating the matter of that address, I often asked myself, is this exactly in the spirit of the patriarch of liberty, Samuel Adams? Is it as he would express it? Will he approve of it? I have felt a great deal for our country in the times we have seen: but individually for no one so much as yourself. When I have been told that you were avoided, insulated, frowned on, I could but ejaculate, 'Father, forgive them, for they know not what they do.' I confess I felt an indignation for you, which for myself I have been able under every trial to keep entirely passive. However, the storm is over, and we are in port. The ship was not rigged for the service she was put on. We will show the smoothness of her motions on her republican tack.

Jefferson was eager to begin setting the government on its new tack, but he was hampered in the months immediately after his inauguration by a Federalist-dominated Congress. The Seventh Congress, elected in the Republican sweep of 1800, would not meet until the following December. Before the Senate adjourned in March, however, Jefferson's first Cabinet appointments were approved: Madison for the State Department and two Massachusetts Republicans, Levi Lincoln and Henry Dearborn, as Attorney General and Secretary of War. Jefferson's Secretary of the Treasury would be Albert Gallatin, the brilliant Swiss immigrant who had succeeded Madison as Republican House leader; but Gallatin's nomination was withheld until the recess so that it would be considered by a more sympathetic Senate. The office of Secretary of the Navy, hardly a prize since Jefferson was known to favor radical reductions in that department, remained vacant until Robert Smith of Baltimore finally accepted in July.

Jefferson's immediate concern, however, was not so much to fill vacancies as to create them. John Adams had spent his last days in office appointing his followers to every unfilled post. A dozen years later, Jefferson recalled his bitterness at this ploy: "The last day of his political power, the last hours, and even beyond the midnight, were employed in filling all offices, & especially permanent ones, with the bitterest federalists, and providing for me the alternative, either to execute the government by my enemies, whose study it would be to thwart & defeat all my measures, or to incur the odium of such numerous removals from office as might bear me down." Jefferson chose the course of removal; he had confided this decision to James Monroe three days after the inauguration.

Washington March 7. 1801.
I have firmly refused to follow the counsels of those who have advised the giving offices to some of their leaders, in order to reconcile. I have given and will give only to republicans, under existing circumstances. But I believe with others that deprivations of office, if made on the ground of political principle alone, would revolt our new converts, and give a body to leaders who now stand alone. Some I know must be made. They must be as few as possible, done gradually, and bottomed on some malversation or inherent disqualification.

In practice this meant that Jefferson would remove few officeholders solely because of their politics, but those few places, and others that became vacant because of resignations or deaths, would be given only to Republicans. Jefferson decided, however, that he could remove immediately any obviously incompetent and corrupt officials and all those Adams had appointed since December. The occasion for presenting his policies publicly came in June when he received a formal remonstrance from Federalists in New Haven. At the urging of local Republicans, he had replaced the recent Adams appointment as collector of customs there with a member of his own party. Jefferson replied to the remonstrance with an indictment of Federalist appointment policies, measures that he said forced him to take steps to give Republicans their "just share."

Washington July 12. 1801
Declarations by myself in favor of *political tolerance,* exhortations to *harmony* and affection in social intercourse, and to respect for the *equal rights* of the minority, have on certain occasions been quoted and misconstrued into assurances that the tenure of offices was to be undisturbed. But could candor apply such a construction? . . . When it is considered that during the late administration

Jefferson's draft form for telling some of Adams's recent appointees that they should regard their appointments "as if never made"

NATIONAL ARCHIVES

326

REMOVALS AND APPOINTMENTS.

The subsequent LIST contains the Names of the FEDERAL RE-PUBLICANS who have been dismissed from office, by the President of the United States, on account of their political opinions; together with the names of the Persons who have been appointed in their places, since the 4th of March, 1801.

1. John Wilkes Kittera, Attorney for the Eastern District of Pennsylvania, *dismissed;* Alexander James Dallas appointed in his room.

2. John Hall, Marshal of the same District, *dismissed;* John Smith appointed in his room.

3. Samuel Hodgdon, Superintendant of Public Stores at Philadelphia, *dismissed;* William Irvine appointed in his room.

4. John Harris, Store-keeper at the same place, *dismissed;* Robert Jones, appointed in his room.

5. Henry Miller, Supervisor of the Revenue of the District of Pennsylvania, *dismissed;* Peter Muhlenberg appointed in his room.

6. J. M. Lingan, Attorney for the District of Columbia, *dismissed;* Daniel Carrol Brent appointed in his room.

7. Thomas Swann, Attorney, *dismissed;* John Thompson Mason appointed in his room.

8. John Pierce, Commissioner of Loans for the State of New-Hampshire, *dismissed;* William Gardiner appointed in his room.

9. Thomas Martin, Collector of the District of Portsmouth, in the same State, *dismissed;* Joseph Whipple appointed in his room.

10. Jacob Sheaffe, Navy Agent at Portsmouth, New-Hampshire, *dismissed;* Woodbury Langdon appointed in his room.

List appended to the New Haven remonstrance of those who had allegedly been removed from office "on account of their political opinions"

those who were not of a particular sect of politics were excluded from all office; when, by a steady pursuit of this measure nearly the whole offices of the US. were monopolized by that sect; when the public sentiment at length declared itself and burst open the doors of honor and confidence to those whose opinions they more approved, was it to be imagined that this monopoly of office was still to be continued in the hands of the minority? Does it violate their *equal rights* to assert some rights in the majority also? Is it *political intolerance* to claim a proportionate share in the direction of the public affairs? Can they not *harmonize* in society unless they have every thing in their own hands? ...

...It would have been to me a circumstance of great relief had I found a moderate participation of office in the hands of the majority. I would gladly have left to time and accident to raise them to their just share. But their total exclusion calls for prompter correctives. I shall correct the procedure: but, that done, return with joy to that state of things, when the only questions concerning a candidate shall be, is he honest, is he capable, is he faithful to the constitution?

After a brief stay at Monticello in April, Jefferson moved into the barren President's House in the new capital, urging his Cabinet members to return to Washington as soon as possible. May brought the first major policy consideration in foreign affairs when reports arrived of new troubles in the Mediterranean. The pirates of Tripoli had resumed raids on American shipping and the Algerians grumbled menacingly at delays in the delivery of bribes promised by the Adams administration. The Cabinet met and lent its advice, and Jefferson reached a frugal but firm decision: cruisers no longer needed to harass the French in the Caribbean would sail to the Mediterranean to guard shipping from the Tripolitans and to deliver part of the overdue "tribute." He summarized this program for Wilson Cary Nicholas, a senator from Virginia.

Washington June 11. 1801.

In March, finding we might with propriety call in our cruisers from the W. Indies, this was done; and as 6. were to be kept armed, it was thought best ... that we should send 3. with a tender into the Mediterranean to protect our commerce against Tripoli. But as this might lead to war, I wished to have the approbation of the new administration....It was the 15th. of May before Mr.

*Jefferson was the first President
to respond to the Barbary pirates
with force; Tripoli declared war
and was bombarded in August, 1804.*

Gallatin's arrival enabled us to decide definitively. It was then decided unanimously...on the 1st. of June they sailed. With respect to Algiers they are in extreme ill humour. We find 3. years arrears of tribute due to them....We have however sent them 30,000. D[ollars] by our frigates as one year's tribute, and have a vessel ready to sail with the stores for another year....We have taken these steps towards supplying the deficiencies of our predecessors merely in obedience to the law; being convinced it is money thrown away, & that there is no end to the demands of these powers, nor any security in their promises. The real alternative before us is whether to abandon the Mediterranean, or to keep up a cruize in it, perhaps in rotation with other powers who would join us as soon as there is peace. But this, Congress must decide.

Jefferson's procedure in dealing with the demands of the Barbary pirates established the routine he would follow during his entire administration. As the Cabinet members reassembled in the fall for the legislative session, Jefferson circulated a letter to them outlining his views on the "mode & degrees of communication" between the President and the heads of departments. Although he couched this directive in tactful phrases, Jefferson made his position clear: the Attorney General and Secretaries would follow the procedures of close consultation instituted by Washington, not the haphazard measures followed by Adams.

Washington Nov. 6, 1801.
Having been a member of the first administration under Gen. Washington, I can state with exactness what our course then was. Letters of business came addressed, sometimes to the President, but most frequently to the

heads of departments. If addressed to himself, he referred them to the proper department to be acted on: if to one of the Secretaries, the letter, if it required no answer, was communicated to the President simply for his information. If an answer was requisite, the Secretary of the department communicated the letter & his proposed answer to the President. Generally they were simply sent back, after perusal, which signified his approbation. Sometimes he returned them with an informal note, suggesting an alteration or a query. If a doubt of any importance arose, he reserved it for conference. By this means, he was always in accurate possession of all facts and proceedings in every part of the Union, and to whatsoever department they related; he formed a central point for the different branches; preserved an unity of object and action among them, exercised that participation in the gestion of affairs which his office made incumbent on him, and met himself the due responsibility for whatever was done. During Mr. Adams's administration, his long and habitual absences from the seat of government rendered this kind of communication impracticable, removed him from any share in the transaction of affairs, and parcelled out the government in fact among four independent heads, drawing sometimes in opposite directions. That the former is preferable to the latter course cannot be doubted. . . .

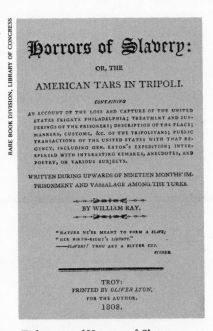

Title page of Horrors of Slavery, *a book in Jefferson's library by a man who had been imprisoned for nineteen months by the Tripolitans*

By the fall, Jefferson had already demonstrated his implementation of republican principles. The Cabinet would be an active group of councilors to the President, not merely a collection of administrators responsible only for their own departments. Incompetent officials would not be tolerated on any level. And frugality would be the new order, not merely because Jefferson abhorred waste but because he saw no room for expensive bureaucracy in a republic. The specific economies Jefferson proposed usually served more than one purpose. The Navy, for instance, had been reduced because he disapproved of large military establishments. The diplomatic service would be cut, he explained to William Short, not so much to save money as to insure America's freedom from European political interests.

Washington Oct. 3. 1801.
If we can delay but for a few years the necessity of vindicating the laws of nature on the ocean, we shall be the more sure of doing it with effect. The day is within

my time as well as yours when we may say by what laws other nations shall treat us on the sea. And we will say it. In the meantime we wish to let every treaty we have drop off, without renewal. We call in our diplomatic missions, barely keeping up those to the most important nations. There is a strong disposition in our countrymen to discontinue even these; and very possibly it may be done. Consuls will be continued as usual. The interest which European nations feel as well as ourselves in the mutual patronage of commercial intercourse, is a sufficient stimulus on both sides to ensure that patronage.

In November, Jefferson received news that seemed to insure peace for those "few years." Napoleon, France's First Consul, had agreed to the Convention of 1800 setting aside the old Franco-American alliance and France and Great Britain had ended their war. European issues need no longer divide American political loyalties. Jefferson would henceforth have a free hand to pursue the program of financial retrenchment and reallocation of national resources that he presented to Congress in his first annual message.

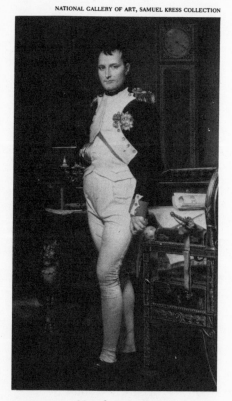

Napoleon by David

Dec. 8. 1801.

When we consider that this government is charged with the external and mutual relations only of these states that the states themselves have principal care of our persons, our property, and our reputation, constituting the great field of human concerns, we may well doubt whether our organisation is not too complicated, too expensive; whether offices or officers have not been multiplied unnecessarily, and sometimes injuriously to the service they were meant to promote. I will cause to be laid before you an essay towards a statement of those who, under public employment of various kinds, draw money from the treasury or from our citizens. Time has not permitted a perfect enumeration, the ramifications of office being too multipled and remote to be completely traced in a first trial. Among those who are dependant on Executive discretion, I have begun the reduction of what was deemed unnecessary.... Considering the general tendency to multiply offices and dependancies, and to increase expence to the ultimate term of burthen which the citizen can bear, it behoves us to avail ourselves of every occasion which presents itself for taking off the surcharge; that it never may be seen here that, after

Albert Gallatin, above; below, Jefferson's copy of a book that extolled "Republican Economy"

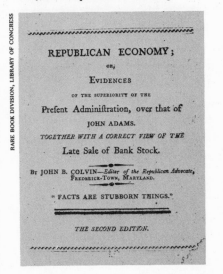

REPUBLICAN ECONOMY;

OR,

EVIDENCES

OF THE SUPERIORITY OF THE

Prefent Adminiftration, over that of

JOHN ADAMS.

TOGETHER WITH A CORRECT VIEW OF THE

Late Sale of Bank Stock.

By JOHN B. COLVIN—*Editor of the Republican Advocate*, FREDERICK-TOWN, MARYLAND.

"FACTS ARE STUBBORN THINGS."

THE SECOND EDITION.

leaving to labour the smallest portion of it's earnings on which it can subsist, government shall itself consume the whole residue of what it was instituted to guard.

[In presenting his economic policy, Jefferson did not advocate breaking faith with financial commitments made in the past, but in two other areas—the Judiciary Act passed early in 1801 and the Naturalization Act—he wanted to undo some of the damage from laws passed during the Adams administration.]

The Judiciary system of the United States, and especially that portion of it recently erected, will of course present itself to the contemplation of Congress. And that they may be able to judge of the proportion which the institution bears to the business it has to perform, I have caused to be procured from the several states, and now lay before Congress, an exact statement of all the causes decided since the first establishment of the courts, and of those which were depending when additional courts and judges were brought in to their aid. . . .

I cannot omit recommending a revisal of the laws on the subject of naturalisation. Considering the ordinary chances of human life, a denial of citizenship under a residence of fourteen years, is a denial to a great proportion of those who ask it: and controuls a policy pursued, from their first settlement, by many of these states, and still believed of consequence to their prosperity. And shall we refuse, to the unhappy fugitives from distress, that hospitality which the savages of the wilderness extended to our fathers arriving in this land? Shall oppressed humanity find no asylum on this globe?

Congress responded enthusiastically to the major portions of Jefferson's program. Federalists found their best issue in his request for repeal of the Judiciary Act—a statute that had expanded federal court jurisdiction and established an expensive judicial bureaucracy. Even this battle was won, despite some embarrassing occasions on which Vice President Burr used his tie-breaking vote to aid the Federalists. Congress restored the naturalization law of 1795—the Sedition Act had already expired—and also abolished the tangled system of internal taxes begun by Hamilton. Once this was done, Treasury Secretary Gallatin was free to present proposals for his own program. His first report was a call for reforms of the sinking fund, the fund set aside for repayment of the national debt. Jefferson congratulated him on the plans to simplify the fund's operation and suggested other modifications in Treasury policy that would make the department more republican and more economical.

Washington Apr. 1. 1802.
I have read and considered your report on the operations of the Sinking fund and entirely approve of it, as the best plan on which we can set out. I think it an object of great importance, to be kept in view, and to be undertaken at a fit season, to simplify our system of finance, and bring it within the comprehension of every member of Congress. Hamilton set out on a different plan. In order that he might have the entire government of his machine, he determined so to complicate it as that neither the President or Congress should be able to understand it, or to controul him. He succeeded in doing this, not only beyond their reach, but so that he at length could not unravel it himself. He gave to the debt, in the first instance, in funding it, the most artificial and mysterious form he could devise. He then moulded up his appropriations of a number of scraps & remnants many of which were nothing at all, and applied them to different objects in reversion and remainder until the whole system was involved in impenetrable fog, and while he was giving himself the airs of providing for the paiment of the debt, he left himself free to add to it continually as he did in fact instead of paying it....

[Jefferson suggested the administration aim at a simple measure for the future reduction or increase of taxes.]

That is, to form into one consolidated mass all the monies recieved into the treasury, and to marshal the several expenditures, giving them a preference of paiment according to the order in which they should be arranged. As for example. 1. the interest of the public debt, 2. such portions of principal as are exigible. 3. the expences of government. 4. such other portions of principal, as... we are still free to pay when we please. The last object might be made to take up the residuum of money remaining in the treasury at the end of every year... and would be the barometer whereby to test the economy of the administration. It would furnish a simple measure by which every one could mete their merit, and by which every one could decide when taxes were deficient or superabundant. If to this can be added a simplification of the form of accounts in the treasury department, and in the organisation of it's officers, so as to bring every thing to a single center, we might hope to see the finances of the Union as clear and intelligible as a merchant's books, so that every member of Congress, and every man of any mind in the Union should be able to comprehend them, to investigate abuses, and consequently to controul them....

[Repeal of internal taxes would allow certain economies within the department as well.]

We shall now get rid of the Commissioner of the internal revenue, and Superintendant of stamps. It remains to amalgamate the Comptroller and Auditor into one, and reduce the register to a clerk of accounts....This constellation of great men in the treasury department was of a piece with the rest of Hamilton's plans. He took his own stand as a Lieutenant General, surrounded by his Major Generals, and stationing his brigadiers and Colonels under the name of Supervisors, Inspectors &c. in the different states. Let us deserve well of our country by making their interests the end of all our plans, and not our own pomp, patronage and irresponsibility.

Robert R. Livingston by Vanderlyn

A month before Congress adjourned in the spring news of events in Europe cast a pall over the optimistic economic program. Six months earlier, when Robert R. Livingston sailed to France as the new American minister, the government had heard rumors of a secret treaty under which Spain had surrendered the enormous Louisiana Territory to France. In April the rumors were confirmed. Although Madison had given Livingston firm instructions before he left, Jefferson felt the situation warranted a sharp reminder of American policy. He sent Livingston an outline of the threats and favors he might offer to save American rights to trade at New Orleans, a privilege that had finally been established by Pinckney's Treaty in 1795. Without New Orleans, American use of the Mississippi was a fiction. If the ambitious Napoleon gained control of the trans-Mississippi West, America's own territory would be in danger.

Washington, April 18, 1802.

The cession of Louisiana and the Floridas by Spain to France works most sorely on the U.S....It compleatly re-

*A British map of the Mississippi,
drawn in 1763 from French surveys*

verses all the political relations of the U. S. and will form a new epoch in our political course. Of all nations of any consideration France is the one which hitherto has offered the fewest points on which we could have any conflict of right, and the most points of a communion of interests. From these causes we have ever looked to her as our *natural friend,* as one with which we never could have an occasion of difference. Her growth therefore we viewed as our own, her misfortunes ours. There is on the globe one single spot, the possessor of which is our natural and habitual enemy. It is New Orleans, through which the produce of three-eighths of our territory must pass to market . . . France placing herself in that door assumes to us the attitude of defiance. Spain might have retained it quietly for years. Her pacific dispositions, her feeble state, would induce her to increase our facilities there, so that her possession of the place would be hardly felt by us, and it would not perhaps be very long before some circumstance might arise which might make the cession of it to us the price of something of more worth to her. Not so can it ever be in the hands of France. The impetuosity of her temper, the energy and restlessness of her character, placed in a point of eternal friction with us, and our character, which though quiet, and loving peace and the pursuit of wealth, is high-minded, despising wealth in competition with insult or injury, enterprizing and energetic as any nation on earth, these circumstances render it impossible that France and the U. S. can continue long friends when they meet in so irritable a position. They as well as we must be blind if they do not see this; and we must be very improvident if we do not begin to make arrangements on that hypothesis. The day that France takes possession of N. Orleans fixes the sentence which is to restrain her forever within her low water mark. It seals the union of two nations who in conjunction can maintain exclusive possession of the ocean. From that moment we must marry ourselves to the British fleet and nation. We must turn all our attentions to a maritime force, for which our resources place us on very high ground: and having formed and cemented together a power which may render reinforcement of her settlements here impossible to France, make the first cannon which shall be fired in Europe the signal for tearing up any settlement she may have made, and for holding the two continents of America in sequestration for the common purposes of the United British and American nations. This is not a state of things we seek or desire. It is one which this measure, if adopted by France, forces on us. . . .

If France considers Louisiana however as indispensable for her views she might perhaps be willing to look about for arrangements which might reconcile it to our interests. If anything could do this it would be the ceding to us the island of New Orleans and the Floridas. . . .

Every eye in the U. S. is now fixed on this affair of Louisiana. Perhaps nothing since the revolutionary war has produced more uneasy sensations through the body of the nation. Notwithstanding temporary bickerings have taken place with France, she has still a strong hold on the affections of our citizens generally. I have thought it not amiss, by way of supplement to the letters of the Secretary of State, to write you this private one to impress you with the importance we affix to this transaction.

Pierre Samuel Du Pont de Nemours

To supplement Livingston's efforts, Jefferson enlisted Pierre Samuel Du Pont de Nemours, a French economist who was returning to the Continent on personal and business matters. Jefferson sent Du Pont a letter and enclosed his instructions to Livingston for Du Pont to read before delivering them. The letter repeated Jefferson's determination to keep Louisiana from Napoleon. The Frenchman's role would be to impress the Consulate with the gravity of the situation.

Washington, Apr. 25. 1802.

I am thus open with you because I trust that you will have it in your power to impress on that government considerations, in the scale against which the possession of Louisiana is nothing. In Europe nothing but Europe is seen, or supposed to have any weight in the affairs of nations. But this little event, of France possessing herself of Louisiana, which is thrown in as nothing, as a mere make-weight in the general settlement of accounts, this speck which now appears as an almost invisible point in the horizon, is the embryo of a tornado which will burst on the countries on both shores of the Atlantic and involve in it's effects their highest destinies. . . . if you can be the means of informing the wisdom of Buonaparte of all it's consequences, you will have deserved well of both countries. Peace and abstinence from European alliances are our objects, and so will continue while the present order of things in America remains uninterrupted.

Although versions of the secret Franco-Spanish treaty on Louisiana had been published in America before the end of the congressional session, Jefferson did not present the problem to the legislature until Livingston or Du Pont could report on their conversations with Napoleon's ministers. It was equally prudent to keep the matter out of politics that summer because congressional elections were approaching. Jefferson could take some wry pride in the nature of the Federalist press campaign, which tried to discredit Republicans by attacking the President. Opposition editors could find little to attack in his record; instead they bombarded him with the most vicious personal slanders he suffered in his long career. The most malicious charge was made in a Richmond newspaper by James Callender, a turncoat Republican journalist whom Jefferson had once befriended. Callender recounted a tale that Jefferson kept a slave, Sally Hemings, as his concubine at Monticello and that she had borne him several children. Sally was the illegitimate offspring of Jefferson's father-in-law and a mulatto slave and thus his dead wife's half sister. Some Jefferson biographers, and Jefferson's Randolph and Eppes descendants, have claimed that Sally's white children were fathered by one of his nephews. For a man who was always reticent about his family life, the situation was most painful. He never commented publicly on this charge, but his bitterness toward the 1802 campaign was plain in a letter to Robert R. Livingston.

MASSACHUSETTS HISTORICAL SOCIETY

Jefferson kept careful records of the clothing given to the slaves at Monticello. Sally Hemings was listed among those receiving Irish linen, calamanco, and flannel.

Washington Oct. 10. 1802.

You will have seen by our newspapers that with the aid of a lying renegade from republicanism, the federalists have opened all their sluices of calumny. They say we lied them out of power, and openly avow they will do the same by us. But it was not lies or arguments on our part which dethroned them, but their own foolish acts, sedition laws, alien laws, taxes, extravagances and heresies. Porcupine their friend [Philadelphia's *Porcupine's Gazette,* published by William Cobbett] wrote them down. Callendar, their new recruit, will do the same. Every decent man among them revolts at his filth; and there cannot be a doubt that were a presidential election to come on this day, they would have but three New England states and about half a dozen votes from Maryland and North Carolina, these two states electing by districts. Were all the states to elect by a general ticket, they would have but 3. out of 16. states. And these 3. are coming up slowly.

The Republicans gained more ground in the elections for the Eighth Congress, which would convene in 1803; but in the meantime Jefferson and Madison still had no news, good or bad, from Livingston's halting negotiations. In November word came from the West that the Spanish Intendant had closed the port of New Orleans to American shipping, in violation of treaty promises. Pressure for an immediate solution to the question of possession of the trans-Mississippi West rose in Congress. There was some indication, however, that the Intendant had acted without his government's knowledge. Jefferson investigated the closing through diplomatic channels and on January 11 nominated James Monroe to join Livingston. The next day the House approved a committee report drafted by Madison, calling for an appropriation of two million dollars "to defray any expenses which may be incurred in relation to the intercourse between the United States and foreign nations." The "expenses," as the House knew from secret sessions, were to finance Monroe and Livingston's joint mission: the purchase of New Orleans and the Floridas. This accomplished, Jefferson wrote Monroe urging him to accept the appointment.

Washington Jan. 13. 1803.

The agitation of the public mind on occasion of the late suspension of our right of deposit at N. Orleans is extreme. In the Western country it is natural and grounded on honest motives. In the seaports it proceeds from a desire for war which increases the mercantile lottery; in the federalists generally and especially those of Congress the object is to force us into war if possible, in order to derange our finances, or if this cannot be done, to attach the Western country to them, as their best friends, and thus get again into power. Remonstrances, memorials &c. are now circulating thro' the whole of the Western country and signing by the body of the people. The measures we have been pursuing being invisible, do not satisfy their minds. Something sensible therefore was become necessary; and indeed our object of purchasing N. Orleans and the Floridas is a measure liable to assume so many shapes, that no instructions could be squared to fit them. It was essential then to send a Minister extraordinary, to be joined with the ordinary one, with discretionary powers, first however well impressed with all our views and therefore qualified to meet and modify to these every form of proposition which could come from the other party. This could be done only in full and frequent oral communications. Having determined on this, there could not be two opinions among the republicans as to the person. You possessed the unlimited con-

The port of New Orleans

fidence of the administration and of the Western people; and generally of the republicans every where; and were you to refuse to go, no other man can be found who does this. The measure has already silenced the feds here. Congress will no longer be agitated by them: and the country will become calm as fast as the information extends over it. All eyes, all hopes are now fixed on you; and were you to decline, the chagrin would be universal, and would shake under your feet the high ground on which you stand with the public. Indeed I know nothing which would produce such a shock. For on the event of this mission depends the future destinies of this republic.

Officially, the administration's goals were limited to the purchase of territories on the Gulf, but the ministers' instructions empowered them to sign a treaty "concerning the enlargement and more effective security of the rights and interests of the United States in the River Mississippi and in the territories eastward thereof." If they could purchase more than Florida and New Orleans with the $9,375,000 the President was willing to spend, he would not be disappointed. Jefferson's interest in the eventual possession of Louisiana was apparent in a message he sent Congress advocating a timely expedition to the West.

MISSOURI HISTORICAL SOCIETY

January 18, 1803.

An intelligent officer, with ten or twelve chosen men, fit for the enterprise, and willing to undertake it, taken from our posts, where they may be spared without inconvenience, might explore the whole line, even to the Western ocean, have conferences with the natives on the subject of commercial intercourse, get admission among them for our traders, as others are admitted, agree on convenient deposits for an interchange of articles, and return with the information acquired, in the course of two summers. Their arms and accoutrements, some instruments of observation, and light and cheap presents for the Indians, would be all the apparatus they could carry, and with an expectation of a soldier's portion of land on their return, would constitute the whole expence. Their pay would be going on, whether here or there. While other civilised nations have encountered great expence to enlarge the boundaries of knowledge, by undertaking voyages of discovery, and for other literary purposes, in various parts and directions, our nation seems to owe to the same object, as well as to its own

Drawing of a salmon trout by Clark from his journal for March, 1806

Charles Willson Peale painted companion portraits of William Clark (opposite) and Meriwether Lewis (above) shortly after their return from the Pacific late in 1806.

interests, to explore this, the only line of easy communication across the continent, and so directly traversing our own part of it. The interests of commerce place the principal object within the constitutional powers and care of Congress, and that it should incidentally advance the geographical knowledge of our own continent, cannot be but an additional gratification. The nation claiming the territory, regarding this as a literary pursuit, which [it] is in the habit of permitting within it's dominions, would not be disposed to view it with jealousy, even if the expiring state of it's interests there did not render it a matter of indifference. The appropriation of two thousand five hundred dollars, 'for the purpose of extending the external commerce of the United States,' while understood and considered by the Executive as giving the legislative sanction, would cover the undertaking from notice.

Congress agreed to the project and the President named his private secretary, Meriwether Lewis, to head the expedition. Once Lewis persuaded his friend and fellow Virginian William Clark to join him, preparations began for one of America's most historic missions of exploration.

The Seventh Congress, elected with Jefferson in 1800, had served the President well in financial policy and diplomatic affairs. The Republicans would dominate the Eighth Congress completely, with an increased House majority and a preponderance of two to one in the Senate. As their party's power ebbed away, Federalists' bitterness increased. Jefferson's selective removal of incumbent officials was almost complete, and the only remaining concentration of opposition power was in the judiciary. Many Federalist judges used their positions to expound political theory. When Justice Samuel Chase of the Supreme Court delivered a highly partisan charge to a grand jury in Baltimore, Jefferson suggested to Maryland Congressman Joseph Nicholson that he initiate impeachment proceedings. Chase was eventually impeached and acquitted.

Washington May 13. 1803.

You must have heard of the extraordinary charge of Chase to the grand jury at Baltimore. Ought this seditious and official attack on the principles of our constitution, and on the proceedings of a state, to go unpunished? And to whom so pointedly as yourself will the public look for the necessary measures? I ask these questions for your consideration. For myself, it is better that I should not interfere.

The symbol for Jefferson of Federalist power in the judiciary was Chief Justice John Marshall. Jefferson's first serious clash with Marshall came over the issue of Adams's "midnight" appointments. William Marbury had been appointed a justice of the peace by Adams on March 2, 1801, but Jefferson had ordered Madison to withhold his signed and sealed commission, which had not been delivered. Citing the Judiciary Act of 1789, Marbury had then petitioned the Supreme Court for a writ of mandamus granting the commission. Marshall dismissed the suit in February, 1803, saying the court lacked jurisdiction and thus avoiding an open confrontation with the executive branch. Yet his decision marked the first occasion on which an act of Congress—the section of the Judiciary Act of 1789 empowering the court to issue such a writ—was held unconstitutional.

On the eve of the Fourth of July came fitting news for the celebration of America's independence: Monroe and Livingston had negotiated a treaty with France that would give America not merely a foothold at New Orleans but possession of the entire province of Louisiana, a tract stretching from the Mississippi to the Rockies. Some High Federalists grumbled at the purchase price, and others objected to buttressing the interests of the West at the expense of the East Coast. But Gouverneur Morris expressed a more general opinion: "I am content to pay my share of fifteen millions, to deprive foreigners of all pretext for entering our interior country." Jefferson wrote proudly to John Dickinson of the accomplishment.

> Monticello Aug. 9. 1803.
> The acquisition of New Orleans would of itself have been a great thing, as it would have ensured to our Western brethren the means of exporting their produce: but that of Louisiana is inappreciable, because, giving us the sole dominion of the Missisipi, it excludes those bickerings with foreign powers, which we know of a certainty would have put us at war with France immediately: and it secures to us the course of a peaceable nation.

Jefferson conceded in a letter to Joseph Priestley that he had not expected the treaty so soon. Napoleon had yielded the territory because of his plans for a new war against Britain. The Louisiana cession would cut France's military expenditures and the purchase price would contribute to her war chest.

> Washington, January 29, 1804.
> I did not expect he would yield till a war took place between France and England, and my hope was to palliate and endure...until that event. I believed the event not very distant, but acknolege it came on sooner than I had expected. Whether, however, the good sense

of Bonaparte might not see the course predicted to be necessary & unavoidable, even before a war should be imminent, was a chance which we thought it our duty to try; but the immediate prospect of rupture brought the case to immediate decision. The *dénoument* has been happy; and I confess I look to this duplication of area for the extending a government so free and economical as ours, as a great achievement to the mass of happiness which is to ensue.

In October Jefferson called an early session of Congress to ratify the treaty, appropriate money for the purchase, and work out the details of government for the territory. He gave the two houses some details of the negotiations and submitted the matter to their wisdom. Acquisition of Louisiana would, he pointed out modestly, "promise, in due season, important aids to our treasury, an ample provision for our posterity, and a wide spread for the blessings of freedom and equal laws." But he did not ignore the circumstances that had made the promise possible—the reopening of war between Britain and France—and he suggested guidelines for maintaining American neutrality in the new dispute.

Oct. 17. 1803.

CULVER PICTURES, INC.

Sculptured group of Monroe and Livingston with the French Minister of Finance, François de Barbé-Marbois, at the signing ceremony

We have seen with sincere concern the flames of war lighted up again in Europe, and nations with which we have the most friendly and useful relations, engaged in mutual destruction. While we regret the miseries in which we see others involved, let us bow with gratitude to that kind providence, which, inspiring with wisdom and moderation our late legislative councils...guarded us from hastily entering into the sanguinary contest, and left us only to look on, and to pity it's ravages. These will be heaviest on those immediately engaged. Yet the nations pursuing peace will not be exempt from all evil. In the course of this conflict, let it be our endeavor, as it is our interest and desire, to cultivate the friendship of the belligerent nations by every act of justice, and of innocent kindness...but to administer the means of annoyance to none; to establish in our harbours such a police as may maintain law and order; to restrain our citizens from embarking individually in a war in which their country takes no part; to punish severely those persons, citizen or alien, who shall usurp the cover of our flag...; to exact from every nation the observance towards our vessels and citizens, of those principles and

341

practices which all civilized people acknowledge; to merit the character of a just nation, and maintain that of an independant one, preferring every consequence to insult and habitual wrong. Congress will consider whether the existing laws enable us efficaciously to maintain this course.... We should be most unwise indeed, were we to cast away the singular blessings of the position in which nature has placed us, the opportunity she has endowed us with of pursuing at a distance from foreign contentions, the paths of industry, peace, and happiness....

While Congress attended to the purchase, Jefferson became embroiled in one of the more lighthearted diplomatic crises of his career. If he was ever proud of causing a minor breach in foreign relations, he would have boasted of this one, for he annoyed the new British minister in Washington, Anthony Merry, by his steadfast adherence to republican principles. Although he appreciated European .graces and saw that the President's House offered its guests dishes prepared by a French chef, Jefferson himself proclaimed that "there is no 'court of the U.S.,' since the 4th of Mar. 1801. That day buried levees, birthdays, royal parades, and the arrogance of precedence in society." On being presented to Jefferson early one November morning at the President's House, Merry was shocked to find him "not merely in undress, but actually standing in slippers down at the heels, and both pantaloons, coat and underclothes indicative of an indifference to appearance."

A month later, the Merrys were invited to a dinner with the President. To Jefferson the evening was a congenial gathering of Cabinet officers and members of the diplomatic corps and their wives. The Merrys, however, obviously expected the dinner to be in their honor and conducted along lines of strict etiquette. When the meal was announced, Jefferson gave his arm to Dolley Madison, his unofficial hostess. Mrs. Merry, whose ideas of diplomatic prerogative were even more rigid than her husband's, was infuriated. Merry wrote indignantly to his government, asking further instructions in dealing with this affront. Jefferson and Madison tried vainly to placate him. Secretly amused by the whole affair, Jefferson wrote Monroe, who had become the American minister in Britain.

Washington Jan. 8. 1804.

We have told him that the principle of society, as well as of government, with us, is the equality of the individuals composing it. That no man here would come to a dinner, where he was to be marked with inferiority to any other. That we might as well attempt to force our

Portrait of Jefferson as President by Charles Fevret de Saint-Mémin

principle of equality at St. James's, as he his principle of precedence here. I had been in the habit, when I invited female company (having no lady in my family) to ask one of the ladies of the 4. secretaries to come and take care of my company; and as she was to do the honors of the table I handed her to dinner myself. That Mr. Merry might not construe this as giving them a precedence over Mrs. Merry, I have discontinued it; and here as well as in private houses, the pele-mele [pell-mell] practice, is adhered to.... With respect to Merry, he appears so reasonable and good a man, that I should be sorry to lose him as long as there remains a possibility of reclaiming him to the exercise of his own dispositions. If his wife perseveres, she must eat her soup at home, and we shall endeavor to draw him into society as if she did not exist.

The Merry incident was one of the last occasions for wry humor Jefferson found in the election year of 1804. As it began, he followed his established practice of ignoring the political process by which he was to be renominated; but his hopes of completely turning his back on the race were complicated by problems with the Vice President. Burr had lost the support of New York Republicans, when he sought Federalist support in the gubernatorial elections, and had alienated party members in Congress by actions such as voting against the repeal of the Judiciary Act. Jefferson found that close association with Burr confirmed Hamilton's claims of his arrogance and ambition, and the President had quietly encouraged Governor George Clinton to remain in office in New York to foil Burr's hopes. Burr was unaware of this, but he did realize that his chances for state or federal elective office were slim and he was becoming desperate. On January 26 he visited Jefferson by appointment, and the President made notes as the Vice President opened with an oversimplified version of his political career and motives.

Anas

Jan. 26. [1804]... he had come to N. Y. a stranger, some years ago; that he found the country in possession of two rich families (the Livingstons and Clintons); that his pursuits were not political, and he meddled not. When the crisis, however, of 1800 came on, they found their influence worn out, and sollicited his aid with the people. He lent it without any views of promotion. That his being named as a candidate for V.P. was unexpected by him. He acceded to it with a view to promote my fame and advancement, and from a desire to be with me, whose company and conversation had always been fascinating to him.... That his attachment to me had been sincere, and was still unchanged... he asked if any change had taken place in mine towards him.... He reminded me of a letter written to him about the time of counting the votes, (say Feb. 1801) mentioning that his election had left a chasm in my arrangements; that I had lost him from my list in the admn. &c. He observed, he believed it would be for the interest of the republican cause for him to retire; that a disadvantageous schism would otherwise take place; but that were he to retire, it would be said he shrunk from the public sentence, which he never would do; that his enemies were using my name to destroy him, and something was necessary from me to prevent and deprive them of that weapon, some mark of favor from me, which would declare to the world that he retired with my confidence.

I answered by recapitulating to him what had been my conduct previous to the election of 1800. That I never had interfered directly or indirectly with my friends or any others, to influence the election either for him or myself; that I considered it as my duty to be merely passive.... That in the election now coming on, I was observing the same conduct....

[Jefferson quickly corrected Burr's version of his letter, which actually dated to December, 1800. He had written Burr only to confirm the precedent set by Washington and Adams of confining the Vice President to domestic duties because of his role as potential successor to the President.]

I should here notice, that Colo. Burr must have thought that I could swallow strong things in my own favor, when he founded his acquiescence in the nomination as Vice-President, to his desire of promoting my honor, the being with me, whose company and conversation had always been fascinating with him, &c. I had never seen Colo. Burr till he came as a member of Senate. His conduct very soon inspired me with distrust. I habitually cautioned Mr. Madison against trusting him too much. I saw afterwards, that under General Washington's and Mr. Adams' administrations, whenever a great military appointment or a diplomatic one was to be made, he came post to Philadelphia to show himself, and in fact that he was always at market, if they had wanted him.

A month later, the Republican caucus in Congress unanimously renominated Jefferson. George Clinton was chosen as the vice-presidential candidate; Aaron Burr received not a single vote. Political wrangles were soon displaced in Jefferson's attention, however, by personal tragedy. In February Mary Jefferson Eppes, often called Polly or Maria, gave birth to her fourth child, only the second to live. The pregnancy had been difficult, and her recovery was slow. On Jefferson's return to Monticello in April, he took personal charge of her treatment and reported the results to James Madison.

Monticello Apr. 9. 1804.

I found my daughter Eppes at Monticello, whither she had been brought on a litter by hand; so weak as barely to be able to stand, her stomach so disordered as to reject almost every thing she took into it, a constant small fever, and an imposthume [abscess] rising in her breast. The indulgence of her friends had permitted her to be uninformed of the importance of strict attention to the necessity of food, and it's quality. I have been able to regulate this, and for some days she has taken food enough to support her, and of the kind only which her stomach bears without rejection. Her first imposthume has broken, but there is some fear of a second: if this latter cause does not more than countervail the effect of her present regimen, I am not without hopes of raising her again, as I should expect that restoring her strength by wine and digestible food, her fever would wear off. Her spirits and confidence are favourably affected by my being with her, and aid the effects of regimen.

NEW-YORK HISTORICAL SOCIETY

Republican placard of 1804 urging election of Jefferson and Clinton

Eight days later, not yet twenty-six years old, Mary died. Her elder sister Martha, a tall, forthright woman, had always been closer to their father than pretty, quiet Polly. But Polly probably bore a stronger physical resemblance to the girls' mother, and her death was a dreadful blow to Jefferson. He had not only lost a daughter but her last illness seemed a repetition of her mother's passing and brought back all the torment he had known at Monticello in the summer of 1782. He shared his wracking grief with his old friend John Page, now Governor of Virginia.

Washington June 25. [18]04.

Others may lose of their abundance; but, I, of my want, have lost, even the half of all I had. My evening prospects now hang on the slender thread of a single life. Perhaps I may be destined to see even this last cord of parental affection broken! The hope with which I had looked forward to the moment when, resigning public cares to younger hands, I was to retire to that domestic comfort from which the last great step is to be taken, is fearfully blighted. When you and I look back on the country over which we have passed, what a field of slaughter does it exhibit. Where are all the friends who entered it with us under all the inspiring energies of health and hope? As if pursued by the havoc of war, they are strowed by the way, some earlier, some later, and scarce a few straglers remain to count the numbers fallen, and to mark yet by their own fall the last footsteps of their party. Is it a desireable thing to bear up thro' the heat of the action, to witness the death of all our companions, and merely be the last victim? I doubt it. We have however the traveller's consolation. Every step shortens the distance we have to go; the end of our journey is in sight, the bed wherein we are to rest, and to rise in the midst of the friends we have lost.

John Page by Charles W. Peale

For a time, it seemed that Jefferson might be consoled for Polly's loss by the renewal of a friendship with a family who had also loved her well, the Adamses. Without her husband's knowledge, Abigail Adams sent Jefferson a letter of condolence, recalling her first meeting with Polly when the child had stopped in London on her way to rejoin her father and sister in Paris in 1787. At first, Jefferson hoped he could reestablish old ties, but the ensuing correspondence with Abigail degenerated into charges and countercharges of political favoritism and personal spite, especially concerning Adams's midnight appointments. Mrs. Adams closed the brief exchange on October 25.

If Jefferson did not regain a friend that summer, he lost a bitter enemy when Alexander Hamilton was slain in a duel with Aaron Burr in July. With Hamilton gone and Burr's career ruined by the scandal, old political alignments and rivalries faded more quickly. In the presidential and congressional elections Jefferson and Clinton carried every state except Connecticut and Delaware. Shortly after returns from Massachusetts were announced, Jefferson wrote joyfully to William Heath, a Continental Army veteran who had fought long for Republican measures in the Bay State.

Washington Dec. 13. [18]04

I sincerely join you in congratulations on the return of Massachusets into the fold of the Union. This is truly the case wherein we may say 'this our brother was dead, and is alive again: and was lost, and is found.' It is but too true that our union could not be pronounced entirely sound while so respectable a member as Massachusets was under morbid affection. All will now come to rights. Connecticut encouraged by her elder sister will rally to catholic principles, will dismount her oligarchy, and fraternize with the great federated family. The new century opened itself by committing us on a boisterous ocean. But all is now subsiding, peace is smoothing our paths at home and abroad, and if we are not wanting in the practice of justice and moderation, our tranquility and prosperity may be preserved, until increasing numbers shall leave us nothing to fear from without.... Should we be able to preserve this state of public happiness and to see our citizens whom we found so divided, rally to their genuine principles, I [shall] hope yet to enjoy the comfort of that general good will which has been so unfeelingly wrested from me, and to sing at the close of my term the nunc demittas Domine with a satisfaction leaving nothing to desire but the last great audit.

Engraving of Hamilton-Burr duel from Lamb's History of New York

For all his letters of congratulations to New England Republicans, Jefferson did not end his first term in a state of unrealistic euphoria. The war in Europe had spread, and the nation again had to reaffirm and defend its neutral status and trade. In January Jefferson sent timely suggestions to Congressman Joseph Nicholson. With his usual thrift, he had decided to ignore the costly and grandiose plans for coastal fortifications adopted by the Adams administration, which he pointed out there was neither time nor money to erect. Instead, he outlined two methods of preventing foreign vessels from threatening towns that lined the harbors.

Washington Jan. 29. [18]05.

If we cannot hinder vessels from entering our harbours, we should turn our attention to the putting it out of their power to lie, or come to, before a town to injure it. Two means of doing this may be adopted in aid of each other. 1. Heavy cannon on travelling carriages, which may be moved to any point on the bank or beach most convenient for dislodging the vessel. A sufficient number of these should be lent to each sea port town, and their militia

Napoleon entering Notre-Dame to be crowned emperor in December, 1804, as Jefferson's first term ended

trained to them. The executive is authorised to do this; it has been done in a small degree, and will now be done more competently.

2. Heavy cannon on floating batteries or boats, which may be so stationed as to prevent a vessel entering the harbor, or force her after entering to depart. There are about 15. harbors in the U.S. which ought to be in a state of substantial defence. The whole of these would require, according to the best opinions 240. gunboats...the whole cost one million of Dollars. But we should allow ourselves 10. years to compleat it unless circumstances should force it sooner....We now possess 10. built and building. It is the opinion of those consulted that 15. more would enable us to put every harbour under our view into a respectable condition: and that this should limit the views of the present year. This would require an appropriation of 60,000. D. and I suppose *that* the best way of limiting it, without declaring the number, as perhaps that sum would build more. I should think it best not to give a detailed report, which exposes our policy too much.

Ominously, Jefferson's first administration of frugality and peace ended with a call for gunboats and cannon. With freedom from the worst effects of European wars, he had been able to put republican principles into effective practice; Gallatin's financial program of reduced expenditures and tax reduction had gone smoothly as wartime trade increased America's customs' receipts; and the West had been secured and extended. But much of Jefferson's success was due to good fortune, which he used skillfully, even brilliantly. He had been given time to lay the foundations for republican government by the accidents of Continental wars and the conflicting needs of kings and emperors. No one could expect that good fortune to continue indefinitely, and Jefferson knew that his administration and the national unity he had won might soon have to prove themselves in a time of trial.

Chapter 12

From Promise to Performance

When Jefferson began his second term in 1805, he had a clear mandate to continue Republican policies. Unlike his election in 1800, his victory in 1804 was not indebted to reaction to the opposition's mistakes. His triumph was a vote of approval for his first administration and a tribute to his ability to implement the policies he had proposed as an alternative to Federalism. But the political winds during his second term would be much less favorable. The "few years" he had thought necessary to consolidate domestic affairs before America could defend her rights abroad would be all too few. The conflict between France and Great Britain developed into the War of the Third Coalition against Napoleon in 1805. British warships had already begun to patrol the American coast in search of deserters from the Royal Navy, and those squadrons were mere harbingers of further harassment of American trade to come.

The pressures of time overshadowed Jefferson's second administration — time to build gunboats for harbor defense, time to receive diplomatic dispatches from abroad, time to rally public opinion or to quiet public outrage, and time to prepare for a challenge to American rights. If it came too soon for effective retaliation, such a challenge would damage the national honor and prestige and impair the commercial privileges that had brought prosperity to merchants and farmers and financial stability to the government. Jefferson confided to his colleagues that he was working under a personal time limit as well. Even before taking his oath of office for the second time, he had decided against accepting a third term, as he explained to John Taylor of Caroline.

> Washington Jan. 6. 1805
> My opinion originally was that the President of the U. S. should have been elected for 7. years, and forever ineligible afterwards. I have since become sensible that 7. years is too long to be irremoveable, and that there should

Jefferson asked for and received authorization from Congress to purchase or construct 257 gunboats; five types can be seen above.

be a peaceable way of withdrawing a man in midway who is doing wrong. The service for 8. years with a power to remove at the end of the first four, comes nearly to my principle as corrected by experience: and it is in adherence to that, that I determine to withdraw at the end of my second term.... Genl. Washington set the example of voluntary retirement after 8. years. I shall follow it. And a few more precedents will oppose the obstacle of habit to any one after a while who shall endeavor to extend his term. Perhaps it may beget a disposition to establish it by an amendment of the constitution. I believe I am doing right therefore in pursuing my principle. I had determined to declare my intention but I have consented to be silent on the opinion of friends, who think it best not to put a continuance out of my power in defiance of all circumstances.

Jefferson knew he could rely on wide popular support during his second term. In notes for his second inaugural address, he defined the contrast between that message and the one he had delivered to Congress four years earlier.

[before March 4, 1805]

The former one was an exposition of the principles on which I thought it my duty to administer the government. The second then should naturally be a Compte rendu, or a statement of facts, shewing that I have conformed to those principles. The former was *promise:* this is *performance.*

The performance had been superb. In his inaugural address Jefferson had only to list his accomplishments to prove that point. He also floated a new proposition: that surplus revenues in the national treasury be put to regular use, in peacetime as a fund for education and internal improvements such as rivers, canals, and roads and in war as an easily tapped source for defense.

[March 4, 1805]

In the transaction of your foreign affairs we have endeavored to cultivate the friendship of all nations, & especially of those with which we have the most important relations. We have done them justice on all occasions; favor, where favor was lawful, cherished mutual interests & intercourse on fair & equal terms....

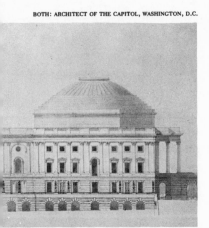

Jefferson made Benjamin H. Latrobe the Surveyor of Public Buildings in 1803; top priority was completion of the south wing of the Capitol. Latrobe's sketch of the ground-floor plan, c. 1804, is below; south elevation, 1810, above.

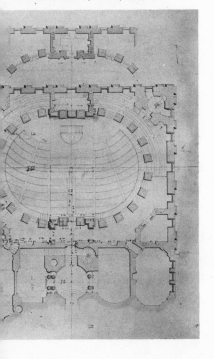

At home, fellow-citizens, you best know whether we have done well or ill. The suppression of unnecessary offices, of useless establishments and expences, enabled us to discontinue our internal taxes. These, covering our land with officers, & opening our doors to their intrusions, had already begun that process of domiciliary vexation, which, once entered, is scarcely to be restrained from reaching successively every article of property & produce....

The remaining revenue, on the consumption of foreign articles, is paid chiefly by those who can afford to add foreign luxuries to domestic comforts. Being collected on our sea-board and frontiers only, & incorporated with the transactions of our mercantile citizens, it may be the pleasure and the pride of an American to ask What farmer, what mechanic, what labourer ever sees a tax-gatherer of the US? These contributions enable us to support the current expences of the government, to fulfill contracts with foreign nations, to extinguish the native right of soil within our limits, to extend those limits, & to apply such a surplus to our public debts, as places at a short day their final redemption. And that redemption once effected, the revenue thereby liberated may, by a just repartition of it among the states, & a corresponding amendment of the constitution, be applied, *in time of peace,* to rivers, canals, roads, arts, manufactures, education, & other great objects within each state. *In time of war,* if injustice by ourselves or others must sometimes produce war, increased as the same revenue will be by increased population & consumption, & aided by other resources reserved for that crisis, it may meet within the year all the expenses of the year without encroaching on the rights of future generations by burthening them with the debts of the past. War will then be but a suspension of useful works; & a return to a state of peace a return to the progress of improvement.

But Jefferson knew that the Republicans' success in uniting the nation had not ended dissension but only modified it. His own party showed the strains of political victory. In opposition, Republicans could not afford the luxury of bickering among themselves; in power, they seemed determined to make up for years of suppressing conflicts of personality and philosophy by publicizing their differences. In the spring of 1805,

Jefferson was particularly concerned by factions in Pennsylvania and New York, key states in Republican control of the Middle States. But, as he explained to Senator George Logan of Pennsylvania, he would wisely choose neutrality for himself in intraparty squabbles as he had for the nation in European conflicts.

Washington May 11. [18]05.

I see with infinite pain the bloody schism which has taken place among our friends in Pensylvania & New York, & will probably take place in other states. The main body of both sections mean well, but their good intentions will produce great public evil. The minority, whichever section shall be the minority, will end in coalition with the federalists, and some compromise of principle; because these will not sell their aid for nothing. Republicanism will thus lose, & royalism gain some portion of that ground which we thought we had rescued to good government. I do not express my sense of our misfortunes from any idea that they are remediable. I know that the passions of men will take their course, that they are not to be controuled but by despotism, & that this melancholy truth is the pretext for despotism. The duty of an upright administration is to pursue it's course steadily, to know nothing of these family dissensions, and to cherish the good principles of both parties.

George Logan

The second term got off to a good start when a treaty was signed in June ending the Tripolitan War. The treaty's terms were favorable to the United States and were the culmination of Jefferson's long resistance to the pirates' depradations on shipping and demands for tribute, although some payments would continue until 1816. A month later, Jefferson's policy of using American neutrality to gain concessions from European powers was severely tested. The challenge came not from the great rivals, France and Great Britain, but from Spain. In the autumn of 1804, James Monroe had gone to Madrid to join Thomas Pinckney in negotiating several disputed matters: the western boundary of Louisiana, possession of the Floridas, and indemnification for American shipping seized by Spain or brought into Spanish ports during the last European war. The American demands were rejected and Monroe returned to London to become the new American minister there, stopping briefly at Paris, where Napoleon supported his ally. By July, Jefferson had received news of the failure. Spurred by Spanish intransigence, the President proposed an overture to Great Britain as a countermeasure to French support of Spain. Madison was surprised by the proposal, and Jefferson wrote to explain his arguments.

Late in 1805, Jefferson received Suliman Mellimelli, an envoy from Tunis who brought presents, which were refused, and demanded tribute, which the President would not pay.

Monticello Aug. 27 [18]05.

I have no idea of committing ourselves immediately, or independantly of our further will, to the war. The treaty should be provisional only, to come into force on the event of our being engaged in war with either France or Spain, during the present war in Europe. In that event we should make common cause, & England should stipulate not to make peace without our obtaining the objects for which we go to war, to wit, the acknolegement by Spain of the rightful boundaries of Louisiana (which we should reduce to our minimum by a secret article) and 2. indemnification for spoliations for which purpose we should be allowed to make reprisal on the Floridas & *retain them* as an indemnification. Our cooperation in the war (if we should actually enter into it) would be sufficient consideration for Great Britain to engage for it's object: and it being generally known to France & Spain that we had entered into treaty with England would probably ensure us a peaceable & immediate settlement of both points.

By the time Jefferson returned to Washington in October, however, an alliance with Great Britain seemed much less feasible. The European war then looked as if it would be a long one, and Jefferson decided to press negotiations again, this time in Paris by the new United States Minister to France, John Armstrong. Jefferson outlined his revised policy to the Secretary of State.

Washington Oct. 23. [18]05.

The probability of an extensive war on the continent of Europe strengthening every day for some time past, is now almost certain. This gives us our great desideratum, time. In truth it places us quite at our ease. We are certain of one year of campaigning at least, and one other year of negociation for their peace arrangements. Should we be now forced into war, it is become much more questionable than it was, whether we should not pursue it unembarrassed by any alliance & free to retire from it whenever we can obtain our separate terms. It gives us time too to make another effort for peaceable settlement. Where shall this be done? Not at Madrid certainly. At Paris: through Armstrong, or Armstrong & Monroe as negociators, France as the Mediator, the price of the Floridas as the means. We need not care who gets that:

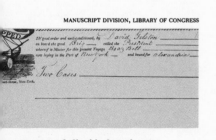

An 1805 bill of lading for two cases of wine ordered by Madison, Jefferson, and a third gentleman

353

*Cartoon of Jefferson, stung by
Napoleon, coughing up two million
dollars for East and West Florida*

and an enlargement of the sum we had thought of may be the bait to France, while the Guadaloupe as the Western boundary may be the soother of Spain providing for our spoliated citizens in some effectual way. We may announce to France that determined not to ask justice of Spain again, yet desirous of making one other effort to preserve peace, we are willing to see whether her interposition can obtain it on terms which we think just; that no delay however can be admitted, & that in the mean time should Spain attempt to change the status quo, we shall repel force by force, without undertaking other active hostilities till we see what may be the issue of her interference.

In November the Cabinet agreed on the terms to be offered by the negotiators in Paris: purchase of the Floridas and part of Texas, with the assumption of Spanish payments for depredations on American shipping as a large portion of the price. That same month Jefferson received word from Armstrong that Talleyrand was willing to force Spain to negotiate. In a confidential message to Congress, Jefferson broadly outlined the policy to be pursued.

[December 6, 1805]

The conduct of France, and the part she may take in the misunderstandings between the US. and Spain, are too important to be unconsidered.... Whatever direction she might mean to give to these differences, it does not appear that she has contemplated their proceeding to actual rupture, or that, at the date of our last advices from Paris, her government had any suspicion of the hostile attitude Spain had taken here. On the contrary we have reason to believe that she was disposed to effect a settlement on a plan analogous to what our ministers had proposed, and so comprehensive as to remove as far as possible the grounds of future collision & controversy on the Eastern as well as Western side of the Missisipi.

The present crises in Europe is favorable for pressing such a settlement; and not a moment should be lost in availing ourselves of it. Should it pass unimproved, our situation would become much more difficult. Formal war is not necessary. It is not probable it will follow. But the protection of our citizens, the spirit and honor of our country, require that force should be interposed to a

*Cartoon of Jefferson encouraging
congressional dogs, including son-
in-law John Eppes, to fight the
bull Spain and take West Florida*

certain degree. It will probably contribute to advance the object of peace.

But the course to be pursued will require the command of means which it belongs to Congress exclusively to yield or to deny. To them I communicate every fact material for their information, & the documents necessary to enable them to judge for themselves. To their wisdom then I look for the course I am to take, and will pursue with sincere zeal that which they shall approve.

What Jefferson really wanted from Congress was authorization for an appropriation of two million dollars to purchase the Floridas, a sum he intended to make known through the House Republican leadership and a committee headed by John Randolph of Roanoke. Randolph balked, however, at what he said was extortion, a payment through France to force cessions from Spain. Not until mid-February were resolutions finally passed for "extraordinary" but unspecified diplomatic expenses.

That was the beginning of Randolph's falling out with the executive branch, a schism among Republicans that damaged the party's prestige and the sense of invincibility that had marked Jefferson's first five years in office. A related matter drew more of Randolph's wrath in January; Jefferson sent another confidential message to Congress concerning the continuing British raids on American shipping and the impressment of American sailors.

Jan. 17. 1806.

The right of a Neutral to carry on commercial intercourse with every part of the dominions of a belligerent, permitted by the municipal laws of the country (with the exception of blockaded ports & Contraband of war), was believed to have been decided between Great Britain & the US. by the sentence of the Commissioners mutually appointed to decide on that & other questions of difference between the two nations; and by the actual paiment of damages awarded by them against Great Britain for the infractions of that right. When therefore it was percieved that the same principle was revived, with others more novel, & extending the injury, instructions were given to the Minister Plenipotentiary of the US. at the court of London, and remonstrances duly made by him on this subject, as will appear by documents transmitted herewith. These were followed by a partial & temporary suspension only, without any disavowal of the principle. He has therefore been instructed to urge this subject anew, to bring it more fully to the bar of

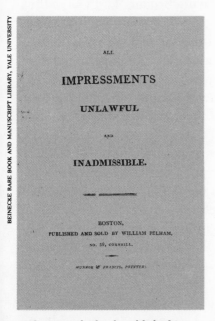

ALL
IMPRESSMENTS
UNLAWFUL
AND
INADMISSIBLE.

BOSTON,
PUBLISHED AND SOLD BY WILLIAM PELHAM,
NO. 59, CORNHILL.

MUNROE & FRANCIS, PRINTERS.

Title page of a book published in Boston in 1804 on impressment

355

reason, & to insist on rights too evident, and too important to be surrendered. In the mean time the evil is proceeding under adjudications founded on the principle which is denied. Under these circumstances the subject presents itself for the consideration of Congress.

On the impressment of our Seamen, our remonstrances have never been intermitted. A hope existed, at one moment, of an arrangement which might have been submitted to. But it soon passed away, & the practice, tho' relaxed at times in the distant seas, has been constantly pursued in those in our neighborhood.

Following this message, Randolph broke completely with the administration. He ridiculed the attempt to protect the interests of eastern merchants and their shipping after declining to use force in the West. "After shrinking from the Spanish jackal," he asked in debate, "do you presume to bully the British lion?" When a program of nonimportation of selected British goods passed the House over Randolph's opposition, his leadership had ended.

Although Jefferson and Madison had not let congressional leaders know precisely what measures they wanted, it was clear that they intended some effective program of commercial retaliation. But they received more than they bargained for. The commercial restrictions were not to go into effect until November, and, in the meantime, they were directed to send a special mission to London to negotiate the dispute with Britain. In theory, the British would be willing to make concessions over the summer rather than face restrictions on their trade with America the following fall and winter. Jefferson chose William Pinkney of Maryland as Monroe's colleague for this assignment. He described the circumstances leading to the mission to Monroe, whose position was especially delicate because Randolph's followers were championing him over Madison as the next Republican leader.

Washington May 4. [18]06.

His course [Randolph's] has excited considerable alarm. Timid men consider it as a proof of the weakness of our government, & that it is to be rent into pieces by demagogues & to end in anarchy. I survey the scene with a different eye, and draw a different augury from it. In a house of Representatives of a great mass of good sense, Mr. R.'s popular eloquence gave him such advantages as to place him unrivalled as the leader of the house: and, altho' not conciliatory to those whom he led, principles of duty & patriotism induced many of them to swallow humiliations he subjected them to, and to vote as was

Late nineteenth-century engraving of an American seaman being impressed

Prime Minister Charles James Fox

right, as long as he kept the path of right himself. The sudden defection of such a man, could not but produce a momentary astonishment & even dismay. But for a moment only. The good sense of the house rallied around it's principles, & without any leader, pursued steadily the business of the session, did it well, & by a strength of vote which has never before been seen.... The augury I draw from this is, that there is a steady, good sense in the legislature and in the body of the nation, joined with good intentions, which will lead them to discern & to pursue the public good under all circumstances which can arise, and that no ignis fatuus will be able to lead them long astray. In the present case, the public sentiment, as far as declarations of it have yet come in, is, without a single exception, in firm adherence to the administration.... The great body of your friends are among the firmest adherents to the administration. And in their support of you will suffer Mr. R. to have no communications with them.... it is unfortunate for you to be embarrassed with such a soi-disant friend. You must not commit yourself to him.

[Jefferson saw advantages for the Monroe-Pinkney mission in the death of William Pitt and the succession of Charles James Fox as Prime Minister.]

The late change in the ministry I consider as ensuring us a just settlement of our differences, and we ask no more. In Mr. Fox personally I have more confidence than in any man in England, and it is founded in what, through unquestionable channels, I have had opportunities of knowing of his honesty & his good sense. While he shall be in the administration, my reliance on that government will be solid. We had committed ourselves in a line of proceedings adapted to meet Mr. Pitt's policy & hostility before we heard of his death, which self-respect did not permit us to abandon afterwards.... It ought not to be viewed by the ministry as looking towards them at all, but merely the consequences of the measures of their predecessors, which their nation has called on them to correct. I hope, therefore, they will come to just arrangements. No two countries upon earth have so many points of common interest and friendship: and their rulers must be great bunglers indeed if with such dispositions, they break them asunder. The only rivalry that can arise is on the ocean. England may by petty larceny thwartings, check us on that element a little, but nothing she can do will retard us there one year's growth.... We ask for peace & justice from all nations, & we will remain uprightly neutral in fact, tho' leaning in belief to the opinion that an English ascendancy on the ocean is safer for us than that of France.

Over the summer of 1806, Jefferson and Madison waited for reports from the two negotiating teams in London and Paris. It was, of course, an election year, and Jefferson wrote to Barnabas Bidwell, a freshman congressman from Massachusetts who had aided the administration against Randolph, encouraging him to seek reelection. Jefferson felt that if Bidwell did not run, the loss of his seat could upset the delicate balance between loyal Republicans and Randolph's followers, the Quids. He may also have hoped that Bidwell would become the leader the executive needed to assure that its measures were not simply abandoned in Congress, even though Randolph described the role as that of a "backstairs counsellor."

Washington July 5. 1806.

I read with extreme regret the expressions of an inclination on your part to retire from Congress. I will not say that this time, more than all others, calls for the service of every man. But I will say there never was a time when the services of those who possess talents, integrity, firmness, & sound judgment were more wanted in Congress. Some one of that description is particularly wanted to take the lead in the H. of R. to consider the business of the nation a[s] his own business, to take it up as if he were singly charged with it and carry it through. I do not mean that any gentleman relinquishing his own judgment should implicitly support all the measures of the administration; but that, where he does not disapprove of them, he should not suffer them to go off in sleep, but bring them to the attention of the house, and give them a fair chance. Where he disapproves, he will of course leave them to be brought forward by those who concur in the sentiment.... When a gentleman, through zeal for the public service, undertakes to do the public business, we know that we shall hear the cant of backstairs' counsellors. But we never heard this while the declaimer [Randolph] was himself, a backstairs' man

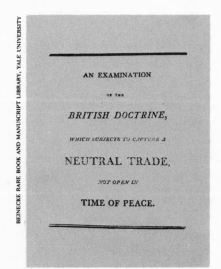

AN EXAMINATION

OF THE

BRITISH DOCTRINE,

WHICH SUBJECTS TO CAPTURE A

NEUTRAL TRADE,

NOT OPEN IN

TIME OF PEACE.

Title page of an 1806 pamphlet by Secretary of State James Madison examining the British attitude toward the neutral carrying trade

A front view of the President's House; the engraving is after a drawing by George Catlin.

as he calls it, but in the confidence & views of the administration, as may more properly & respectfully be said. But if the members are to know nothing but what is important enough to be put into a public message, & indifferent enough to be made known to all the world, if the Executive is to keep all other information to himself, & the House to plunge on in the dark, it becomes a government of chance & not of design.... The last session of Congress was indeed an uneasy one for a time: but as soon as the members penetrated into the views of those who were taking a new course, they rallied in as solid a phalanx as I have ever seen act together.... They want only a man of business and in whom they can confide, to conduct things in the house; and they are as much disposed to support him as can be wished. It is only speaking a truth to say that all eyes look to you.... Perhaps I am not entitled to speak with so much frankness; but it proceeds from no motive which has not a right to your forgiveness. Opportunities of candid explanation are so seldom afforded me, that I must not lose them when they occur.

Rumors of Republican disunion were the Federalists' best weapons in an election year, and Randolph had played into their hands. By October, when Jefferson returned to Washington to begin preparing for the congressional session, the opposition press had extended their time-honored campaign to his Cabinet. Wearily the President wrote to Gallatin of reports that there was disagreement between them. His assurances were unnecessary, for the Treasury Secretary never doubted the President's support, but Jefferson welcomed any opportunity to affirm faith in his colleagues that fall when there was reason to distrust so many Republicans.

Washington Oct. 12. [18]06.

You witnessed in the earlier part of the administration the malignant & long continued efforts which the federalists exerted, in their newspapers, to produce misunderstanding between Mr. Madison & myself. These failed compleatly. A like attempt was afterwards made through other channels to effect a similar purpose between Genl. Dearborn & myself, but with no more success. The machinations of the last session to put you at cross questions with us all were so obvious as to be seen at the first glance of every eye. In order to destroy one member of the administration, the whole were to be set

Public Men, SULLIVAN

Blennerhassett's Island, in the Ohio River, was the staging area for Burr's ill-fated expedition.

to loggerheads to destroy one another. I observe in the papers lately new attempts to revive this stale artifice, & that they squint more directly towards you & myself. I cannot therefore be satisfied till I declare to you explicitly, that my affections and confidence in you are nothing impaired, & that they cannot be impaired by means so unworthy the notice of candid & honorable minds. I make the declaration that no doubts or jealousies, which often beget the facts they fear, may find a moment's harbor in either of our minds.... Our administration now drawing towards a close, I have a sublime pleasure in believing it will be distinguished as much by having placed itself above all the passions which could disturb it's harmony, as by the great operations by which it will have advanced the well-being of the nation.

More alarming than any Federalist tales of defections in the Cabinet were the well-confirmed reports of treasonous activities by Jefferson's former Vice President, Aaron Burr. An ambitious politician denied office by his state and nation, Burr had turned to fantastic schemes in the West. Rumors of his plans, which included recruiting an expedition against Spanish territory in the Southwest and Mexico, had come to Jefferson's attention earlier in the year, but there was little that could be done against Burr until he took concrete, provable action. General James Wilkinson, a co-conspirator in the early stages of the intrigues, offered the proof. Whether Wilkinson experienced an attack of conscience or a sudden realization that the expedition was doomed, he became Burr's chief attacker. The General's dispatch to Jefferson, detailing Burr's plans to lead his expedition down the Ohio and Mississippi and possibly seize New Orleans, reached Washington at the end of November. After conferring with the Cabinet, Jefferson issued a proclamation against the expedition, calling for the support of government officials and private citizens in quelling the grandiose scheme. Neither in the proclamation nor in his message to Congress five days later did he mention Burr's name. But the fact of Burr's involvement was no secret, and in private Jefferson wrote bitterly of his former Vice President to John Langdon, a New Hampshire Republican.

Washington Dec. 22. [18]06.

Our prospects are great if we can preserve external & internal peace. With England I firmly expect a friendly arrangement. With Spain we shall possibly have blows; but they will hasten, instead of preventing a peaceable settlement. The most instant pressure is now from among ourselves. Our Cataline is at the head of an armed body (we know not it's strength) and his object is to siese N. Orleans, from thence attack Mexico, place himself on the throne of Montezuma, add Louisiana to his empire, & the Western states from the Alleganey if he can. I do not believe he will attain the crown; but neither am I certain the halter will get it's due. A few days will let us see whether the Western states suppress themselves this insurrectionary enterprize, or we shall be obliged to make a great national armament for it. In the end, I am satisfied it will exhibit to the world another proof that the people of the US. are qualified for self government. Our friends, the federalists, chuckle at all this: but in justice I must add we have found some faithful among those in the West.

Congress buzzed over Burr's expedition and seemed to have little time for other matters. Jefferson and Madison may have been relieved at the legislators' lack of curiosity in the progress of negotiations abroad: Armstrong and James Bowdoin had failed to reach any understanding with the Spanish in Madrid, and the Monroe-Pinkney mission had been jeopardized by the death of Charles James Fox in September. But the President was not pleased by congressional indifference to his pleas for military preparedness in the event of diplomatic failure. His annual message covered such diverse matters as the progress of the Lewis and Clark expedition and the approach of the year 1808 when Congress could end the slave trade. It closed with a request for a firm but typically republican program.

Dec. 2. [18]06.

The expedition of Messrs. Lewis & Clarke, for exploring the river Missouri, and the best communication from that to the Pacific ocean, has had all the success which could have been expected. They have traced the Missouri nearly to it's source, descended the Columbia to the Pacific ocean, ascertained with accuracy the geography of that interesting communication across our continent, learnt the character of the country, of it's commerce and inhabitants, and it is but justice to say that Messrs. Lewis & Clarke, and their brave companions, have, by this arduous service, deserved well of their country....

I congratulate you, fellow-citizens, on the approach of the period at which you may interpose your authority constitutionally, to withdraw the citizens of the United states from all further participation in those violations of human rights, which have been so long continued on

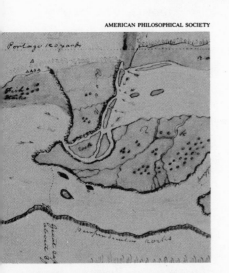

Detail of a map drawn by William Clark showing portages around the "Great Falls" of the Columbia River

361

the unoffending inhabitants of Africa, & which the morality, the reputation & the best interests of our country have long been eager to proscribe. Although no law you may pass can take prohibitory effect till the first day of the year 1808. yet the intervening period is not too long to prevent by timely notice, expeditions which cannot be compleated before that day....

...such is the situation of the nations of Europe, & such too the predicament in which we stand with some of them, that we cannot rely with certainty on the present aspect of our affairs. That may change from moment to moment, during the course of your session, or after you shall have separated. Our duty is therefore to act upon things as they are, & to make a reasonable provision for whatever they may be. Were armies to be raised whenever a speck of war is visible in our horizon, we never should have been without them. Our resources would have been exhausted on dangers which have never happened, instead of being reserved for what is really to take place. A steady, perhaps a quickened pace, in preparations for the defense of our Sea-port towns & waters, an early settlement of the most exposed and vulnerable parts of our country, a militia so organised that it's effective portions can be called to any point in the Union, or Volunteers, instead of them, to serve a sufficient time, are means which may always be ready, yet never preying on our resources until actually called into use. They will maintain the public interests, while a more permanent force shall be in a course of preparation. But much will depend on the promptitude with which these means can be brought into activity. If war be forced upon us in spite of our long & vain appeals to the justice of nations, rapid & vigorous movements in it's outset, will go far towards securing us in it's course & issue, and towards throwing it's burthens on those who render necessary the resort from reason to force.

William Pinkney

Jefferson's hopes for a peaceful settlement with Great Britain were dealt a blow in early February, 1807, when Madison received a report from Monroe indicating that he and Pinkney had agreed to omit any articles on impressment from the treaty. Jefferson hurriedly summoned the Cabinet, which decided not to notify the Senate and sent Monroe and Pinkney explicit instructions not to abandon the impressment issue. But the instructions were several weeks too late. Later in February, Madison received Monroe and Pinkney's announcement that they had signed a treaty on December 31 that would be "satisfactory." On March 3 a copy of the treaty itself arrived: not only was impressment relegated to a nonbinding note that said Britain would exercise caution, but Britain made no concessions on the seizure of neutral shipping and reserved a right to expand her policing of such trade.

That evening, the last of the session, a congressional delegation visited Jefferson to ask if there were any matters he wished to submit before adjournment. Suffering again from "periodical headache" Jefferson replied "Certainly not" to a pointed question as to whether the Monroe-Pinkney treaty might be ready for consideration. Congress adjourned, and Jefferson was left to recover from his illness and try to make peace with James Monroe, a proud man who would not look kindly on the inevitable rejection of the treaty he had signed.

Washington Mar. 21. 1807.

...I percieve uncommon efforts, and with uncommon wickedness are making by the Federal papers to produce mischief between myself personally and our negociators and also to irritate the British government, by putting a thousand speeches in my mouth, not one word of which I ever uttered. I have therefore thought it safe to guard you by stating the view which we have given out on the subject of the treaty, in conversation and otherwise; for ours, as you know, is a government which will not tolerate the being kept entirely in the dark, and especially on a subject so interesting as this treaty.... depend on it, my dear Sir, that it will be considered as a hard treaty when it is known. The British commissioners appear to have screwed every article as far as it would bear, to have taken every thing, and yielded nothing.... If the treaty cannot be put into an acceptable form, then the next best thing is to back out of the negociation as well as we can, letting that die away insensibly, but in the meantime agreeing informally that both parties shall act on the principles of the treaty, so as to preserve that friendly understanding which we so sincerely desire, until the one or the other may be disposed to yield the points which divide us. This will leave you to follow your desire of coming home as soon as you see that the amendment of the treaty is desperate. The power of continuing the negociations will pass over to Mr. Pinkney who, by procrastinations, can let it die away, and give us time, the most precious of all things to us.

Arrest of Burr in February, 1807, just before he tried to flee across the boundary into West Florida

The failure of the Monroe-Pinkney mission, and the political use the Federalists would make of it if the two diplomats did not revise the agreement over the summer, was but one of the threats to Republicanism that spring. Aaron Burr, arrested just above the border of Spanish Florida, had been brought to Richmond for trial on treason charges. The fact that Burr had laid the groundwork for the last stages of his buccaneering enterprise on an island within Virginia jurisdiction determined the site of the court proceedings. A trial in Richmond meant that John Marshall, Adams's appointee as Chief Justice, would preside on circuit duty. When Jefferson learned that Marshall had ordered proceedings to begin before the government could prepare its case, and had released Burr on ten-thousand-dollar bail, he lashed out against Burr, Marshall, and their Federalist adherents in a letter to William Branch Giles.

Monticello Apr. 20. [18]07.

That there should be anxiety & doubt in the public mind in the present defective state of the proof is not wonderful; and this has been sedulously encouraged by the tricks of the judges to force trials before it is possible to collect the evidence dispersed through a line of 2000. miles from Maine to Orleans. The federalists too give all their aid, making Burr's cause their own, mortified only that he did not separate the union or overturn the government, & proving that had he had a little dawn of success they would have joined him to introduce his object, their favorite monarchy, as they would any other enemy, foreign or domestic, who could rid them of this hateful republic, for any other government in exchange. ...We have set on foot an enquiry through the whole of the country which has been the scene of these transactions, to be able to prove to the courts, if they will give time, or to the public by way of communication to Congress, what the real facts have been. For obtaining this we are obliged to appeal to the patriotism of particular persons in different places, of whom we have requested to make the enquiry in their neighborhood, and on such information as shall be voluntarily offered. Aided by no process or facilities from the *federal* courts, but frowned on by their new born zeal for the liberty of those whom we would not permit to overthrow the liberties of their country, we can expect no revealments from the accomplices of the chief offender. Of treasonable intentions the judges have been obliged to confess there is probable appearance. What loophole they will find in it when it comes to trial, we cannot foresee....

Chief Justice John Marshall

*Detail from contemporary cartoon
shows the British* Leopard *firing
on the* Chesapeake, *June 22, 1807.*

If there ever had been an instance in this or the preceding administrations of federal judges, so applying principles of law as to condemn a federal, or acquit a republican offender, I should have judged them in the present case with more charity. All this however will work well. The nation will judge both offender, & judges for themselves. If a member of the Executive or Legislature does wrong, the day is never far distant when the people will remove him. They will see then and amend the error in our constitution which makes any branch independant of the nation, they will see that one of the great co-ordinate branches of the government, setting itself in opposition to the other two, and to the common sense of the nation, proclaims impunity to that class of offenders which endeavors to overturn the constitution, and are themselves protected in it by the constitution itself: for impeachment is a farce which will not be tried again. If their protection of Burr produces this amendment, it will do more good than his condemnation could have done.

Burr was acquitted by the jury in Richmond, after Marshall issued an opinion strictly construing the treason law; but the former Vice President was forced to flee the country to avoid further prosecution and the wrath of the public. The twisted logic by which some Federalists made "Burr's cause their own" was of less concern to Jefferson than the continuing Federalist domination of the bench. "This insurrection," he wrote, "will probably shew that the fault in our constitution is not that the Executive has too little power, but that the Judiciary either has too much, or holds it under too little responsibility." Indignant as he was at Federalist attempts to capitalize on Burr's case, Jefferson's real work after the close of the congressional session was to insure that negotiations in London took "a little nap" while the British government found reasons to conciliate America.

That hope was gone by July. On June 22 the British ship *Leopard*, one of a squadron off Hampton Roads, Virginia, had demanded that the American warship *Chesapeake* stop to be searched for British deserters among her crew. When the *Chesapeake*'s captain refused, the *Leopard* opened fire, killing three American sailors before the captain finally surrendered. After removing four supposed deserters, the *Leopard* allowed the *Chesapeake* to put in to shore. On June 25 members of the Cabinet were ordered to meet "without a moment's avoidable delay," and Jefferson prepared for their approval a proclamation calling for national unity and banning British ships from American waters. The *Anas* recorded subsequent meetings.

BY THOMAS JEFFERSON,

PRESIDENT OF THE U. STATES OF AMERICA,

A Proclamation.

During the wars which, for some time, have unhappily prevailed among the powers of Europe, the United States of America, firm in their principles of peace, have endeavored by justice, by a regular discharge of all their national and social duties, and by every friendly office their situation has admitted, to maintain, with all the belligerents, their accustomed relations of friendship, hospitality, and commercial intercourse.— Taking no part in the questions which animate these powers against each other, nor permitting themselves to entertain a wish but for the restoration of general peace, they have observed with good faith the neutrality they assumed, and they believe that no instance of a departure from its duties can be justly imputed to them by any nation. A free use of their harbors and waters, the means of refitting and of refreshment, of succour to their sick and suffering, have, at all times, and on equal principles, been extended to all, and this too amidst a constant recurrence of acts of insubordination to the laws, of violence to the persons, and of trespasses on the property of our citizens, committed by officers of one of the belligerent parties received among us. In truth these abuses of the laws of hospitality have, with few exceptions, become habitual to the commanders of the British armed vessels hovering on our coasts, and frequenting our harbors. They have been the subject of repeated representations to their government. Assurances have been given that proper orders should restrain them within the limit of the rights and of the respect due to a friendly nation: but those orders and assurances have been without effect; no instance of punishment for past wrongs has taken place.

Part of the President's July 8, 1807, proclamation following the British firing on the Chesapeake

Anas

July the 2nd [1807]. Present all the Heads of Department and Attorney General. The Proclamation of this day unanimously agreed to.

A copy of the proclamation to be enclosed to the Governors.

Recall all our vessels from the Mediterranean, by a vessel to be sent express.

Send the Revenge to England, with despatches to our Minister, demanding satisfaction for the attack on the Chesapeake, in which must be included. 1. A disavowal of the Act and of the principle of searching a public armed vessel. 2. A restoration of the men taken. 3. A recall of Admiral Barclay [George Berkeley, the commander of the British fleet off the coast who had ordered the attack].... The vessels recalled from the Mediterranean are to come to Boston. When may be further orders.

July the 4th. Present the same. Agreed that a call of Congress shall issue the fourth Monday of August (24th) to meet the fourth Monday in October (26th) unless new occurrences should render an earlier call necessary. Mr. Smith wished an earlier call.

July the 5th. Present the same. It was agreed to call on the Governors of the States to have their quotas of 100,000 militia in readiness. The object is to have the portions on the sea-coast ready for any emergency, and for those in the North we may look to a winter expedition against Canada.

July the 7th. Present the Secretaries of State and Navy and Attorney General. Agreed to desire Governor of Virginia to order such portion of Militia into actual service as may be necessary for defense of Norfolk, and of the gunboats at Hampton and in Matthews County.

Again Jefferson's strategy was to try to buy time and to refrain from committing the nation to war. On July 11 he outlined the three principles on which he and the Cabinet had acted to Barnabas Bidwell.

Washington July 11. [18]07.

You have long ago learnt the atrocious acts committed by the British armed vessels in the Chesapeake & it's neighborhood. They cannot be easily accomodated, altho' it is believed that they cannot be justified by orders from

their government. We have acted on these principles. 1.
to give that government an opportunity to disavow &
make reparations.   2. to give ourselves time to get in the
vessels, property and seamen now spread over the ocean.
3. to do no act which might compromit Congress in their
choice between war, non-intercourse or any other measure. We shall probably call them some time in October,
having regard to the return of the healthy season, and to
the reciept of an answer from Great Britain, before which
they could only act in the dark. In the mean time we shall
make all the preparations which time will permit, so as
to be ready for any alternative.

The *Chesapeake-Leopard* affair had provoked a mood
of unqualified national indignation, but Jefferson was aware that public
opinion and alignments within his party could change at any moment. In
triumph, Republicanism had absorbed the rivalries and potential for division
formerly expressed in two-party battles. Jefferson described this phenome-
non to Thomas Cooper, a friend of Joseph Priestley's.

Washington July 9. [18]07.
I had always expected that when the republicans should
have put down all things under their feet, they would
schismatise among themselves. I always expected too
that whatever names the parties might bear, the real
division would be into moderate and ardent republicanism. In this division there is no great evil, not even if
the minority obtain the ascendancy by the accession of
federal votes to their candidate: because this gives us
one shade only, instead of another, of republicanism.
It is to be considered as apostacy only when they purchase the votes of federalists with a participation in
honor and power. The gross insult lately recieved from
the English has forced the latter into a momentary coalition with the mass of republicans. But the moment we
begin to act, in the very line they have joined in approv-
ing, all will be wrong, and every act the reverse of what
it should have been: still it is better to admit their
coalescence, & leave to themselves their shortlived
existence.

Even after his return to Monticello in August, Jefferson
kept in touch with Cabinet officers and governors concerned with planning

the fortification of key harbors and enforcing the ban on British ships. By October, when Congress met in special session, no word had come of British reaction to the *Chesapeake* incident. The day before presenting his annual message, Jefferson wrote confidentially to his son-in-law, Thomas Mann Randolph, of the calm mood that had succeeded the cries for war of the preceding summer.

French cartoon of the Berlin Decree showing pace Britain could expect to receive goods from its colonies during the blockade by France

Washington Oct. 26. [18]07.
At present we have nothing from Europe. The two houses have assembled earlier than usual. There was a quorum of the H. of R. here on Saturday.... The members, as far as I can judge are extremely disposed for peace: and as there is no doubt Gr. Br. will disavow the act of the Leopard, I am inclined to believe they will be more disposed to combat her practice of impressment by a non-importation law than by arms. I am at the same time not without all hope she may relinquish the pretension to impressment on our agreeing not to employ her seamen, which it is our interest to agree to. If we resort to non-importation, it will end in war and give her the choice of the moment of declaring it. Altho' I think it well that our constituents should know what is probable, yet I must not be quoted. You will be free however to mention these as your own opinions or as what you collect from your correspondence.

By mid-December, Jefferson and Madison had unofficial but reliable texts of the newest commercial restrictions on American shipping. Britain, although willing to disavow the *Leopard's* attack on the *Chesapeake,* would not abandon impressment. And, by orders in council of November 11, the Tory government had barred any vessels from the Continent that had not first paid customs duties in British ports and obtained clearance papers. To balance this, Napoleon had withdrawn his statement that American ships would be exempt from his Berlin Decree of 1806, a decree placing the British Isles under blockade and authorizing the seizure of any ships that defied the blockade. If American ships bound for Europe did not stop at British ports, they would be seized by the Royal Navy; if they did put in at British ports, they would be subject to capture by Napoleon. In the preliminary draft of a message to Congress, Jefferson indignantly summarized the situation.

[before December 17, 1807]
The sum of these mutual enterprizes on our national rights is that.... The whole world is thus laid under interdict by these two nations, and our vessels, their car-

goes & crews, are to be taken by the one or the other, for whatever place they may be destined, out of our own limits. If therefore on leaving our harbors we are certainly to lose them, is it not better, as to vessels, cargoes & seamen, to keep them at home? This is submitted to the wisdom of Congress, who alone are competent to provide a remedy.

Instead of submitting the original version, Jefferson sent a brief message that left no doubt of what he wanted from the two houses: a complete embargo on trade from American ports.

Dec. 17. 1807

The communications now made, showing the great and increasing dangers with which our vessels, our seamen, and merchandize, are threatened on the high seas & elsewhere, from the belligerent powers of Europe, and it being of the greatest importance to keep in safety these essential resources, I deem it my duty to recommend the subject to the consideration of Congress, who will doubtless perceive all the advantages which may be expected from an inhibition of the departure of our vessels from the ports of the United States.

Neither Randolph's Quids nor New England Federalists could block the request; the Embargo Act became law four days later. No American ships could sail to foreign ports; those engaged in the coastal trade were required to post bond to insure that they would not venture into international trade under the guise of interstate commerce. Although foreign ships were not barred from the United States, it was obvious that few would risk the voyage since they would be forbidden to carry any cargoes back across the Atlantic. Jefferson had played his last card in the game of keeping America at peace: a demand that her citizens sacrifice convenience, and even their livelihoods, in the national interest. It would be his final opportunity to win the dangerous contest. In December, in response to addresses from the state legislatures urging him to another term, he had made public the decision he had reached three years earlier.

[Washington,] Dec. 10. [18]07.

That I should lay down my charge at a proper period is as much a duty as to have borne it faithfully. If some termination to the services of the Chief magistrate be not fixed by the constitution, or supplied by practice, his office, nominally for years, will, in fact, become for life;

and history shews how easily that degenerates into an inheritance. Believing that a representative government, responsible at short periods of election, is that which produces the greatest sum of happiness to mankind, I feel it a duty to do no act which shall essentially impair that principle; and I should unwillingly be the person who, disregarding the sound precedent set by an illustrious predecessor, should furnish the first example of prolongation beyond the second term of office.

Truth also requires me to add that I am sensible of that decline which advancing years bring on; and feeling their Physical, I ought not to doubt their Mental effect. Happy if I am the first to percieve and to obey this admonition of nature, and to sollicit a retreat from cares too great for the wearied faculties of age.

The knowledge that this would be his last year in office increased Jefferson's desire to prove the energy of republican government, but his task was even more difficult because it was an election year. The unity Jefferson had hoped to create within the nation seemed to disappear within his own party. On January 23 the Republican caucus in Congress nominated Madison for President and George Clinton for Vice President, but it was well known that supporters of Monroe and Clinton would contest Madison's right to the candidacy. Almost a month later Jefferson wrote sadly to Monroe, bemoaning his rivalry with Madison and warning his old friend of the bitter nature of national political contests.

Washington, Feb. 18. [18]08.

I see with infinite grief a contest arising between yourself and another who have been very dear to each other, and equally so to me. I sincerely pray that these dispositions may not be affected between you: with me I confidently trust they will not. For independantly of the dictates of public duty which prescribe neutrality to me, my sincere friendship for you both will ensure it's sacred observance. I suffer no one to converse with me on the subject. I already percieve my *old* friend Clinton estranging himself from me. No doubt lies are carried to him, as they will be to the other two candidates.... The object of the contest is a fair & honorable one, equally open to you all; and I have no doubt the personal conduct of each will be so chaste as to offer no ground of dissatisfaction with each other. But your friends will not be as delicate. I know too well from experience the progress of political

Two halves of an 1807 Federalist cartoon: Washington (left) is characterized by books labeled order, law, and religion; Jefferson by sophisms, the Notes on Virginia, Tom Paine, Condorcet, *and* Voltaire

controversy, and the exacerbation of spirit into which it degenerates, not to fear for the continuance of your mutual esteem. One piquing thing said draws on another, that a third, and always with increasing acrimony, until all restraint is thrown off, and it becomes difficult for yourselves to keep clear of the toils in which your friends will endeavor to interlace you.... With respect to myself, I hope they will spare me. My longings for retirement are so strong that I with difficulty encounter the daily drudgeries of my duty. But my wish for retirement itself is not stronger than that of carrying into it the affections of all my friends. I have ever viewed Mr. Madison and yourself as two principal pillars of my happiness. Were either to be withdrawn, I should consider it as among the greatest calamities which could assail my future peace of mind. I have great confidence that the candor & high understanding of both will guard me against this misfortune, the bare possibility of which has so far weighed on my mind, that I could not be easy without unburthening it.

Monroe would not be dissuaded. His bitterness at the rejection of his treaty had been carefully nurtured by the Quids since his return, and he saw his candidacy as a matter of personal vindication. Despite his personal preference for Madison, Jefferson did not interfere in the race. His own contest was with the enforcement of the embargo. In mid-March he presented the Secretary of State with his views on the value of that weapon as a temporary policy.

[Washington,] Mar. 11. 1808.

I take it to be an universal opinion that war will become preferable to a continuance of the embargo after a certain time. Should we not then avail ourselves of the intervening period to procure a retraction of the obnoxious decrees peaceably if possible? An opening is given us by both parties sufficient to form a basis for such a proposition. I wish you to consider, therefore, the following course of proceeding, to wit.

To instruct our ministers at Paris & London, by the next packet, to propose immediately to both those powers a declaration on both sides that these decrees & orders shall no longer be extended to vessels of the US. in which case we shall remain faithfully neutral: but, without assuming the air of menace, to let them both percieve that if they do not withdraw these orders &

371

decrees, there will arrive a time when our interests will render war preferable to a continuance of the embargo: that when that time arrives, if one has withdrawn & the other not, we must declare war against that other; if neither shall have withdrawn, we must take our choice of enemies between them. This it will certainly be our duty to have ascertained by the time Congress shall meet in the fall or beginning of winter, so that taking off the embargo they may decide whether war must be declared & against whom.

As demonstrated by this letter, Jefferson realized that the embargo could not continue beyond the next congressional session. By then its merits in diplomatic negotiations would be known and continuation would be pointless. He soon found that an effective embargo, at least in some parts of the Union, might not last even that long. Opposition to enforcement was particularly strong in Massachusetts despite its Republican governor, James Sullivan; messages like this one to the Secretary of the Navy, Robert Smith, were common in the summer of 1808.

Monticello, Aug. 9. [18]08.

I have some apprehension the tories of Boston &c. with so poor a head of a governor may attempt to give us trouble. I have requested Genl. Dearborn to be on the alert, and fly to the spot where any open & forcible opposition shall be commenced and to crush it in embryo. I am not afraid but that there is sound matter enough in Massachusets to prevent an opposition to the laws by force.

Jefferson confided to Albert Gallatin, "This embargo law is certainly the most embarrassing one we have ever had to execute. I did not expect a crop of so sudden and rank growth of fraud and open opposition by force could have grown up in the United States." Opposition was most marked in New England but sprang up as well in northern New York, where the Great Lakes and the St. Lawrence River offered avenues for illicit trade. Jefferson wrote firmly to New York Governor Daniel Tompkins.

Monticello Aug. 15. [18]08.

The case of opposition to the embargo laws on the Canada line, I take to be that of distinct combinations of a number of individuals to oppose by force and arms the execution of those laws, for which purpose they go armed, fire upon the public guards, in one instance at least have

Detail of an 1808 caricature showing the supposed influence of Napoleon on Jefferson; the drawing is by an unknown cartoonist who always signed his name as "Peter Pencil."

wounded one dangerously, and rescue property held under these laws. This may not be an insurrection in the popular sense of the word, but being arrayed in war-like manner, actually committing acts of war, and persevering systematically in defiance of the public authority, brings it so fully within the legal definition of an insurrection, that I should not hesitate to issue a proclamation were I not restrained by motives of which Y[our] E[xcellency] seems to be apprised. But as by the laws of New York an insurrection can be acted on without a previous proclamation I should concieve it perfectly correct to act on it as such, and I cannot doubt it would be approved by every good citizen. Should you think proper to do so, I will undertake that the necessary detachments of militia called out in support of the laws, shall be considered as in the service of the US. and at their expence. And as it has been intimated to me that you would probably take the trouble of going to the spot yourself, I will refer to your own discretion the measures to be taken, & the numbers to be cal[led] out at different places....I think it so important in example to crush these audacious proceedings, and to make the offenders feel the consequences of individuals daring to oppose a law by force, that no effort should be spared to compass this object.

Such defiance of the embargo could render it useless. Radical Federalists in the Northeast seemed to have adopted that course from the beginning, Jefferson wrote Dr. Michael Leib.

Washington June 23. [18]08.
They are endeavoring to convince England that we suffer more by the embargo than they do, & that if they will but hold out a while, we must abandon it. It is true the time will come when we must abandon it. But if this is before the repeal of the orders of council, we must abandon it only for a state of war. The day is not distant, when that will be preferable to a longer continuance of the embargo. But we can never remove that, & let our vessels go out & be taken under these orders, without making reprisal. Yet this is the very state of things which these Federal monarchists are endeavoring to bring about; and in this it is but too possible they may succeed. But the fact is that if we have war with England it will be solely produced by their maneuvres.

In truth, the embargo was having a greater effect at home that summer than it was abroad. Britain suffered little; France, whose navy was weak, had already lost much of her trade with America before the Embargo Act. In his last annual message on November 8, Jefferson outlined the situation to Congress but offered no recommendations for further action. He was reluctant to press his own views, for he knew he would be "but a spectator" to any programs enacted. He explained his position to Levi Lincoln, his former Attorney General.

Public Men, SULLIVAN

Levi Lincoln

> Washington Nov. 13. [18]08.
> The congressional campaign is just opening: three alternatives alone are to be chosen from. 1. embargo. 2. war. 3. submission & tribute. And, wonderful to tell, the last will not want advocates. The real question however will lie between the two first, on which there is considerable division. As yet the first seems most to prevail; but opinions are by no means yet settled down. Perhaps the advocates of the 2d. may, to a formal declaration of war, prefer *general* letters of mark & reprisal, because on a repeal of their edicts by the belligerent, a revocation of the letters of mark restores peace without the delay, difficulties & ceremonies of a treaty. On this occasion I think it is fair to leave to those who are to act on them, the decisions they prefer, being to be myself but a spectator. I should [not] feel justified in directing measures which those who are to execute them would disapprove. Our situation is truly difficult. We have been pressed by the belligerents to the very wall, & all further retreat impracticable.

Jefferson, quite properly, did not feel he should direct the setting of policies, but Madison, now the President-elect, found it difficult to do so from the Cabinet. Congress floundered without effective leadership for the next two months. At the end of January, Jefferson wrote to Monroe of what the eventual legislative action might be.

> Washington Jan. 28. [18]09.
> The course the Legislature means to pursue may be inferred from the act now passed for a meeting in May, & a proposition before them for repealing the embargo in June & then resuming & maintaining by force our right of navigation....Final propositions will therefore be soon despatched to both the belligerents through the resident ministers, so that their answers will be recieved before the meeting in May, & will decide what is to be

A cartoon depicting Madison and Jefferson dragging American ship into port on Napoleon's orders

done. This last trial for peace is not thought desperate. If, as is expected, Bonaparte should be successful in Spain,... it may induce both powers to be more accommodating with us.... Otherwise we must again take the tented field as we did in 1776. under more inauspicious circumstances. There never has been a situation of the world before, in which such endeavors as we have made would not have secured our peace. It is probable there never will be such another. If we go to war now, I fear we may renounce for ever the hope of seeing an end of our national debt. If we can keep at peace 8. years longer, our income, liberated from death, will be adequate to any war, without new taxes or loans, and our position & increasing strength will put us hors d'insulte from any nation. I am now so near the moment of retiring, that I take no part in affairs beyond the expression of an opinion. I think it fair that my successor should now originate those measures of which he will be charged with the execution & responsibility, and that it is my duty to clothe them with the forms of authority. Five weeks more will relieve me from a drudgery to which I am no longer equal, and restore me to a scene of tranquility, amidst my family & friends, more congenial to my age and natural inclinations.

But Jefferson's inference was drawn too early. New England Federalists mobilized opposition to the continuation of the embargo beyond the winter congressional session. In Connecticut the governor issued a declaration echoing the Kentucky Resolutions of 1798, a hint that the northern states might also consider nullifying distasteful federal statutes. The Essex Junto, a group of New Englanders who had explored secession as a solution to sectional grievances in 1804, were willing to take that course again in 1809 and led the anti-embargo forces in Congress. In a later letter to William Branch Giles, Jefferson recalled a meeting with Congressman John Quincy Adams of Massachusetts during that bitter session. Adams was reluctant to intrude on Jefferson's time, knowing the strained relations between his parents and the President, but the matter he had to communicate was too important to be concealed.

Monticello Dec. 25. [18]25.

He made some apologies for the call on the ground of our not being then in the habit of confidential communications, but that that which he had then to make involved too seriously the interest of our country not to

375

overrule all other considerations with him, and make it his duty to reveal it to myself particularly. I assured him there was no occasion for any apology for his visit.... He spoke then of the dissatisfaction of the Eastern portion of our confederacy with the restraints of the embargo then existing and their restlessness under it. That there was nothing which might not be attempted, to rid themselves of it. That he had information of the most unquestionable certainty that certain citizens of the Eastern states (I think he named Massachusets particularly) were in negotiation with Agents of the British government, the object of which was an agreement that the New England states should take no further part in the war then going on; that without formally declaring their separation from the union of the States, they should withdraw from all aid and obedience to them; that their navigation and commerce should be free from restraint and interruption by the British; that they should be considered and treated by them as Neutrals and as such might conduct themselves towards both parties; and, at the close of the war, be at liberty to rejoin the Confederacy. He assured me that there was eminent danger that the Convention would take place; that the temptations were such as might debauch many from their fidelity to the union; and that, to enable it's friends to make head against it, the repeal of the embargo was absolutely necessary. I expressed a just sense of the merit of this information, and of the importance of the disclosure to the safety & even the salvation of our country. And, however reluctant I was to abandon the measure, (a measure which, persevered in a little longer, we had subsequent and satisfactory assurance would have effected it's object completely) from that moment, and influenced by that information, I saw the necessity of abandoning it, and instead of effecting our purpose by this peaceful weapon, we must fight it out or break the Union. I then recommended to my friends to yield to the necessity of a repeal of the embargo, and to endeavor to supply it's place by the best substitute in which they could procure a general concurrence.

Two cartoons by Peter Pencil made in 1809: "Non Intercourse or Dignified Retirement" (right) shows Jefferson in ragged clothing, "stript...rather than submit to London or Parisian Fashions!"; in "Intercourse or Impartial Dealings" (above), George III wields a club while Napoleon steals his purse.

And thus Jefferson abandoned the embargo. Republicans in Congress were released from any ties of party discipline so that they might vote as they wished in the matter. With repeal certain Madison tried, too late, to exert influence in Congress. He managed to persuade the legislature to enact a Nonintercourse Act that would take effect when the embargo ended and reopen trade with all nations except France and Britain. But the Secretary of State failed to win a system of "letters of marque and reprisal" allowing merchant ships to arm in defense of their rights. The President-elect was given only weak support for the continuing battle ahead.

As Jefferson ended his Presidency, he saw his dreams of winning recognition of commercial rights through peaceful measures destroyed. The embargo had "Federalized" New England and had brought no concessions from Britain. On February 28 the President wrote his son-in-law of the substitution of nonintercourse for the embargo and remarked on the plans to hold meetings in his honor along the road to Monticello the next month.

Washington Feb. 28. [18]09.

By yesterday's mail I learn that it would be the desire of many of the good citizens of our county to meet me on the road on my return home, as a manifestation of their good will. But it is quite impossible for me to ascertain the day on which I shall leave this. The accumulated business at the close of a session will prevent my making any preparation for my departure till after the 4th. of March. After that, the arrangement of papers and business to be delivered over to my successor, the winding up my own affairs & clearing out from this place will employ me for several days, (I cannot conjecture even how many,) so as to render the commencement, and consequently the termination of my journey, altogether uncertain. But it is a sufficient happiness to me to know that my fellow citizens of the county generally entertain for me the kind sentiments which have prompted this proposition, without giving to so many the trouble of leaving their homes to meet a single individual. I shall have opportunities of taking them individually by the hand at our courthouse & other public places & of exchanging assurances of mutual esteem. Certainly it is the greatest consolation to me to know that in returning to the bosom of my native country, I shall be again in the midst of their kind affections: and I can say with truth that my return to them will make me happier than I have been since I left them.

In his letter to Randolph, Jefferson only hinted at his weariness and desire to escape the demands of his office. He was more frank in writing to Samuel Du Pont de Nemours four days later.

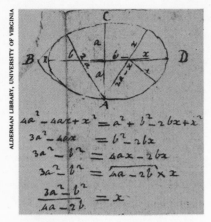

$$4a^2 - 4ax + x^2 = a^2 + b^2 - 2bx + x^2$$
$$3a^2 - 4ax = b^2 - 2bx$$
$$3a^2 - b^2 = 4ax - 2bx$$
$$3a^2 - b^2 = \overline{4a - 2b} \times x$$
$$\frac{3a^2 - b^2}{4a - 2b} = x$$

*Jefferson's formula for drawing
an ellipse, another example
of his continuous interest in "the
tranquil pursuits of science"*

Washington Mar. 2. [18]09.

Within a few days I retire to my family, my books, & farms & having gained the harbor myself, I shall look on my friends still buffeting the storm, with anxiety indeed, but not with envy. Never did prisoner, released from his chains, feel such relief as I shall on shaking off the shackles of power. Nature intended me for the tranquil pursuits of science, by rendering them my supreme delight. But the enormities of the times in which I have lived have forced me to take a part in resisting them, and to commit myself on the boisterous ocean of political passions. I thank god for the opportunity of retiring from them without censure, and carrying with me the most consoling proofs of public approbation.

Like many another American President, Jefferson had lost his fight for the goal he had voiced in 1805: "at the end of a second term, [to] carry into retirement all the favor which the first has acquired." The achievements of his first term would not be erased, but the effort to purchase time in the second administration had failed, and each month he bought came at the cost of some sectional interest or political allegiance. In later years Jefferson emphasized that the embargo had not been given a fair trial, that the trade ban would have succeeded had it continued longer. By early 1809 the British had begun to feel the effects of the loss of American commerce and public opinion had at last begun to work on their government. But Jefferson himself had envisioned the policy as only a temporary measure. Unfortunately, its effects were felt slowly in Europe, but immediately in America.

Jefferson was nevertheless hopeful of his friend Madison's chances. "I leave everything in the hands of men so able to take care of them," he wrote shortly before leaving Washington that spring, "that if we are destined to meet misfortunes it will be because no human wisdom could avert them." The Treasury was sound; the federal bureaucracy was reformed; the rich, expanding West was unchallenged by foreign kings or emperors. Thanks to Jefferson's eight years in office, no Republican President would ever again have to prove that his party and its principles could govern America justly and energetically.

Chapter 13

Thomas Jefferson Survives

S hortly after returning to Monticello in March, 1809, Jefferson outlined his expectations for retirement in an address to his neighbors in Albemarle. He longed for "the enjoyment of an affectionate intercourse" with "neighbors and friends, and the endearments of family love," and looked forward to "repose and safety under the watchful cares, the labors and perplexities of younger and abler minds." He had sacrificed family and friends to help build the nation; he had neglected his own lands and crops to help build a republican system of government. No one better deserved years of peaceful retirement, but this, too, was denied him. Jefferson's last seventeen years were to be as full of challenge, hard work, and frustrating disappointments as any period in his life. Jefferson left the capital confident that Madison would preserve his public policies. One guest at the new President's inaugural ball remarked on Jefferson's pride in his younger friend. "I do believe," she wrote, "father never loved son more than he loves Mr. Madison." She also commented on Jefferson's obvious physical exhaustion, "looking as if he could scarcely stand." His weariness owed much to the strain of the last two years in office. He returned to Virginia at age sixty-five, suffering from rheumatism and headaches and weakened by an infected tooth. The Presidency had proved financially demanding as well, and he was burdened with substantial debts.

In the first winter of his retirement, Jefferson told his grandson, Thomas Jefferson Randolph, that he was busier in some ways than he had been when President. He found ample time, nevertheless, to reply to Thaddeus Kosciusko, the Polish patriot who had aided the American cause in Virginia during the Revolution. On hearing from his old comrade for the first time in decades, Jefferson answered with a long summary of American politics and closed with "a word as to myself," a portrait of daily life at Monticello.

Monticello Feb. 26. [18]10.

...in the bosom of my family, and surrounded by

my books, I enjoy a repose to which I have been long a stranger. My mornings are devoted to correspondence. From breakfast to dinner, I am in my shops, my garden, or on horseback among my farms; from dinner to dark I give to society and recreation with my neighbors and friends; and from candlelight to early bed-time I read. My health is perfect; and my strength considerably reinforced by the activity of the course I pursue; perhaps it is as great as usually falls to the lot of near 67. years of age. I talk of ploughs and harrows, seeding and harvesting, with my neighbors, and of politics too, if they chuse, with as little reserve as the rest of my fellow citizens, and feel at length the blessing of being free to say and do what I please, without being responsible for it to any mortal. A part of my occupation, and by no means the least pleasing, is the direction of the studies of such young men as ask it. They place themselves in the neighboring

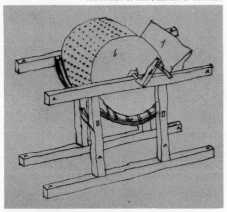

Jefferson's sketch of corn sheller he ordered for Monticello; it was designed by Paul Pillsbury in 1803.

The ex-President's response, on April 3, 1809, to an address of welcome from Albemarle residents

village, and have the use of my library and counsel, and make a part of my society. In advising the course of their reading, I endeavor to keep their attention fixed on the main objects of all science, the freedom and happiness of man. So that coming to bear a share in the councils and government of their country, they will keep ever in view the sole objects of all legitimate government.

Jefferson's early years of retirement were a period of personal happiness. His public career had taken him away from his own daughters during their childhood, and he seemed determined to make up for that loss by giving every minute he could to his grandsons and grand-daughters—one Eppes and, by 1818, eleven Randolphs. Virginia Randolph Trist later recalled those happy days after her grandfather retired.

St. Servan, France, May 26th, 1839.
When he walked in the garden and would call the children to go with him, we raced after and before him, and we were made perfectly happy by this permission to accompany him. Not one of us, in our wildest moods, ever placed a foot on one of the garden-beds, for that would violate one of his rules, and yet I never heard him utter a harsh word to one of us, or speak in a raised tone of voice, or use a threat. He simply said, "Do," or "Do not"....

One of our earliest amusements was in running races on the terrace, or around the lawn. He placed us according to our ages, giving the youngest and smallest the start of all the others by some yards, and so on; and then he raised his arm high, with his white handkerchief in his hand, on which our eager eyes were fixed, and slowly counted three, at which number he dropped the handkerchief, and we started off to finish the race by returning to the starting-place and receiving our reward of dried fruit—three figs, prunes, or dates to the victor, two to the second, and one to the lagger who came in last.

Two of the Randolphs' eleven children who lived with their grandfather at Monticello were Thomas Jefferson and Cornelia.

Another source of personal happiness came as the result of intervention by Dr. Benjamin Rush. The Philadelphia physician-politician had maintained close ties with both Jefferson and John Adams and was determined that the two resume their friendship. Jefferson explained to Rush that his public differences with Adams were no barrier to their private friendship but that he believed Adams had been privy to the letters he had exchanged with Abigail Adams in 1804 and had endorsed her bitter criticism of his administration. The misunderstanding seemed insuperable until the summer of 1811 when Edward Coles, Madison's secretary, and his brother John Coles visited Quincy. Some months later reports of their conversations reached Jefferson and confirmed Mrs. Adams's contention that Adams had had no part in his wife's political remarks. From his estate at Poplar Forest, Jefferson wrote Rush that henceforth the doctor might feel free to play peacemaker, as he had tried to do previously by encouraging Jefferson to write to Adams.

Dr. Benjamin Rush by St. Mémin

Poplar Forest Dec. 5. [18]11.
Two of the Mr. Coles, my neighbors and friends...took a tour to the Northward during the last summer. In Boston they fell into company with Mr. Adams, & by his invitation passed a day with him at Braintree. He spoke out to them every thing which came uppermost, & as it occurred to his mind, without any reserve, and seemed most disposed to dwell on those things which happened during his own administration....Among many other topics, he adverted to the unprincipled licentiousness of the press against myself, adding, 'I always loved Jefferson, and still love him'—This is enough for me. I only needed this knolege to revive towards him all the affections of the most cordial moments of our lives....I wish therefore but for an apposite occasion to express to Mr. Adams my unchanged affections for him. There is an awkwardness which hangs over the resuming a correspondence so long discontinued, unless something could arise which should call for a letter. Time and chance may perhaps generate such an occasion, of which I shall not be wanting in promptitude to avail myself.

Rush went to work quickly. He wrote Adams, quoting Jefferson's letter, but Adams was not fooled. "I perceive plainly enough," he told Rush, "that you have been teasing Jefferson to write to me, as you did me some time ago to write to him." He left the doctor in suspense, merely conceding that "time and chance...or possibly design, may produce ere long a letter between us." Adams did not wait for time or chance, and on New Year's Day, 1812, he dispatched a short message to Monticello, ostensibly covering "a Packett containing two Pieces of Homespun lately produced in this quarter" by one who "was honoured in his youth with some of your Attention and much of your kindness." Although the homespun did not arrive with the letter, Jefferson sat down immediately to reply, opening with a description of the progress of textile manufactures in Virginia and moving on to the resumption of their friendship.

Monticello Jan. 21. 1812.

A letter from you calls up recollections very dear to my mind. It carries me back to the times when, beset with difficulties & dangers, we were fellow laborers in the same cause, struggling for what is most valuable to man, his right of self-government. Laboring always at the same oar, with some wave ever ahead threatening to overwhelm us & yet passing harmless under our bark, we knew not how, we rode through the storm with heart & hand, and made a happy port. Still we did not expect to be without rubs and difficulties; and we have had them....

But whither is senile garrulity leading me? Into politics, of which I have taken final leave. I think little of them & say less. I have given up newspapers in exchange for Tacitus & Thucydides, for Newton & Euclid; & I find myself much the happier. Sometimes indeed I look back to former occurrences, in remembrance of our old friends and fellow laborers, who have fallen before us. Of the signers of the Declaration of Independance I see now living not more than half a dozen on your side of the Potomak, and, on this side, myself alone. You & I have been wonderfully spared, and myself with remarkable health, & a considerable activity of body & mind....I have heard with pleasure that you also retain good health, and a greater power of exercise in walking than I do. But I would rather have heard this from yourself, & that, writing a letter, like mine, full of egotisms, & of details of your health, your habits, occupations & enjoiments, I should have the pleasure of knowing that, in the race of life, you do not keep, in it's physical decline, the same distance ahead of me which you have done in political honors & atchievements. No circumstances have lessened the interest I feel in these particulars respecting yourself; none have suspended for one moment my sincere esteem for you; and I now salute you with unchanged affections and respect.

Abigail Adams (top), after retiring with her husband to their handsome home at Braintree, renamed Quincy

The messenger who took Jefferson's letter to the post office returned with the "homespun" sent by Adams: a two-volume set of

John Quincy Adams's *Lectures on Rhetoric and Oratory.* Delighted by the joke, Jefferson congratulated his friend on his son's work and added: "A little more sagacity of conjecture in me...would have saved you the trouble of reading a long dissertation on the state of real homespun in our quarter." Jefferson and Adams assured each other that they were tired of politics, and their correspondence scrupulously avoided any topics that might reopen old wounds, including an approaching war with Great Britain. British intransigence on impressment and interference with neutral shipping had continued during Madison's first three years, and despite all his efforts to avoid it, he asked Congress to declare war in June, 1812. At first, this struggle for a second "weaning from British principles," as Jefferson described it, went well for his family. Wartime demand for foodstuffs gave him encouraging profits the first year, but a British blockade in the spring of 1813 left Jefferson with hundreds of barrels of unsold flour in Richmond warehouses. He had corresponded with Madison frequently since his retirement, offering advice on problems with Great Britain, occasional suggestions for appointments, and news of agricultural matters of interest to both planters. He used their close friendship in 1813 to plead almost desperately for a military effort to disrupt the British blockade, which was proving disastrous to Virginia's economy.

Monticello May 21. [18]13.

We have never seen so unpromising a crop of wheat as that now growing. The winter killed an unusual proportion of it, and the fly is destroying the remainder. We may estimate the latter loss at one-third at present, and fast increasing from the effect of the extraordinary drought. With such a prospect before us, the blockade is acting severely on our past labors. It caught nearly the whole wheat of the middle and upper country in the hands of the farmers and millers, whose interior situation had prevented their getting it to an earlier market. From this neighborhood very little had been sold. When we cast our eyes on the map, and see the extent of country from New York to North Carolina inclusive whose produce is raised on the waters of the Chesapeak... and consider it's productiveness in comparison with the rest of the Atlantic States, probably a full half, and that all this can be shut up by two or three ships of the line, lying at the mouth of the bay, we see that an injury so vast to ourselves and so cheap to our enemy must for ever be resorted to by them, and constantly maintained. To defend all the shores of those waters in detail, is impossible. But is there not a single point where they may be all defended by means to which the magnitude of the

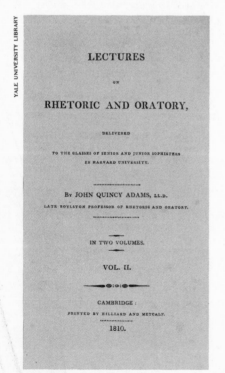

LECTURES

ON

RHETORIC AND ORATORY,

DELIVERED

TO THE CLASSES OF SENIOR AND JUNIOR SOPHISTERS
IN HARVARD UNIVERSITY.

By JOHN QUINCY ADAMS, LL.D.
LATE BOYLSTON PROFESSOR OF RHETORIC AND ORATORY.

IN TWO VOLUMES.

VOL. II.

CAMBRIDGE:
PRINTED BY HILLIARD AND METCALF.
1810.

Title page of the second volume of John Quincy Adams's Lectures on Rhetoric and Oratory, *1810*

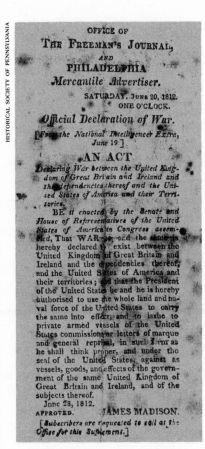

Broadside of declaration of war

object gives a title? I mean at the mouth of the Chesapeak. Not by ships of the line, or frigates; for I know that with our present enemy we cannot contend in that way. But would not a sufficient number of gunboats, of *small* draught, stationed in Lynhaven river, render it unsafe for ships of war either to ascend the Chesapeak or to lie at it's mouth? . . .

. . . The importance of keeping open a water which covers, wholly or considerably, five of the most productive States, containing threefifths of the population of the Atlantic portion of our union, and of preserving their resources for the support of the war, as far as the state of war, and the means of the Confederacy will admit; and especially if it can be done for less than is contributed by the union for more than one single city, will justify our anxieties to have it effected. And should my views of the subject be even wrong, I am sure they will find their apology with you in the purity of the motives of personal & public regard which induce a suggestion of them. In all cases I am satisfied you are doing what is for the best as far as the means put into your hands will enable you; and this thought quiets me under every occurrence and under every occurrence I am sincerely, affectionately & respectfully your's.

Madison did not share Jefferson's faith in gunboats, and frigates from the small navy could not be spared; the war continued to take its toll. In this context of conflict, the forbidden topic of politics became unavoidable between Monticello and Braintree. In May, 1813, Adams saw a copy of the *Memoirs of the Late Reverend Theophilus Lindsay,* an acquaintance of his London years, which contained outspoken letters Jefferson had written Joseph Priestley after the bitterly contested electoral battle of 1801. Adams demanded an explanation of remarks in the letters that seemed directed at him. The time had come for mutual explanation.

Monticello June 27. [18]13.

The same political parties which now agitate the U.S. have existed thro' all time. Whether the power of the people, or that of the aristoi should prevail, were questions which kept the states of Greece and Rome in eternal convulsions; as they now schismatize every people whose minds and mouths are not shut up by the gag of a despot. . . . To come to our own country, and to the times when you and I became first acquainted, we well remember the violent parties which agitated the old Congress, and their bitter contests. There you & I were together, and the Jays, and the Dickinsons, and other anti-independants were arrayed against us.... When our present government was in the mew, passing from Confederation to Union, how bitter was the schism between the Feds and Antis. Here you and I were together again.... But as soon as it was put into motion, the line of division was again drawn; we broke into two parties, each wishing to give a different direction to the government; the one to strengthen the most popular branch, the other the more permanent branches, and to extend their permanence. Here you & I separated for the first time: and as we had been longer than most others on the public theatre, and our names therefore were more familiar to our countrymen, the party which considered you as thinking with them, placed your name at their head; the other, for the same reason, selected mine. But neither decency nor inclination permitted us to become the advocates of ourselves, or to take part personally in the violent contests which followed. We suffered ourselves, as you so well expressed it, to be the passive subjects of public discussion. And these discussions, whether relating to men, measures, or opinions, were conducted by the parties with an animosity, a bitterness, and an indecency, which had never been exceeded.... Shall we, at our age, become the Athletae of party, and exhibit ourselves, as gladiators, in the Arena of the newspapers? Nothing in the universe could induce me to it. My mind has been long fixed to bow to the judgment of the world, who will judge me by my acts, and will never take counsel from me as to what that judgment shall be. If your objects and opinions have been misunderstood, if the measures and principles of others have been wrongfully imputed to you, as I believe they have been, that you should leave an explanation of them, would be an act of justice to yourself.

An 1814 cartoon depicts John Bull offering terms of capitulation to some weak-kneed Americans.

The friendship not only survived the introduction of politics but was strengthened. Jefferson accepted the challenge of mutual self-explanation so enthusiastically that he told Adams of a subject he had concealed even from his family. He sent Adams his "Syllabus" of the teachings of Christ, a digest of basic Christian tenets compared with the beliefs of others, such as the ancients and the Jews, which he had prepared many years before. In discussing the Syllabus, Jefferson demonstrated that he was not an unbeliever but an opponent of organized religions and the priests and theologians who made a mystery of basic morality.

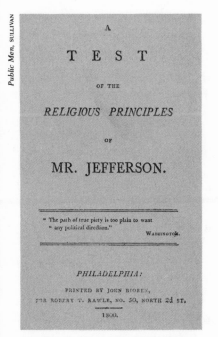

A

T E S T

OF THE

RELIGIOUS PRINCIPLES

OF

MR. JEFFERSON.

" The path of true piety is too plain to want
" any political direction."
WASHINGTON.

PHILADELPHIA:

PRINTED BY JOHN BIOREN,
FOR ROBERT T. RAWLE, NO. 50, NORTH 2d ST.

1800.

One of the many pamphlets that had attacked Jefferson's religious views in the campaign of 1800

Monticello Oct. 12. [18]13.

It was the reformation of this 'wretched depravity' of morals which Jesus undertook. In extracting the pure principles which he taught, we should have to strip off the artificial vestments in which they have been muffled by priests, who have travestied them into various forms, as instruments of riches and power to them.... We must reduce our volume to the simple evangelists, select, even from them, the very words only of Jesus, paring off the Amphibologisms into which they have been led by forgetting often, or not understanding, what had fallen from him, by giving their own misconceptions as his dicta, and expressing unintelligibly for others what they had not understood themselves. There will be found remaining the most sublime and benevolent code of morals which has ever been offered to man. I have performed this operation for my own use, by cutting verse by verse out of the printed book, and arranging, the matter which is evidently his, and which is as easily distinguishable as diamonds in a dunghill. The result is an 8vo. [octavo] of 46. pages of pure and unsophisticated doctrines, such as were professed & acted on by the *unlettered* apostles, the Apostolic fathers, and the Christians of the 1st. century.

The war dragged on, but by the summer of 1814, Jefferson was spending much of his time on a project that was to demand his attention for the rest of his life. Earlier in the year his nephew, Peter Carr, and other citizens of Albemarle County had begun to organize a private secondary school in the Charlottesville neighborhood. When Jefferson was named to the academy's board, he set to work using the scheme as the basis for his dream of giving Virginia a comprehensive system of education. On September 7 he sent Carr a plan he had drafted at the request of the other trustees "adapted, in the first instance to our slender funds, but susceptible of being enlarged." The new institution was to be considered in terms of the general needs of the state, not as an isolated preparatory school for young gentlemen.

Monticello Sept. 7. [18]14.

In the first place, we must ascertain with precision the

object of our institution, by taking a survey of the general field of science, and marking out the portion we mean to occupy at first, and the ultimate extension of our views beyond that, should we be enabled to render it, in the end, as comprehensive as we would wish.

I. Elementary Schools.

... The mass of our citizens may be divided into two classes, the laboring & the learned. The laboring will need the first grade of education to qualify them for their pursuits and duties: the learned will need it as a foundation for further acquirements....

II. General Schools.

At the discharge of the pupils from the elementary schools, the two classes separate: & those destined for labor will engage in the business of agriculture, or enter into apprenticeships...; their companions, destined to the pursuits of science, will proceed to the College, which will consist of 1st. General schools and, 2d. of Professional schools. The General schools will constitute the second grade of education.

The learned class may still be subdivided into two sections. 1. Those who are destined for learned professions as means of livelihood; and. 2. the Wealthy, who possessing independant fortunes may aspire to share in conducting the affairs of the nation, or to live with usefulness & respect in the private ranks of life.... All the branches, then, of useful science, ought to be taught in the general schools, to a competent degree....

III. Professional Schools.

At the close of this course the Students separate, the wealthy retiring with a sufficient stock of knolege to improve themselves to any degree to which their views may lead them, and the Professional section to the Professional Schools constituting the IIId. Grade of education, and teaching the particular sciences which the individuals of this section mean to pursue.... In these Professional schools each science is to be taught in the highest degree it has yet attained. They are to be in the

Ist. Department, the Fine arts....

IId. Department, Architecture, military and naval; Projectiles, Rural economy..., technical philosophy, the Practice of Medecine, Materia Medica, Pharmacy and

The burning of Washington, 1814

Surgery. In the

IIId. Department, Theology & Ecclesiastical history; Law municipal and foreign....

On this survey of the field of science, I recur to the question, what portion of it we mark out for the occupation of our Institution? With the 1st. grade of education we shall have nothing to do. The sciences of the 2d. grade are our first object....

To implement his plans, Jefferson drafted a bill for the incorporation of the planned academy as Central College, but the Virginia legislature ignored the measure that winter. In wartime, the state's lawmakers had little time for public education, and in September, 1814, the return of peace and prosperity seemed more distant than ever. In late August, British troops had landed on American soil and marched on the capital. Washington was occupied and its public buildings burned. In a typical gesture, Jefferson offered the government his most precious possession to soften a national loss: his own library to restock the Library of Congress. On September 21 he wrote to Samuel Harrison Smith, who was the chairman of the library committee for the Library of Congress, to arrange for the sale of his books.

Monticello, September 21, 1814.

I learn from the newspapers that the vandalism of our enemy has triumphed at Washington over science as well as the arts, by the destruction of the public library....

I presume it will be among the early objects of Congress to re-commence their collection. This will be difficult while the war continues, and intercourse with Europe is attended with so much risk. You know my collection, its condition and extent. I have been fifty years making it, and have spared no pains, opportunity or expense, to make it what it is.... I had standing orders during the whole time I was in Europe, on its principal book-marts... for such works relating to America as could not be found in Paris. So that in that department particularly, such a collection was made as probably can never again be effected.... During the same period, and after my return to America, I was led to procure, also, whatever related to the duties of those in the high concerns of the nation. So that the collection, which I suppose is of between nine and ten thousand volumes, while it includes what is chiefly valuable in science and literature generally, extends more particularly to whatever belongs to the American statesman. In the diplomatic and parliamentary branches, it is particularly full. It is long since I have been sensible it ought not to continue private property, and had provided that at my death, Congress should have the refusal of it at their own price. But the loss they have now incurred, makes the present the proper moment for their accommodation, without regard to the small remnant of time and the barren use of my enjoying it.

Congress authorized almost twenty-four thousand dollars for the purchase in December, and the income, though far less than the books were worth, was welcome and timely for Jefferson. That same month the Treaty of Ghent was signed, ending the war. It came just in time to quell secessionist threats in New England, but the peace left America in a severe economic depression that pressed heavily on farmers of the South and West. Jefferson pushed overseers and servants to harvest crops that might help him recover from the debts burdening his acres. But he was over seventy, increasingly troubled by rheumatism and other ills of old age, and in 1815 his eldest grandson, Thomas Jefferson Randolph, assumed responsibility for much of the estate. America's finances were no better, and the creation of banks as a prescription for all economic ills had new popularity. In his annual message of December, 1815, James Madison recommended "consideration" of a "national bank." As Congress debated provisions of the Second Bank of the United States, Jefferson wrote to fellow Virginian, Colonel Charles Yancey.

Monticello Jan. 6. [18]16

Like a dropsical man calling out for water, water, our deluded citizens are clamoring for more banks, more banks. The American mind is now in that state of fever which the world has so often seen in the history of other nations. We are under the bank-bubble, as England was under the South sea bubble, France under the Misisipi bubble, and as every nation is liable to be, under whatever bubble design or delusion may puff up in moments when off their guard. We are now taught to believe that legerdemain tricks upon paper can produce as solid wealth as hard labor in the earth. It is vain for common sense to urge that *nothing* can produce but *nothing:* that it is an idle dream to believe in a philosopher's stone which is to turn every thing into gold, and to redeem man from the original sentence of his maker, 'in the sweat of his brow shall he eat his bread'. . . . I am willing to swim or sink with my fellow citizens.... But my exhortation would rather be 'not to give up the ship.'

The Second Bank of the United States became a reality, nevertheless, adding its branches to scores of state-chartered banks which had grown up over the nation. Instead of peaceful, prosperous retirement, Jefferson was engaged in a fight to recover from losses incurred during years of naval war. In 1816 he and Adams debated the question whether they would choose to live their lives over again. In his first comments on this query, Jefferson seemed ready to answer in the affirmative. "I think with you," he wrote Adams, "that it is a good world on the whole, that it has been framed on a principle of benevolence, and more pleasure than pain dealt out to us." But on reconsidering the matter a few months later, he qualified the statement.

Monticello Aug. 1. [18]16.

...Would I agree to live my 73. years over again for ever? I hesitate to say...from 25. to 60. I would say Yes; and might go further back, but not come lower down. For, at the latter period, with most of us, the powers of life are sensibly on the wane, sight becomes dim, hearing dull, memory constantly enlarging it's frightful blank and parting with all we have ever seen or known, spirits evaporate, bodily debility creeps on palsying every limb, and so faculty after faculty quits us, and where then is life?... There is a ripeness of time for death, regarding others as well as ourselves, when it is reasonable we should drop off, and make room for another growth.... I enjoy good health; I am happy in what is around me. Yet I assure you I am ripe for leaving all, this year, this day, this hour.

Gilbert Stuart's striking portrait of John Adams the year before he died

Duties as planter and head of a family were not the only ones Jefferson bore in those years. Adams's estimate of the number of books he read each year filled Jefferson with envy. He wrote his friend of the drain on his precious time caused by the innumerable and unsolicited letters he answered each day.

Monticello Jan. 11. [18]17.

Forty three volumes read in one year, and 12. of them quartos! Dear Sir, how I envy you! Half a dozen 8vos. in that space of time are as much as I am allowed. I can read by candlelight only, and stealing long hours from my rest; nor would that time be indulged to me, could I, by that light, see to write. From sun-rise to one or two aclock, and often from dinner to dark, I am drudging at the writing table. And all this to answer letters into which neither interest nor inclination on my part enters; and often for persons whose names I have never before heard. Yet, writing civilly, it is hard to refuse them civil answers. This is the burthen of my life, a very grievous one indeed, and one which I must get rid of.

The next year brought a more pleasant "burthen." In February, 1816, the legislature had agreed to Jefferson's bill to incorporate the academy at Charlottesville as Central College. The charter was a broad one, even if funds for expanding the academy were small. Fortunately the Board of Visitors was more distinguished than the endowment; Jefferson could look forward to the aid of his friends Monroe and Madison. James Monroe had become Madison's Secretary of State in 1810 and had won the 1816 presidential election handsomely. In May Jefferson cheerfully described to Adams the academic work facing the new President and the retiring executive.

Album of Virginia BY ED. BEYER 1858

Plans for the University of Virginia were agreed upon at Rockfish Gap.

Monticello. May 5. [18]17.

I do not entertain your apprehensions for the happiness of our brother Madison in a state of retirement. Such a mind as his, fraught with information, and with matter for reflection, can never know ennui. Besides, there will always be work enough cut out for him to continue his active usefulness to his country. For example, he and Monroe (the president) are now here on the work of a collegiate institution to be established in our neighborhood, of which they and myself are three of six Visitors. This, if it succeeds, will raise up children for Mr. Madison to employ his attentions thro' life. I say, if it succeeds; for we have two very essential wants in our way 1. means to compass our views & 2dly. men qualified to fulfill them. And these you will agree are essential wants indeed.

Land had been purchased west of Charlottesville for the college, and even before the first cornerstone was laid, Jefferson planned to turn it into a state university. When the legislature incorporated Central College, it had directed the trustees of the Literary Fund, an agency responsible for distributing funds to charity schools, to prepare a statewide educational plan. On September 9 Jefferson sent Joseph Cabell, his ally in the legislature, a scheme for local tax support of elementary schools that would free the Literary Fund for higher education. He included the suggestion that Central College's Visitors surrender their institution "for use as the University of Virginia, which shall be established on the said lands."

Cabell was not able to gain everything he and Jefferson sought, but he did win the state's commitment to the creation of the University of Virginia. There would be an income of only fifteen thousand dollars for the school, not the entire Literary Fund, and the legislature had not selected a site. But Jefferson was named to the commission to select the location, and at meetings at Rockfish Gap early in August, 1818, he skillfully persuaded his colleagues to recommend the Central College campus. That winter Cabell shepherded the proposal for a Charlottesville campus through the legislature. Inadequately financed, the state university would be the only part of Jefferson's educational plan, his "bantling of forty years," to become a reality in his lifetime. But its location at Charlottesville meant that he could supervise its development, and he became the first Rector of the state university.

There had always been an element of local pride in Jefferson's wish to see a coherent system of education in Virginia; he had envisioned it as a model for other states and for all Americans. Events in 1819 and 1820 provided additional justification for his plan. First the financial panic of 1819, with stock market failures and bank closings, bore out his warnings of the results of the "bank-bubble" and catering to mercantile interests. The panic was a personal disaster as well, for he had countersigned loans amounting to twenty thousand dollars for Wilson Cary Nicholas at the Bank of the United States. Nicholas's bankruptcy left Jefferson responsible for the debt, a financial burden he was never able to discharge. Jefferson's distrust of the North increased, and he saw the university as a way to insulate young Southerners from the influences of that region. This feeling was confirmed in 1820 when he saw northern "consolidation," his term for the amalgamation of federal power at the expense of states' rights, triumph in the Missouri Compromise. Under this agreement, Maine and Missouri were admitted to the Union simultaneously to preserve the balance of slave and free states, and Congress banned slavery from the Louisiana Territory north of the line 36°30'. Jefferson attacked the compromise in a letter to John Holmes, a member of the Massachusetts Senate, because it imposed the morality of one section on another and infringed on the rights of individual citizens.

> Monticello Apr. 22. [18]20.
>
> I had for a long time ceased to read newspapers or pay any attention to public affairs, confident they were in good hands, and content to be a passenger in our bark to the shore from which I am not distant. But this momentous question, like a fire bell in the night, awakened and filled me with terror. I considered it at once as the

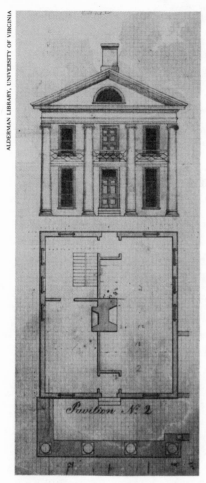

One of the pavilions Jefferson designed as residences for professors at the university

knell of the Union. It is hushed, indeed, for the moment. But this is a reprieve only, not a final sentence. A geographical line, coinciding with a marked principle, moral and political, once concieved and held up to the angry passions of men, will never be obliterated; and every new irritation will mark it deeper and deeper. I can say with conscious truth that there is not a man on earth who would sacrifice more than I would, to relieve us from this heavy reproach, in any *practicable* way. The cession of that kind of property, for so it is mis-named, is a bagatelle which would not cost me a second thought, if, in that way, a general emancipation and *expatriation* could be effected: and, gradually, and with due sacrifices, I think it might be. But, as it is we have the wolf by the ear, and we can neither hold him, nor safely let him go. Justice is in one scale, and self-preservation in the other.... An abstinence too from this act of power, would remove the jealousy excited by the undertaking of Congress, to regulate the condition of the different descriptions of men composing a state. This certainly is the exclusive right of every state, which nothing in the constitution has taken from them and given to the general government....

I regret that I am now to die in the belief that the useless sacrifice of themselves, by the generation of '76. to acquire self government and happiness to their country, is to be thrown away by the unwise and unworthy passions of their sons, and that my only consolation is to be that I live not to weep over it.

The chance for the creation of a great southern university to compete with the colleges of the North nearly died in the winter of 1820–21. The legislature allowed the Visitors to borrow sixty thousand dollars from the Literary Fund, but that was only enough for completion of housing for students and professors. Another loan was needed to begin construction of the library. Jefferson wrote another Visitor, James Breckinridge, of his "deep affliction" at news the university might be denied new funds.

Monticello Feb. 15. [18]21.
The reflections that the boys of this age are to be the men of the next; that they should be prepared to recieve the holy charge which we are cherishing to deliver over to them; that in establishing an institution of wis-

Jefferson in 1821 by Thomas Sully

dom for them we secure it to all our future generations . . . ; these are considerations which will occur to all; but all, I fear, do not see the speck in our horizon which is to burst on us as a tornado, sooner or later. The line of division lately marked out between different portions of our confederacy, is such as will never, I fear, be obliterated, and we are now trusting to those who are against us in position and principle, to fashion to their own form the minds & affections of our youth. If, as has been estimated, we send 300,000. D. a year to the Northern seminaries, for the instruction of our own sons, then we must have there at all times 500. of our sons imbibing opinions and principles in discord with those of their own country. This canker is eating on the vitals of our existence, and if not arrested at once will be beyond remedy. We are now certainly furnishing recruits to their school.

Jefferson's friends in the legislature won again; the Visitors were allowed to borrow another sixty thousand dollars. Slowly, tantalizingly, the campus at Charlottesville took shape. Jefferson brooded over the carvings on marble columns, canvassed the states for prospective faculty members, and accepted the fact that he had but a few years in which to see his dream realized. In January, 1821, he turned to a long neglected task: recording the facts of his life. He began his *Autobiography* with this explanation: "At the age of 77, I begin to make some memoranda and state some recollections of dates & facts concerning myself, for my own more ready reference & for the inform[atio]n of my family." He knew that the number who could share his memories of those dates and facts was shrinking, and in June, 1822, Jefferson wrote Adams of the sad cycle of senility and death in their revolutionary circle.

Monticello June 1. [18]22.

The papers tell us that Genl. Starke is off at the age of 93. Charles Thomson [Secretary of the Continental Congress] still lives at about the same age, chearful, slender as a grasshopper, and so much without memory that he scarcely recognises the members of his household. An intimate friend of his called on him not long since: it was difficult to make him recollect who he was, and sitting one hour, he told him the same story 4. times over. Is this life? . . . It is at most but the life of a cabbage, surely not worth a wish. When all our faculties have left, or are leaving us, one by one, sight, hearing, memory,

A bird's-eye view, which may have been drawn by Cornelia Randolph, of the university's lawns and ranges, pavilions, "hotels" for "dieting the students" and connecting dorms

every avenue of pleasing sensation is closed, and athumy, debility and mal-aise left in their places, when the friends of our youth are all gone, and a generation is risen around us whom we know not, is death an evil?

Adams replied in an unusually lighthearted vein. Jefferson's letter, he wrote, was "the best letter that ever was written by an Octogenearian." He told of his own failing eyesight but boasted that he teased others to read to him "most unmercifully and tyrannically, against their consent." Adams's letter dispelled Jefferson's uncharacteristically gloomy mood, and he offered to break his lifelong rule of keeping his personal correspondence confidential. If Adams would consent to publish their recent exchange of letters, the public might take pity on them both.

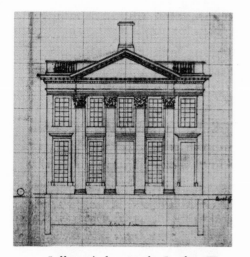

Jefferson's drawing for Pavilion III using the Corinthian order

Monticello June 27. [18]22.

I do not know how far you may suffer as I do, under the persecution of letters, of which every mail brings a fresh load....I happened to turn to my letter-list some time ago, and a curiosity was excited to count those recieved in a single year....I found the number to be 1267. many of them requiring answers of elaborate research, and all to be answered with due attention and consideration. Take an average of this number for a week or a day, and I will repeat the question suggested by other considerations in mine of the 1st. Is this life?...It occurs then that my condition of existence, truly stated in that letter, if better known, might check the kind indiscretions which are so heavily oppressing the departing hours of life. Such a relief would to me be an ineffable blessing. But yours of the 11th. equally interesting and affecting, should accompany that to which it is an answer. The two taken together would excite a joint interest, and place before our fellow-citizens the present condition of two antient servants, who having faithfully performed their

40. or 50. campaigns, stipendiis omnibus expletis [after all their military duty had been completed], have a reasonable claim to repose from all disturbance in the Sanctuary of Invalids and Superannuates.

Construction was complete for all the university buildings except the library by the fall of 1822, and to build it, the Visitors sought another loan. To allow hiring of professors and payment of operating expenses, they asked that the legislature convert earlier loans to outright grants so that repayment of interest and principal would not be a drain on yearly income. Once again, Joseph Cabell did battle in the state legislature. He did not share Jefferson's belief that all the Visitors' demands would be met and asked the Rector to state his priorities. Jefferson's continuing ill health, aggravated by a fall in which he broke his left arm, did not keep him from preparing this concise, practical statement for Cabell's use in December.

Monticello Dec. 28. [18]22

If the remission of the principal debt, and an accomodation of the cost of the library cannot both be obtained, which would be most desirable? Without any question, the latter. Of all things the most important is the completion of the buildings. The remission of the debt will come of itself.... The great object of our aim from the beginning has been to make this establishment the most eminent in the United States, in order to draw to it the youth of every state, but especially of the South and West. We have proposed therefore to call to it characters of the first order of science from Europe as well as our own country; and, not only by their salaries, and the comforts of their situation, but by the distinguished scale of it's structure and preparation.... Had we built a barn for a College and log-huts for accommodations, should we ever have had the assurance to propose to an European Professor of that character to come to it? Why give up this important idea, when so near it's accomplishment that a single lift more effects it?... The opening of the institution in a half-state of readiness would be the most fatal step which could be adopted. It would be an impatience defeating it's own object....

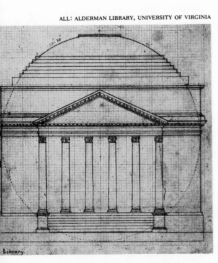

ALL: ALDERMAN LIBRARY, UNIVERSITY OF VIRGINIA

Elevation of Rotunda, which housed the library, as drawn by the Rector

Jefferson never completely recovered from the accident that cost him the use of his left arm. His senses were as keen as ever, but his physical stamina was severely limited. The year 1823 was not an easy one on other scores. The legislature had granted the Visitors another loan but did nothing to relieve them of the payment of old debts. The year was brightened by an appeal from James Monroe. Unlike Madison, Monroe had seldom sought Jefferson's advice, but in October he asked both ex-Presidents for their counsel on the latest diplomatic turn: Britain's suggestion that she and the United States issue a joint condemnation of the efforts of the Quadruple Alliance to reconquer the Spanish American colonies, which had won their freedom and independence. The fate of these new republics had long troubled Jefferson, and he had discussed their problems in a letter to Lafayette a decade earlier.

DIPLOMATIC RECEPTION ROOMS, U.S. DEPARTMENT OF STATE

James Monroe by Thomas Sully, 1820

Monticello Nov. 30. [18]13

I join you sincerely, my friend in wishes for the emancipation of South America. That they will be liberated from foreign subjection I have little doubt. But the result of my enquiries does not authorise me to hope they are capable of maintaining a free government. Their people are immersed in the darkest ignorance, and brutalised by bigotry & superstition. . . . Their efforts I fear therefore will end in establishing military despotism in the several provinces. . . . But their future wars & quarrels among themselves will oblige them to bring the people into action & into the exertion of understandings. Light will at length beam in on their minds and the standing example we shall hold up, serving as an excitement as well as a model for their direction may in the long run qualify them for self government.

When Monroe wrote in October to ask whether the present situation warranted an exception to the rule of America's splendid diplomatic isolation, Jefferson answered in the affirmative.

Monticello Oct. 24. [18]23.

The question . . . is the most momentous which has ever been offered to my contemplation since that of independance. That made us a nation, this sets our compass, and points the course which we are to steer thro' the ocean of time opening on our view. . . . Our first and fundamental maxim should be, never to entangle ourselves in the broils of Europe; our 2d. never to suffer Europe to intermeddle with Cis-Atlantic affairs. America, North & South, has a set of interests distinct from those of Europe, and peculiarly her own. She should therefore have a system of her own, separate and apart from that of Europe. While the last is laboring to become the dom-

Francis Walker Gilmer

icil of despotism, our endeavor should surely be to make our hemisphere that of freedom. One nation, most of all, could disturb us in this pursuit; she now offers to lead, aid, and accompany us in it. . . . With her then we should the most sedulously nourish a cordial friendship; and nothing would tend more to knit our affections than to be fighting once more side by side in the same cause. Not that I would purchase even her amity at the price of taking part in her wars. But the war in which the present proposition might engage us, should that be it's consequence, is not her war, but ours. It's object is to introduce and establish the American system, of ousting from our land all foreign nations, of never permitting the powers of Europe to intermeddle with the affairs of our nations. It is to maintain our own principle, not to depart from it.

This philosophy found official expression in December when the Monroe Doctrine was proclaimed. The independence of the two American continents had been declared. The next year, 1824, Jefferson brooded over the coming presidential elections. For the first time since 1800 Republican unity was in question; no fewer than four candidates competed for party support. The election was bound to reflect the growing division between North and South, free and slave states, and Jefferson wrote Lafayette of his fear that "the question will be ultimately reduced to the northernmost and southernmost candidate." Jefferson was busy that spring with the university. He compiled a catalogue of 6,860 volumes that should be purchased for the library—an astounding intellectual feat. News that the Virginia legislature had decided to forget the interest on the three loans freed enough income to allow the Visitors to recruit a faculty in earnest. Jefferson had difficulty attracting American scholars of the "first grade" for the professorships, and since he would not settle for second-rate men, was forced to look in Europe. Francis Walker Gilmer, described by Jefferson as "the best-educated subject we have raised since the Revolution," sailed to Britain to recruit teachers from Oxford, Cambridge, and Edinburgh with this letter of introduction to Richard Rush, the American minister in London.

Monticello Apr. 26. [18]24.

I have heretofore informed you that our legislature had undertaken the establishment of an University of Virginia. . . . and we propose to open it at the beginning of the next year. We require the intervening time for seeking out, and engaging Professors. As to these, we have determined to recieve no one who is not of the first order of science in his line; and as such in every branch cannot be obtained with us, we propose to seek some of them at least in the countries ahead of us in science, and preferably in Great Britain, the land of our own language, habits, and manners. But how to find out those who are of the first grade of science, of sober and correct habits and morals, harmonising tempers, talents for communication is the difficulty. Our first step is to send a special agent to the Universities of Oxford, Cambridge & Edinburgh, to make the selection for us....We do not certainly expect to obtain...men of the first eminence, established there in reputation and office, and with emoluments not to be bettered anywhere. But we know that there is another race, treading on their heels, preparing to take their places, and as well, and sometimes better qualified to fill them. These while unsettled, surrounded by a crowd of competitors, of equal claims and perhaps superior credit and interest, may prefer a comfortable certainty here to an uncertain hope there, and a lingering delay even of that. From this description we expect we may draw professors equal to those of the highest name.

John Quincy Adams

In the autumn, Jefferson learned that the school would be honored by a visit from Lafayette. "What recollections, dear friend, will this call up to you and me! What a history have we to run over...," he wrote in October. Lafayette reached Monticello three weeks later and was the guest of honor at a banquet held in the unfinished Rotunda of the university. Because Jefferson was too weak to read the brief speech he had prepared, another guest delivered his tribute to "our benefactor in peace as well as in war." The speech concluded with a plea for the university: "Could I live to see it once enjoy the patronage & cherishment of our public authorities with undivided voice, I should die without a doubt of the future fortunes of my native state." That wish seemed near fulfillment, for Gilmer had returned from Europe with commitments from five British scholars; a sixth professor was found in New York City. Delays in the professors' arrival threatened the scheduled opening on February 1, but Jefferson seemed relieved that the event was at last in sight.

An indecisive vote in the Electoral College brought John Quincy Adams to the Presidency that month; Jefferson contented himself with a gracious note of congratulations to the new President's father. As one visitor remarked of Jefferson that winter, "in politics, his interest seems nearly gone." He was, he wrote John Adams, "comforted and protected from other solicitudes by

Pictorial Field Book of the War of 1812 (Extra Illustrated) BY BENSON J. LOSSING, 1868

the cares of our University." Slowly, but unmistakably Jefferson's health failed. An illness, variously described as urinary disease or diabetes, developed in the late winter of 1825, just as the university finally opened its doors to pupils and faculty. Despite his weakness, Jefferson sent word to Madison of the school's progress.

> Monticello Mar. 22. [18]25.
>
> Our Students are at present between 50. & 60, and are coming in 2. or 3. every day. We hear of many on the road who cannot come on, the Richmond and Frederick stages having ceased to run. Some of them hire horses and get on. The schools of antient & modern languages and Mathematics have a little over 30. each, Nat. Philosophy fewer, because few come well enough prepared in Mathematics to enter that school to any advantage. They are half idle all, for want of books, Hilliard's supply shipped from Boston...being not yet arrived.

The ailing Rector was not left in peace, however, as his dream of a university came to pass. Thomas Mann Randolph, Martha Jefferson's brilliant and charming husband, had become a victim of the mental instability that crippled so many members of his family. Randolph had served as Governor of Virginia from 1819 to 1822 but suffered financial difficulties and found it difficult to live in the shadow of his father-in-law. By 1825 he was completely alienated from his wife and children and tended to blame his wife's family for his financial disgrace. In June Jefferson tried unsuccessfully to placate the son-in-law he had welcomed so happily thirty-five years before.

Engraving of Monticello drawn for a mid-nineteenth-century magazine

> Monticello June 5. [18]25.
>
> Your situation is painful, but neither novel nor infrequent. It is indeed that of a great portion of our countrymen, brought on them, not by their own errors, but by that of our legislators, in subjecting the proportions between the money of the country, and it's other property to the gambling operations of money brokers....I hope that to your other pains has not been added that of moment's doubt that you can ever want a necessary or comfort of life while I possess any thing. All I have is destined to the comfortable maintenance of yourself and the family, and to a future provision for them. I have no other use for the property. Abandon then, dear Sir, to the will of the law the afflicting concerns, which have been hitherto but sources of pain and labour to you. Restore yourself to the bosom of your family & friends.

In August, a friend noticed for the first time that Jefferson's memory failed occasionally. Even so, the "men and gentlemen" of the university plagued their aging Rector. On the evening of October 1 students rioted. When the Visitors met two days later to consider the situation, Jefferson rose to speak, but as one student recalled, "he had not gone far before his feelings overcame him, and he sat down, saying that he would leave to abler hands the task of saying what he wished to say." The guilty students were so moved that they stepped forward to confess. Jefferson recounted the story to Joseph Coolidge, husband of his granddaughter Ellen.

The descendants of Jefferson still possess this scrap of paper which announces the marriage of Ellen Wayles Randolph to Joseph Coolidge.

Engraving of the University of Virginia after an 1826 map, showing major buildings completed

Monticello Oct. 13. [1825].

The University had gone on with a degree of order and harmony which had strengthened the hope that much of self government might be trusted to the discretion of the Students of the age of 16. and upwards, until the 1st. instant. In the night of that day a party of 14. students, animated first with wine, masked themselves so as not to be known, and turned out on the lawn of the University, with no intention, it is believed, but of childish noise and uproar. Two professors hearing it went out to see what was the matter. They were received with insult, and even brick-bats were thrown at them. Each of them seised an offender, demanded their names (for they could not distinguish them under their disguise) but were refused, abused, and the culprits calling on their companions for a rescue, got loose and withdrew to their chambers. The Faculty of Professors met the next day, called the whole before them, and in an address, rather harsh, required them to denounce the offenders. They refused, answered the address in writing and in the rudest terms, and charged the Professors themselves with false statements. 50 others, who were in their rooms, no ways implicated in the riot and knowing nothing about it, immediately signed the answer, making common cause with the rioters, and declaring their belief of their assertions in opposition to those of the Professors.... The Visitors called the whole body of Students before them; exhorted them to make known the persons masked, the innocent to aid the cause of order, by bearing witness to the truth, and the guilty to relieve their innocent brethren from censures which they were conscious that themselves alone deserved. On this the fourteen maskers stepped forward and avowed themselves the persons guilty of whatever had passed, but denying that any trespass had been committed.

402

In this last year of Jefferson's life, even the most innocuous matter turned into a drain on his failing strength. In October, J.H.I. Browere visited Monticello to make a life mask of the former President. Browere had promised that the procedure would take only twenty minutes, but the operation involved hours of agony for Jefferson as the artist used "freely the mallet and chisel" to remove the plaster in which he had coated Jefferson's head. Jefferson remarked to Madison that "there became real danger that the ears would tear from the head sooner than from the plaster. I now bid adieu for ever to busts and even portraits." As his life was ending, Jefferson's letters were often directed to saying what had been too long unsaid and doing what he had left undone. In December, for instance, he sent an unusually explicit statement of his political views to Governor William Branch Giles. John Quincy Adams's first annual message alarmed Jefferson and other Old Republicans; indeed, Adams's policies would soon divide the party into Federal Republicans and Democratic Republicans. The President's obvious commitment to a federal program of internal improvements convinced Jefferson that "consolidation" had triumphed. He counseled patience and perseverance instead of armed resistance to such measures, but his letter to Giles betrayed his suspicion that dissolution of the Union might be necessary.

Monticello Dec. 26. [18]25.

Take together the decisions of the federal court, the doctrines of the President, and the misconstructions of the constitutional compact, acted on by the legislature of the federal branch, and it is but too evident, that the three ruling branches of that department are in combination to strip their colleagues, the State authorities, of the powers reserved by them and to exercise themselves all functions foreign and domestic.... And what is our resource for the preservation of the constitution? Reason and argument? You might as well reason and argue with the marble columns encircling them. The Representatives chosen by ourselves? They are joined in the combination; some from incorrect views of government, some from corrupt ones, sufficient, voting together, to outnumber the sound parts; and, with majorities only of 1, 2, or 3, bold enough to go forward in defiance. Are we then *to stand to our arms, with the hot-headed Georgian* [William H. Crawford]? No. That must be the last resource, not to be thought of until much longer and greater sufferings. If every infraction of a compact of so many parties is to be resisted at once, as a dissolution of it, none can ever be formed which would last one year. We must have patience and long endurance then with our brethren

Browere's life mask of Jefferson

while under delusion; give them time for reflection and experience of consequences; keep ourselves in a situation to profit by the chapter of accidents; and separate from our companions only when the sole alternatives left are the dissolution of our union with them, or submission to a government without limitation of powers. Between these two evils, when we must make a choice, there can be no hesitation.

The next month Jefferson undertook a desperate project to provide for his family. Payments on Nicholas's debts and installments on his own mortgaged acres had drained his income each year. He had tried over and over again to sell land to wipe out his debts and establish some funds on which Martha and her children could draw after his death, but Jefferson found no buyers. Virginia's agriculture no longer seemed a wise investment to those who had seen so many planters struggle for years with falling prices and increased taxes. In January, 1826, Thomas Jefferson Randolph rode to Richmond with instructions to seek legislative authorization for a lottery in which the prize would be his grandfather's lands and slaves. Despite the aid of such devoted friends as Joseph Cabell, young Randolph met strong opposition; lotteries were rarely granted to individuals. Jefferson wrote to Cabell of his desire to "save the house of Monticello and a farm adjoining to end my days in and bury my bones." To his grandson, who had worked so long and valiantly to protect his interest, Jefferson sent his thanks.

Monticello Feb. 8. [18]26.

For myself I should not regard a prostration of fortune, but I am over whelmed at the prospect of the situation in which I may leave my family. My dear & beloved daughter, the cherished companion of my early life and nurse of my age and her children, rendered as dear to me as if my own from having lived with them from their cradle, left in a comfortless situation hold up to me nothing but future gloom. And I should not care were life to end with the line I am writing, were it not that . . . I may yet be of some avail to the family. Their affectionate devotion to me makes a willingness to endure life a duty as long as it can be of any use to them. Yourself particularly, dear Jefferson, I consider as the greatest of the God-sends which heaven has granted to me. Without you, what could I do under the difficulties now invironing me? . . . Perhaps however even in this case I may have no right to complain, as these misfortunes have been held back for my last days when few remain to

A ticket for the Jefferson Lottery

me.... And should this my last request be granted, I may yet close with a cloudless sun a long and serene day of life.

The legislature was generous neither to Jefferson nor to his university. On February 17 he wrote Madison of the vote against additional funds for completion of buildings at Charlottesville and the failure of his plan for a lottery. The letter grew in length and became Jefferson's valedictory to his trusted friend at Montpelier, his comrade and confidante for fifty years.

Extract of Jefferson's will (copied by his grandson Thomas Jefferson Randolph) giving "to my friend James Madison of Montpellier my gold mounted walking staff...."

Monticello Febr. 17. [18]26.

The friendship which has subsisted between us, now half a century, and the harmony of our political principles and pursuits, have been sources of constant happiness to me thro' that long period. And if I remove beyond the reach of attentions to the University, or beyond the bourne of life itself, as I soon must, it is a comfort to leave that institution under your care.... It has also been a great solace to me to believe that you are engaged in vindicating to posterity the course we have pursued for preserving to them, *in all their purity,* the blessings of self-government, which we had assisted too in acquiring for them. If ever the earth has beheld a system of administration, conducted with a single and steadfast eye to the general interest and happiness of those committed to it, one which, protected by truth, can never know reproach, it is that to which our lives have been devoted. To myself you have been a pillar of support thro' life. Take care of me when dead, and be assured that I shall leave with you my last affections.

Not long afterward, the lottery was finally approved by the legislature. When newspapers began to carry offers of tickets in the "Jefferson Lottery," however, private subscribers promised funds in his support, and the lottery was suspended. On March 19 Jefferson made his will, carefully drafting its provisions so that Martha's husband would be unable to touch the funds her father had fought so desperately to give her. A few days later, young Randolph prepared for a visit to Boston and Jefferson gave him a letter of introduction to Adams. Perhaps guessing that it was the last he would write his old friend, Jefferson drafted a touching note which Adams described as "a cordial to me."

Jefferson's design for tombstone and the inscription he desired

Monticello Mar. 25. [18]26.

Dear Sir

My grandson Th: Jefferson Randolph, being on a visit to Boston, would think he had seen nothing were he to leave it without having seen you.... Like other young people, he wishes to be able, in the winter nights of old age, to recount to those around him what he has heard and learnt of the Heroic age preceding his birth, and which of the Argonauts particularly he was in time to have seen. It was the lot of our early years to witness nothing but the dull monotony of colonial subservience, and of our riper ones to breast the labors and perils of working out of it. Theirs are the Halcyon calms succeeding the storm which our Argosy had so stoutly weathered. Gratify his ambition then by recieving his best bow, and my solicitude for your health by enabling him to bring me a favorable account of it. Mine is but indifferent, but not so my friendship and respect for you.

Th. J.

Jefferson's indifferent health failed further after his grandson's departure. Soon he could hardly walk and by the last week of June, he was confined to bed. To the end, nonetheless, he met his duties as elder statesman and symbol of America's heritage. On June 24 he replied to an invitation to attend the celebration of the fiftieth anniversary of the Declaration of Independence at Washington. In declining the honor, Jefferson labored carefully over the precise wording of what was to be his last public statement.

Monticello June 24. [18]26.

I should, indeed, with peculiar delight, have met and exchanged there, congratulations personally, with the small band, the remnant of that host of worthies, who joined with us, on that day, in the bold and doubtful election we were to make for our country, between submission, or the sword; and to have enjoyed with them the consolatory fact that our fellow citizens, after half a century of experience and prosperity, continue to approve the choice we made. May it be to the world, what I believe it will be... the Signal of arousing men to burst the chains, under which Monkish ignorance and superstition had persuaded them to bind themselves, and to assume the blessings & security of self government.... All eyes are opened, or opening to the rights of man. The general spread of the light of science has already laid open to every view the palpable truth that the mass of mankind has not been born, with saddles on their backs, nor a favored few booted and spurred, ready to ride them legitimately, by the grace of god. These are grounds of hope for others. For ourselves let the annual return of this day, for ever refresh our recollections of these ri[ghts,] and an undiminished devotion to them.

The anniversary of the Fourth of July obsessed Jefferson in his last days. On July 2 he lapsed into a coma, only to wake briefly on the evening of the third to ask: "Is it the Fourth?" His physician answered that it soon would be. Shortly before one o'clock on the afternoon of July 4, 1826, Jefferson died. Later that day John Adams passed away, leaving as his last words: "Thomas Jefferson survives." The next day Jefferson was buried in a quiet ceremony at Monticello. His grandson arranged for the simple marker his grandfather had designed. The stone was not to list a single office he had held, only "The following inscription, & not a word more 'Here was buried Thomas Jefferson Author of the Declaration of American Independance, of the Statute of Virginia for religious freedom, & Father of the University of Virginia.' because by these, as testimonials that I have lived, I wish most to be remembered."

These accomplishments reflected what Jefferson felt were the most important events of the long struggle he had led toward the triumph of republican principles. Certainly he could be forgiven the suspicion that the American nation of the second quarter of the nineteenth century would have little regard for his labors in public office. The private subscriptions did not fully materialize, and his daughter and grandchildren were left in want. Many of Jefferson's dreams would become real, however. Although Jefferson only freed five of his own slaves at his death, all slaves would eventually be freed, at great cost to the Union he cherished. Public education would become commonplace. And one hundred and fifty years after his death, those who fought impersonal, unresponsive government, those who defended the rights of conscience against bigotry and prejudice, and those who simply said that government must benefit the governed, not the governors, would call themselves "Jeffersonians."

A modest man who detested hero worship, Jefferson would have cared little that men fought for these principles in his name. His struggles were vindicated merely because the battle continued and because his example and words proved useful to later generations who carried on his jealous guardianship of the nation's honor and her citizens' rights. It was for this that Jefferson had risked his way of life and his family's estates: men were freer because he had lived. He needed no other monument.

407

Selected Bibliography

Adams, Henry. *History of the United States During the Administrations of Jefferson and Madison.* 9 vols. New York: Charles Scribner's Sons, 1891–93.

Berman, Eleanor D. *Thomas Jefferson among the Arts.* New York: Philisophical Library, 1947.

Boorstin, Daniel. *The Lost World of Thomas Jefferson.* New York: Holt, 1948.

Bowers, Claude G. *Jefferson and Hamilton: The Struggle for Democracy in America.* Boston: Houghton Mifflin, 1925.

Brodie, Fawn M. *Thomas Jefferson, An Intimate History.* New York: W. W. Norton, 1974.

Cabell, N.F., ed. *Early History of the University of Virginia, as Contained in the Letters of Thomas Jefferson and Joseph C. Cabell.* Richmond: J.W. Randolph, 1856.

Cappon, Lester J., ed. *The Adams-Jefferson Letters: The Complete Correspondence between Thomas Jefferson and Abigail and John Adams.* Chapel Hill: University of North Carolina Press, for the Institute of Early American History and Culture, 1959.

Cunningham, Noble E., Jr. *The Jeffersonian Republicans in Power: The Formation of Party Organization, 1789–1801.* Chapel Hill: University of North Carolina Press, 1957.

—————. *The Jeffersonian Republicans in Power: Party Operations, 1801–1809.* Chapel Hill: University of North Carolina Press, 1963.

Dumbauld, Edward. *Thomas Jefferson: American Tourist.* Norman: University of Oklahoma Press, 1946.

Fleming, Thomas. *The Man from Monticello.* New York: Morrow, 1969.

Jefferson, Thomas. *The Commonplace Book of Thomas Jefferson: A Repertory of His Ideas on Government.* Edited by Gilbert Chinard. Baltimore: Johns Hopkins Press, 1926.

—————. *Thomas Jefferson's Farm Book.* Edited by Edwin M. Betts. Princeton: Princeton University Press, for the American Philosophical Society, 1953.

—————. *Thomas Jefferson's Garden Book, 1766–1824.* Edited by Edwin M. Betts. Philadelphia: American Philosophical Society, 1944.

—————. *Family Letters of Thomas Jefferson.* Edited by Edwin M. Betts and J.A. Bear, Jr., Columbia: University of Missouri Press, 1966.

—————. *Notes on the State of Virginia.* Edited by William Peden. Chapel Hill: University of North Carolina Press, 1955.

—————. *The Papers of Thomas Jefferson.* Edited by Julian P. Boyd and others. 19 vols. to date. Princeton: Princeton University Press, 1950 –.

—————. *The Writings of Thomas Jefferson.* Edited by A.A. Lipscomb and A.E. Bergh. 20 vols. Washington: Thomas Jefferson Memorial Foundation, 1905.

—————. *The Writings of Thomas Jefferson.* Edited by Paul Leicester Ford. 10 vols. New York: G. P. Putnam's Sons, 1892–99.

Kimball, Fiske. *Thomas Jefferson, Architect.* 2d ed. New York: Da Capo, 1968.

Koch, Adrienne and Peden, William, eds. *The Life and Selected Writings of Thomas Jefferson.* New York: Random House (The Modern Library), 1944.

Madison, James. *The Papers of James Madison.* Vols. 1–7, edited by William T. Hutchinson and William M.E. Rachal et al. Vol. 8 –, edited by Robert A. Rutland and William M. E. Rachal et al. Chicago: University of Chicago Press, 1962 –.

Malone, Dumas. *Jefferson and His Time.* 5 vols. to date: *Jefferson the Virginian; Jefferson and the Rights of Man; Jefferson and the Ordeal of Liberty; Jefferson the President: First Term, 1801–1805; Jefferson the President: Second Term, 1805–1809.* Boston: Little Brown, 1948–74.

Martin, Edwin T. *Thomas Jefferson, Scientist.* New York: Henry Schuman, 1952.

Padover, Saul K. *Jefferson.* New York: Harcourt, Brace & Co., 1942.

Peterson, Merrill D. *Thomas Jefferson and the New Nation.* New York: Oxford University Press, 1970.

—————. *The Jefferson Image in the American Mind.* New York: Oxford University Press, 1960.

Randall, Henry S. *The Life of Thomas Jefferson.* 3 vols. 1858. Reprint. New York: Da Capo, 1972.

Randolph, Sarah N. *The Domestic Life of Thomas Jefferson.* New York: Harper & Bros., 1871.

Schachner, Nathan. *Thomas Jefferson, A Biography.* New York: Appleton-Century-Crofts, 1951.

Weymouth, Lally, ed. *Thomas Jefferson, The Man... His World... His Influence.* New York: G. P. Putnam's Sons, 1973.

White, Leonard D. *The Jeffersonians: A Study in Administrative History, 1801–1829.* New York: Macmillan, 1951.

Acknowledgments

Unless otherwise specifically credited below, all documents reproduced in this volume are from the Thomas Jefferson Papers, Library of Congress, Washington, D.C., the greatest collection of Jefferson documents in existence. The sources of other documents reprinted in this volume are as follows:

Alderman Library, University of Virginia, Charlottesville, page 397
Historical Society of Pennsylvania, Philadelphia, pages 280(middle), 399(bottom)–400
Houghton Library, Harvard University, Cambridge, Mass., page 402
Massachusetts Historical Society, Boston, pages 54(bottom), 285(bottom)–286(top)
National Archives, Washington, D.C., pages 66(bottom)–70
New-York Historical Society, New York, N.Y., page 250
New York Public Library, New York, N.Y., pages 268(bottom)–269, 326(top)
Pierpont Morgan Library, New York, N.Y., pages 234, 256(bottom)–257(top), 280(bottom)
United States Naval Academy Museum, Annapolis, Md., pages 347(bottom)–348

In addition, some documents were reprinted from the following published works:

Jefferson, Thomas. *Notes on Virginia.* London, 1787. Pages 18(bottom)–19, 78–79(center), 82–84, 88(bottom)–90, 107(bottom)–108, 132(bottom)–135, 148
La Rochefoucauld-Liancourt, François, A.F., Duc de. *Travels Through the United States of North America.* 2 vols. London, 1799. Pages 261(bottom)–262(top)
Randall, Henry S. *The Life of Thomas Jefferson.* 3 vols. New York, 1858. Pages 274(bottom)–275(top)
Randolph, Sarah N. *The Domestic Life of Thomas Jefferson.* New York, 1871. Page 381

The principal sources of information contained in the Introduction were the prefatory remarks written by Julian P. Boyd for Volume 1 of *The Papers of Thomas Jefferson,* an essay on the provenance of the Jefferson papers by Paul G. Sifton of the Library of Congress, and *The Jefferson Image in the American Mind* by Merrill D. Peterson.

The Editors wish to express their appreciation to the many institutions and individuals who have made available their pictorial materials for use in this volume. In particular the Editors are grateful to:

Alderman Library, University of Virginia, Charlottesville
American Antiquarian Society, Worcester, Mass.
American Philosophical Society, Philadelphia
Bibliothèque Nationale, Paris
The College of William and Mary, Williamsburg, Va.
Historical Society of Pennsylvania, Philadelphia
Independence National Historical Park Collection, Philadelphia
Library of Congress, Manuscript and Rare Book Divisions, Washington, D.C.
Maryland Historical Society, Baltimore
Massachusetts Historical Society, Boston
Musée Carnavalet, Paris
New-York Historical Society, New York, N.Y.
New York Public Library, New York, N.Y.
Princeton University Library, Princeton, N.J.
Thomas Jefferson Memorial Foundation, Charlottesville, Va.
Virginia Historical Society, Richmond
Yale University Art Gallery, New Haven, Conn.
Yale University Libraries, New Haven, Conn.

Finally, the Editors would like to thank Barbara Nagelsmith in Paris, John D. Knowlton in Washington, D.C., and Ruth W. Lester, Assistant Editor of *The Papers of Thomas Jefferson,* Princeton, for advice and assistance in obtaining pictorial material, Susan Sheldon for editing and proofreading, and Lynn Seiffer for research.

Index

Boldface indicates pages on
which illustrations appear.

your draughts will be most nego[ciated]

necessaries for yourself & your me[n]

United States that these draughts

are made prayable. I also ask [if]

nation with which we have interco[urse]

-plies which your necessities may

retribution. and our own Consuls in fo[reign]

hereby instructed & required to be a[iding]

necessary for procuring your retur[n]

entire satisfaction & confidence to th[e]

Jefferson, President of the United St[ates]

for you

general credit, with my own hand.

To

Capt. Meriwether Le[wis]